T-72
MAIN BATTLE TANK

T-72
MAIN BATTLE TANK

James Kinnear and Stephen L. Sewell

OSPREY PUBLISHING
Bloomsbury Publishing Plc
Kemp House, Chawley Park, Cumnor Hill, Oxford OX2 9PH, UK
Bloomsbury Publishing Ireland Limited,
29 Earlsfort Terrace, Dublin 2, Ireland
Bloomsbury Publishing Inc.
1359 Broadway, 12th Floor, New York, NY 10018, USA
E-mail: info@ospreypublishing.com
www.ospreypublishing.com

OSPREY is a trademark of Osprey Publishing Ltd

First published in Great Britain in 2026

© Osprey Publishing Ltd, 2026

For legal purposes the Acknowledgements on p. 9 constitute an extension of this copyright page.

All rights reserved. No part of this publication may be: i) reproduced or transmitted in any form, electronic or mechanical, including photocopying, recording or by means of any information storage or retrieval system without prior permission in writing from the publishers; or ii) used or reproduced in any way for the training, development or operation of artificial intelligence (AI) technologies, including generative AI technologies. The rights holders expressly reserve this publication from the text and data mining exception as per Article 4(3) of the Digital Single Market Directive (EU) 2019/790.

A catalogue record for this book is available from the British Library

ISBN: HB 9781472871800; eBook 9781472871770; ePDF 9781472871787; XML 9781472871794

26 27 28 29 30 10 9 8 7 6 5 4 3 2 1

Cover, page design and layout by Stewart Larking
Index by Mark Swift
Printed by Repro India Ltd
Artwork by Andrey Aksenov
Front cover: Upper image: An early T-72 (Obiekt-172M) during the public debut of the T-72 'Ural' MBT on Red Square on 7 November 1977 (see page 32). Lower image: Russian T-72 tanks in Chechnya, fitted with KMT series mine ploughs and rollers. (Photo by IVAN SHLAMOV/AFP via Getty Images)

PICTURE CREDITS
All pictures, including those on the front and back cover, are from the authors' collections unless otherwise noted. In particular, the authors would like to express their appreciation to Andrey Aksenov, John Ham, Alexander Koshchavtsev, Alexander Morzhitsky, Sergei Popsuevich and Igor Zheltov. Artworks are by Andrey Aksenov and are credited where they appear. Thanks also go to the Museum of Russian Military History, Padikovo, and the Muzei Tekhniki (Vadim Zadorozhny Museum) at Arkhangelskoe, both located in the suburbs of Moscow, for permission to photograph their preserved tanks in detail.

NOTE ON THE TRANSLATION AND PRONUNCIATION OF RUSSIAN LANGUAGE
The Russian alphabet has more characters than the Latin-based English language, and the Russian language is also grammatically complex, and subject to varying translations depending on context, gender, time period and the nationality of the translator. Therefore, it is not always possible to directly translate Russian terms or names into English, and the various means of doing so are contentious and often arbitrary. Transliterations of some Russian terms have also been simplified in this book without the contentious punctuation marks sometimes used to denote soft and hard signs, as although perceived correct by those with an academic but no practical experience of the language, use outside an academic environment makes the subsequent English translation of a living Russian language difficult to read. An example is Ob'iekt (object) that has been simplified as Obiekt for consistency with previously published books. As these books are technical histories rather than studies of Russian grammar, the authors trust that this simplification of translation and transliteration makes the books easier to read than would be the case if all the punctuation marks were included.

Osprey Publishing supports the Woodland Trust, the UK's leading woodland conservation charity.

To find out more about our authors and books visit **www.ospreypublishing.com**. Here you will find extracts, author interviews, details of forthcoming events and the option to sign up for our newsletter.

For product safety related questions contact productsafety@bloomsbury.com

CONTENTS

	Introduction	6
Chapter 1:	The Concept of 'Wartime Mobilization'	10
Chapter 2:	Development of the T-72 Main Battle Tank	30
Chapter 3:	Description of the T-72 Tank and its Variants	58
Chapter 4:	Derivative Vehicles	134
Chapter 5:	Combat Use	182
Chapter 6:	Manual Extracts	208
Chapter 7:	Walkarounds	220
Chapter 8:	Foreign Production and Service	234
Chapter 9:	Ukrainian Post-Soviet Service and Variants	244
Chapter 10:	T-72 Tanks Preserved in Museums	258
	Conclusion	268
	Appendices	272
	Artwork	304
	Bibliography	306
	Index	311

INTRODUCTION

A T-72B1 on parade in Red Square, Moscow, 7 November 1986. The additional turret frontal armour and radiation lining are evident in this view.

The T-72 was amazing for two achievements: it became the best-known second-generation post-war Soviet tank in the world, and it accomplished that despite the fact that it was never supposed to have existed in the first place.

Like the preceding T-54, T-55 and T-62 models, the T-72 was seen abroad in NATO countries as the standard that all NATO tanks had to surpass on the battlefield. Approximately 22,000 T-72 tanks were built by the USSR over its 17-year production run, and as with the T-55, the tank was released for export, starting in 1978. The tank served in a number of countries for many years after the fall of the USSR and remains in widespread service today, including on both sides of the current conflict in Ukraine. Poland, Czechoslovakia and Yugoslavia built modifications of the tank, and China and North Korea used its design features to build their own follow-on tank projects.

Unlike the previous tanks produced by Nizhny Tagil, however, the T-72 was looked upon by the Ministry of Defence Production (MOP) and its allies as an 'inferior' or even 'stolen' design that did not deserve to be placed in production at all. The chief opponent to the tank was Dmitriy Fedorovich Ustinov, head of the Technical Council of the Council of Ministers and a Deputy Premier and Secretary of the Politburo, and from 1976 – three years after the T-72 entered series production despite his efforts – Minister of Defence. He preferred the Kharkov-designed T-64 series on a personal level, and was unapologetic about his demands to see that tank be the only one to see service as the second-generation full series production post-war Soviet main battle tank.

The Soviet Army, the 'заказчик' (client or customer), having learned many difficult and bloody lessons during the Great Patriotic War, had, however, a totally different view. The T-64 was a capricious and unreliable tank over its first 15 years of existence, and based on their experiences with the legendary T-34 in the war they wanted a main battle tank that was simpler, more reliable, cheaper to mass produce, and faster to get into production in large numbers. Led by Minister of Defence Marshal of the Soviet Union Andrey Grechko (who was Minister of Defence from 1967 to 1976 as the T-72 was being developed and ultimately entered production and service), they backed the preferred upstart from the Urals.

The T-72 tank built on the reputations of the previous Nizhny Tagil tanks and used many of their base components, such as the latest iterations of the V-2 series diesel engine of T-34 lineage. Compared with its two competitors – the earlier, but fussy and complex T-64 or the slightly later turbine-powered T-80 with its insatiable fuel requirements – the T-72 was what the Soviet Army and the General Staff really wanted in the way of a main battle tank (MBT). Albeit the T-72 had less sophisticated systems than either of those tanks, it was easier to teach to recruits over a five-month training schedule in what was a conscript-based army. And the fully equipped Soviet-produced versions of the T-72 tank were a match for any foreign tank of the time, and no slouch in combat. Even today the T-72 can present a good account of itself in the hands of a competent and well-trained crew.

But, not for the first time with Soviet tanks, when the T-72 entered combat in the hands of what were known at the time as Third World armies, the tank did not live up to its potential, and appeared to be an easy target. While admittedly the export versions of the T-72 were down-rated with fewer features than the Soviet ones – homogenous armour protection and more restricted ammunition types being the main differences – loss rates were high and only permitted Western forces or their allies to crow about what a poor opponent the tank was. While patently not true, it certainly appeared to be the received wisdom from a foreign viewpoint. The tank's one true weakness turned out to be its higher-powered version of the V-2 diesel, the V-46, and the 7-speed transmission it inherited from the T-64 which made it very tiring to drive in over long periods, especially in hilly terrain.

Soviet T-72B1 tanks during winter manoeuvres. T-72B and B1 tanks fitted with 'Kontakt-1' ERA blocks were labelled 'BV' abroad, but this is not a Soviet or Russian designation.

Due to the bad publicity received by the T-72 in some foreign conflicts and the resulting lack of interest in the tank from a sales aspect in the period immediately following the break-up of the Soviet Union, President Boris Yeltsin after coming to office in 1991 renamed the final Soviet-era production model, the T-72BM or T-72BU, as the T-90 'Vladimir' or 'the first Russian main battle tank'. But over the past 35 years that tank has been developed as its own specific design. It has been sold abroad together with sales of excess Soviet-era domestic versions, and these tanks are formidable opponents on the battlefields of what is termed today the Global South.

As with the previous books in this series following the development of post-war Soviet armour, this book is based on existing research undertaken by Russian armour historians and veterans of the Soviet tank industry now available in the unclassified world. While there are other versions of the tank that have been built in Poland, Czechoslovakia and Yugoslavia, this book concentrates on the tanks originally built in the Soviet Union and later upgraded by the Russian Federation or Ukraine as the main post-Soviet inheritors of significant numbers of the tank, with major tank rebuild facilities capable of modernizing the original design.

To this day Soviet and Russian post-World War II state archives are essentially barred to Western researchers, so the efforts of the following individuals are greatly appreciated. Most of them will be identifiable from the bibliography used in the research for this book. As with any such work, the result is based on the collective efforts of many individuals who provided archive and photographic material, as well as correcting errors and omissions. Thanks in particular go to Andrey Aksenov, Mikhail Baryatinsky, Alexander Koshchavtsev, Andrey Malyshev, Andrey Malyshev, Viktor Maskovsky, Alexander Morzhitsky, Esa Muikku, Felix Oganesyan, Yuri Pasholok, Sergei Popsuevich, Sergei Suvorov and Igor Zheltov. Credit must also be given to acknowledged experts in the field such as Steve Zaloga for his pioneering research and work on the study of Soviet and Russian tanks. Special thanks go to the ownership and staff of the Museum of National Military History in Padikovo and the Muzei Tekhniki (the Vadim Zadorozhny Museum) in Arkhangelskoe for allowing unrestricted access to their respective T-72 (M-1978) and T-72A (M-1987) tanks, and to Esa Muikku for providing myriad clarifications from his direct experience of operating and maintaining the Finnish Army T-72 tank fleet. All of these people have provided both information and advice on approaching this subject on a purely goodwill basis.

T-72B3M tanks during the Victory Parade on Red Square, Moscow, 9 May 2019.

CHAPTER 1
THE CONCEPT OF 'WARTIME MOBILIZATION'

The Obiekt-166M was an UVZ KB modernization of the T-62 developed and tested between 1963 and 1965. The tank featured the same 115mm U5-TS smoothbore armament, but a modified hull, V-36F diesel (multifuel) engine, modified running gear layout with the distinctive future T-72 road wheels, and other changes. Pictured is the Obiekt-166M1 in the Kubinka back yard in the 1990s.

REFLECTIONS ON THE GREAT PATRIOTIC WAR

After World War II – known as the Great Patriotic War in the Soviet Union – came to a close, the leadership of the country vowed to never be caught off guard and unprepared again for a major war.

They also considered, as had been the case in the 1930s, the technical advantages of foreign designs and thinking, as had been delivered during the war as Lend-Lease equipment from the USA and the Commonwealth. The standard Soviet tank of World War II, the T-34, was a rugged vehicle with wide tracks and a powerful diesel engine, but had relatively basic fire controls, optics and communications equipment. The M4 Medium Tank – the Sherman – was much more sophisticated with better designed and finished components, VHF FM radio sets with much better reception for commanders, vertical axis gun stabilizers and built-in auxiliary power units. The T-34 was, however, eminently suitable for Soviet conditions, in that it was finely engineered only where necessary, with the emphasis being on production output for a tank with a short combat life expectation, which could be operated and maintained by crews with limited training.

Post-war development of Soviet tanks, armoured and softskin vehicles took advantage of the best aspects of foreign technology that had been provided via Lend-Lease during the war, a practice that had been prevalent in the 1930s when foreign tank design features were readily adopted and adapted for local manufacturing, operational service and climatic conditions. Post-war ZiS-151 and ZiL-157 trucks took a great deal of their technology from the US GMC CCKW-353 and Studebaker US6 trucks, and the first Soviet post-war series production tank, the T-54,* moved to use a VHF FM radio as well as eventually receiving first a single axis and then dual axis gun stabilizer. Soviet designers also added in a new system being introduced in Western tanks – infrared night sights and searchlights – and one of their own creation, an underwater driving system for river crossing.

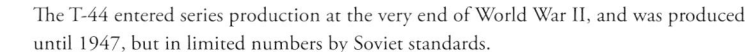

*   The T-44 entered series production at the very end of World War II, and was produced until 1947, but in limited numbers by Soviet standards.

During the 1950s Soviet design emphasized range and firepower. Tanks were fitted with 100mm rifled guns and with a fuel capacity that gave them a road range of up to 700km versus Western tanks, which were armed with 83.4 or 90mm guns and had petrol engines delivering road ranges of only about 160km. An overwhelming consideration in Soviet tank design was also the requirement for them to be 'soldier proof' – i.e. simple enough for tank troops to learn to operate and maintain in just five months of training during the first six months of their standard two-year conscription service. The rudimentary characteristics of Soviet tank designs were quite deliberate, in keeping with the operational and training requirements of a conscript-based army.

SETTING THE STAGE FOR THE SECOND GENERATION OF POST-WAR TANKS

By the late 1950s, there were three established Soviet tank design bureaus run by the following personnel:

- The Leningrad 'Kirov' Factory group (Leningradskiy Zavod imeni Kirova or LKZ), chief designer Zhosef Kotin and deputy chief designer Nikolay Popov;
- The Kharkov Transport Machinery Construction Factory (Kharkovskiy Transportniy Mashinostroitelniy Zavod imeni Malysheva or KhZTM), chief designer Aleksandr Morozov and deputy chief designer Yakov Baran, factory manager O.V. Soich;
- The Ural Railway Wagon Construction Factory (Uralskiy Vagonstroitelniy Zavod imeni Dzerhinskogo or UVZ in Nizhny Tagil), chief designer Leonid Kartsev and deputy chief designer Valeriy N. Venediktov, factory manager I. V. Okunev.

All of them had an understandably great sense of self-confidence in the superiority of their own designs – probably Kotin more so than the others – and all of them felt they were the right men to build the next generation of Soviet medium tanks, or Noviy Sredniy Tank (NST). Starting in 1953 the Central Committee of the Communist Party (Politburo) and Council of Ministers of the USSR (TsK KPSS i SM SSSR, abbreviated to SM SSSR in all further references) tasked all three groups with designing a new Soviet medium tank armed with a high-power 100mm gun and better armoured than the T-54 then in production. Kotin was still convinced of the superiority of heavy tanks in which his design bureau dominated, and thereby did not take up the challenge, but Morozov and Kartsev accepted for their respective plants.

The Obiekt-167 was a further development of the Obiekt-166M, with the same 115mm U5-TS armament (but the 125mm D-81 gun planned for series production), a V-26 engine developing 700hp and six road wheel stations.

Neither the Kharkov (Obiekt-430) nor the Nizhny Tagil (Obiekt-140) projects for the NST were approved and accepted for service. But while Kartsev withdrew saying that neither tank was a sufficient advance on the T-54 – and earning the wrath of the SM SSSR in the process for not being a team player – Morozov advised he could make massive improvements on the Obiekt-430 and meet the requirements.

On 30 November 1960 Marshal Blagonravov, Chief of the Main Armoured Vehicle Directorate (Glavniye Bronetankoviye Upravleniye or GBTU) approved the proposal for the Obiekt-432 tank. This tank was a radical departure from all past Soviet tanks and was designed by Morozov to combine the firepower and protection of a heavy tank with the weight and mobility of a medium tank. This concept intrigued the General Staff and the Scientific and Technical Council of the SM SSSR as well as the Military Industrial Commission then headed by Dmitriy Ustinov.* Ustinov had worked his way up through the party ranks and was a Deputy Premier of the USSR, which gave him great leverage over which weapons systems were accepted for production and service. The final go-ahead came on 17 February 1961, with Central Committee of the Communist Party and Council of Ministers of the USSR (TsK KPSS i SM SSSR) Resolution No. 141-58 which accepted the new Obiekt-432 medium (main battle) tank into service on the basis of the Obiekt-430. The same resolution cancelled further development of the Obiekt-277 (LKZ Leningrad) and Obiekt-770 (ChTZ Chelyabinsk) heavy tanks, and with that the further development of the heavy tank in the Soviet Union.

* The Military Industrial Commission, headed by Ustinov, would play a significant and consistent role in the hindrance of the development of the T-72 versus its competitors, as will be seen later.

The concept for the Obiekt-432 tank was quite radical. It had a composite armour glacis (steel/fibreglass/steel) sloped at 68 degrees from the vertical with the driver-mechanic now located in the centre of the hull. The turret was also made with composite armour (in this case steel/aluminium/steel) and fitted with a totally new gun, the 115mm smoothbore 'Molot'. There were two versions of the weapon, the 2A20 using unitary ammunition then undergoing trials in what became the T-62 tank, and the 2A21 which used separate loading ammunition with partially combustible case propellant. The main reason for this selection was that it also had a 30-round mechanical autoloader situated around the circumference of the rotating turret floor; projectiles were stowed under the floor and the propellant stowed stub casing end-up around it. Morozov dubbed this the 'cabin autoloader'.

This signified a major change in that it eliminated one of the four standard crewmen in Soviet tanks – the loader. This also meant the tank could have a smaller turret. The turret was fitted with a cross-turret coincidence rangefinder with twin heads as well as two-axis gun stabilization.

As well as these changes, the tank also adopted a novel new power plant and running gear system. The engine selected was the brand new 5TDF two-cycle engine, a five-cylinder/ten-piston opposed piston design using extraction cooling via the exhaust drawing cooling air through the radiators and out of the exhaust aperture. It had drive shafts coming out of both ends of the crankshaft and power was sent through two combination 7-speed transmissions and final drives to the drive wheels. Cast aluminium internally amortized road wheels were used, together with lightweight cast tracks. The result was a tank with nearly the same firepower of a heavy tank (115mm vs. 122mm), better armour protection than either the IS-3 or T-10 heavy tank, and an all-up weight of around 36 metric tons.

An Obiekt-167T during winter trials, powered by a GTD-3T gas-turbine engine. The Obiekt-167 prototype testbed did not ultimately enter series production, but via a combination of technical modifications and political machinations it became the basis for the later Obiekt-172M (T-72).

The running gear used on the forthcoming T-72 is evident on this surviving Obiekt-167 prototype at the Kubinka Tank Museum.

LEFT
The same Obiekt-167 located at Patriot Park in 2016, with its distinctive turret mounted 9M14 'Malyutka' ATGM launcher. (Andrey Aksenov)

Ustinov in particular became personally enamoured with this tank and eagerly followed each phase of its development. But with all of these innovations came a myriad of what the Russians call 'detskiy bolezni' (children's diseases) or teething troubles. However, even though the prototypes had significant technical issues, in 1963 Ustinov and Minister of Defence Production S. A. Zverev ordered Obiekt-432 into production – over the objections of Minister of Defence Grechko.

Between 1963 and 1968 1,297 Obiekt-432 (i.e. the early T-64)* tanks were built, with improvements from year to year such as a redesigned hull, addition

---

* Development of the T-64 and later rival T-72 and T-80 'triad' was very much an ongoing effort, hence the 'Obiekt' development designations were retained even as the tanks were in early series production. The series production 'Obiekt-172M' thereby initially retained its development designation while in service.

of OPVT (Oborudovaniya dlya Podvodnogo Vozhdeniya Tanka – equipment for underwater tank driving) and infrared equipment, external stowage bins, and other detail changes. But the tanks still suffered from massive problems with unreliable engines, fragile tracks, capricious mechanical loaders, and poor design features. The first models had two 'cheek' armour panels next to the glacis which were found in testing to vector incoming rounds into the turret race, so a modified glacis and front upper hull were added.

Undeterred, Morozov began redesigning the tank in late 1967 and came up with a new variant he dubbed Obiekt-434. This tank improved on the notorious failings of the Obiekt-432 tank in many areas. One of the main ones was a redesigned turret with a longer cross-turret rangefinder as well as a new commander's weapons station/cupola, the 1EhTs29. This combined the commander's sight and viewer with a remote control 12.7mm 'Utes' heavy machine gun replacing the older DShKM gun used on the T-54 and later on the T-55 and T-62.

But the main improvement was to its armament. Obiekt-434 now mounted the new 125mm 2A26 (D-81) smoothbore gun and a modified autoloader that now only carried 28 rounds, but stowed 15 more rounds of 125mm ammunition inside the tank's fighting compartment. Prototypes began testing in January 1968 and, while still having major problems, were an improvement on the Obiekt-432.

Several things had however been boiling in the background that would have a major impact on the future of the Kharkov tank design bureau. The sequence of events began on 17 February 1961, with Resolution 141-58 of the SM SSSR to work on Obiekt-432 armed with the 2A21 gun and the 5TDF two-cycle diesel engine. At the same time, following Marshal of the Ground Forces V. Ya Chuikov's demand for the introduction of the 115mm gun into service as quickly as possible, the UVZ-designed replacement, the T-55 tank armed with the 2A20 version of the 115mm gun (firing unitary ammunition), was accepted for service in accordance with Resolution No. 729-305 of the SM SSSR on 12 August 1961 as the T-62 Medium Tank. The T-62 tank was however only considered an interim solution – and accordingly dubbed a 'tank destroyer' in many documents – and not the ultimate service tank.

Since the 1930s the Soviet Union had developed the concept of parallel high-risk and low-risk competitive developments as regards tank and armoured vehicle design. This was coupled with an industrial concept of 'doubler plants' whereby a plant built ostensibly for the assembly of one type of equipment could be used to produce the design of another plant or design bureau, either to increase overall production or to make up for the loss of a plant due to enemy action. The Chelyabinsk (ChTZ) and Stalingrad (STZ) plants were for instance built as tractor assembly plants, but both would convert to tank

ALL ABOVE The Obiekt-172 was the original UVZ KB redesign of one of two T-64A tanks delivered from Kharkov in order that it be modified for assembly at Nizhny Tagil, powered by a ChTZ-assembled V-45 diesel engine. The tank was modified per instructions, but in the meantime UVZ worked on redesigning the tank, taking into account the 'rodnaya' (native) Obiekt-167 design, which was more to their liking. The official Obiekt-172 modifications as formally required, particularly to the engine compartment, are evident from these photographs taken during initial trials.

RIGHT A surviving Obiekt-172 prototype, located at the Kubinka Tank Museum. Note the T-64 running gear and road wheels.

BELOW The smooth and uncluttered glacis of the original Obiekt-172, with a single vision device protection splash strip.

production in 1941. The practicality behind this philosophy was demonstrated in the summer of 1941, at which time the T-50 light, T-34M medium and KV-3 heavy tanks were due to replace the T-26, T-34 and KV-1 in production. As of 22 June 1941, series production preparation for all new tank developments was frozen in lieu of concentrating on the increased (or replacement) production of existing and proven tank designs. This allowed the Soviet government to produce large numbers of T-34s and reasonable numbers of KV-1s, even allowing for the autumn 1941 relocation of the tank factories in Kharkov and Leningrad beyond the Ural Mountains. The Soviet philosophy of 'doubler plants' such that tank production could be increased for wartime mobilization or maintained at another location due to loss of production at one plant in case of major war remained in place throughout the post-1945 Cold War. This philosophy was also in the background of the 'high-risk, low risk' individual tank developments that were competitively undertaken in the post-war era. The T-55 vs T-62 'competition' of the late 1950s was soon to be repeated by the T-64 vs T-72 'competition' of the late 1960s and early 1970s, made more complex and piquant by the slightly later introduction of a third tank (the T-80) for good measure. That philosophy was almost sunk in the T-72 development story due to a combination of technical issues, political infighting between individuals and their respective chains of command, and a not inconsequential mix of personal egos among those well connected with, or integral to, the leadership of the country.

On 27 December 1962 Ustinov ordered all tank plants to switch from their own designs and to henceforth only build the Obiekt-432 series tanks, with the T-55 to be phased out in 1964 and T-62 production halted in 1966. All support vehicles such as bridge-layers, engineer vehicles and recovery vehicles were also to change over to the Obiekt-432 chassis.

However, getting the Obiekt-432 tanks to operate reliably was an issue that Kharkov was having difficulty in fully resolving. Engine failures, mechanical loader failures, and problems with the ultra-light running gear all prevented the tanks from demonstrating service requirement levels. Nevertheless, on 19 April 1964, Ustinov issued an order that no criticism of the Obiekt-432 tank or its engine would be accepted as it went through trial-and-error improvements. Very few improvements were however actually made to Obiekt-432 durability or performance. On 22 December 1965, Minister of Defence Production (MOP) S. A. Zverev warned Morozov that 'in 1937 people were shot for this level of work'.

Given the build complexity of the T-64 tank, Ustinov agreed with the various scientific technical councils and the GBTU that 'wartime mobilization' efforts would have to be carried out in order to be able to produce variants of the tank at a much faster pace. These were to be simplified and use more common parts – the big difference being a switch to the older V-2 type four-stroke diesel engine, which had proven highly reliable. Even though simplified to speed production, they were not to be the down-rated export versions of weapons designed for use in the then-designated Third World. An order was given on 11 June 1965 to work on Obiekt-432 tanks fitted with a V-2 type engine; Kharkov was to work on Obiekt-436 with a V-36 engine, and Nizhny Tagil was to work on Obiekt-438 with a V-45 engine.

Meanwhile, two more advanced designs were being developed. Kharkov was working on the Obiekt-434, an improved Obiekt-432 tank with the new 125mm D-81 gun, while Nizhny Tagil was working on its own Obiekt-167M tank. While the former was only a slightly improved Obiekt-432 design with a new mechanical loader only carrying 28 125mm rounds versus 30 115mm rounds, Obiekt-167M was an improved development of the T-62 tank with a new suspension with six road wheels, three return rollers, and mounting either the 115mm 2A21 gun or the 125mm D-81 gun, but with a new cassette-type autoloader of 19 rounds capacity called 'Zhelud'.

The MOP concluded that the V-36 engine was insufficiently developed, and on 15 August 1966 ordered Kharkov to change over to use the new V-45 engine. This new prototype was designated the Obiekt-439. Testing of the Obiekt-436 continued in the interim however, with acquired experience resulting in further changes as Kharkov worked to utilize its own domestic engine types.

ALL ABOVE These images show the UVZ-modified Obiekt-172M during trials in 1971. The Obiekt-172M marked the UVZ departure from the original T-64A design, which would after some significant political machinations result in the series production T-72 MBT. Note the rear turret bulge added to the borrowed T-64A turrets used on early prototypes. (Alexandr Koshchavtsev)

The SM SSSR finally accepted the Obiekt-432 tank for service as the T-64 main battle tank (MBT) in accordance with Resolution No. 982-321 dated 30 December 1966. The very next day, the SM SSSR tasked Kharkov to look into using the safer UVZ 'Zhelud' cassette autoloader, but Morozov categorically refused to even consider it.

Almost immediately after the decision was taken to accept the Obiekt-432 into service as the T-64 MBT, both UVZ in Nizhny Tagil and LKZ in Leningrad were tasked with preparing and testing designs for wartime mobilization tanks. UVZ was to build the V-2-engined model, while LKZ, backed by Ustinov, was tasked with investigating turbine engines. All of the tank factories had tested turbine engines adapted from helicopter turbo-shaft engines, and had found they could be made to work in a tank. But the design bureaus at Kharkov and Nizhny Tagil felt they were too complex, expensive and fuel thirsty to make a suitable engine for tanks to use in combat. Only the KB at LKZ in Leningrad, aware that the US was now dabbling in such engines, felt it could be made into a viable power plant, and was thus tasked with fulfilling the design undertaking.

UVZ in Nizhny Tagil and LKZ in Leningrad accordingly submitted their designs. Following evaluation, the Kharkov Obiekt-438 project was approved on 20 March 1968 by the MOP for production at UVZ in Nizhny Tagil to meet the requirements of a 'mobilization tank'. At this time Obiekt-438 was apparently re-designated Obiekt-172. LKZ in Leningrad received permission from the MOP on 16 April 1968 to develop its turbine-powered version and designated it Obiekt-219. Kharkov was to build five Obiekt-434 and two Obiekt-436 tanks for trials and send two pre-production Obiekt-434 tanks to UVZ in Nizhny Tagil for the latter plant to also prepare for series production of the tank.

It is important to note the recurring importance of the aforementioned 'doubler plant' concept in the development of the future T-72. When the 'resolved' full series production T-64A was taken into service on 15 August 1968 per a Resolution of the SM SSSR as the Soviet Union's new principal MBT, the State-level intent at that time was that this tank be produced at KhZTM (the Malyshev plant) in Kharkov, but also at Uralvagonzavod (UVZ) in Nizhny Tagil as a 'doubler' or 'wartime mobilization' plant, with UVZ tanks to be powered by the then-current ChTZ Chelyabinsk-built V-45 (V-2-45) engine design, as KhZTM would not have the capacity to produce engines for two assembly plants. On 12 May 1970 a Resolution of the SM SSSR confirmed this intent, later followed in accordance with Soviet norms by Ministry of Defence (MO) approval. Meantime, UVZ was instructed to prepare the original Obiekt-172 prototype (with its T-64 running gear) fitted with the V-45 engine ready for series production at UVZ in 1972. While development, rivalry and intrigue continued between the plants, their directors, chief designers and the MO and MOP hierarchy in Moscow, UVZ was

A surviving Obiekt-172M, with the chassis incorporating the UVZ-developed Obiekt-167 type running gear as used on the future series production T-72 MBT.

clearly aware that if their own Obiekt-designs were not accepted for production and service, the plant would become secondary in all respects to KhZTM in Kharkov. Meantime, Kharkov would test their Obiekt-435 with a V-45 engine, with that prototype being sent to Nizhny Tagil when the T-64A was taken into service in 1969. Behind the individual tank development histories and above the technical fray, the Soviet Union was regardless ensuring 'doubler plant' additional ramp-up capacity in the event of war. This factor also continually underlined much of the background behind rival design bureau and tank plant management thinking.

On 20 May 1968 the Obiekt-434 tank was accepted for service armed with the 125mm smoothbore D-81 gun as the T-64A in accordance with Resolution No. 360-137ss of the TsK KPSS i SM SSSR, and two new T-64A tanks were sent to UVZ for familiarization, evaluation and engine installation conversion. While most of the designers liked the overall arrangement of the tank, none of them liked its general technical solutions. They disliked the engine as being too demanding and fussy for reliable service in a tank, as well as too 'peakish' and with a too narrow power band to provide sufficient range of power output for support vehicle derivatives like the existing T-55-based IMR engineer vehicle or MTU bridge-launcher. In addition, UVZ engineers did not like the 'extraction' cooling system without the use of a fan to ensure constant air flow, and the other system was judged prone to overheating at the halt or during underwater river crossing.

Leonid Kartsev, as a Great Patriotic War tank veteran, personally found the 'cabin' autoloader to be a fatal flaw in the tank as it caused two main problems. Firstly, all of the propellant was exposed to any sort of flash damage inside the fighting compartment. The indigenous UVZ 'Zhelud' autoloader used cassettes stowed under the floor of the turret with no exposed propellant (although any spare ammunition beyond the 19 rounds in the 'Zhelud' was stowed around the inside of the fighting compartment). The UVZ-developed autoloader was also safer and less likely to jam or cause injury to the crew members by the mechanism grabbing their uniform sleeves or projectiles bouncing off the loading tray, problems inherent in the early T-64 mechanical loader.

Another problem was that for the first time in Soviet armour design the driver-mechanic was isolated from the rest of the crew and could not get out of his position due to the autoloader. An incident was reported during fording exercises where the tank began to flood and the driver, wearing his heavy winter coveralls, could not get past the ammunition to exit the tank from the turret and drowned. The 'Zhelud' autoloader kept the floor flat if a bit higher and the driver could easily wriggle out to escape via a turret hatch.

None of the designers liked the lightweight running gear of the T-64, with its relatively narrow tracks. Most of the designers had personal wartime experience of service in tank units that had to fight or train in European Russia, and knew that the use of large wide road wheels and wide tracks provided sufficient flotation over soft and marshy soil when running the tanks cross country. The narrow road wheels on the T-64 also left the tank vulnerable to thrown tracks when running at speed cross country, and the lightweight links were also prone to snapping. The initial torsion bar suspension had the same problem, with fragile bars.

The UVZ engineers initially did as requested and grafted a new rear end onto the T-64A hull with new mounts for an experimental V-45K (up-rated V-2 type engine of 730hp) mounted transversely in the engine bay. The modification used a normal T-55-type 'guitara' transfer case to provide power to a newly designed distribution case that provided power to the twin 7-speed transmissions from the T-64A. It was fitted with the usual UVZ type of air cleaner, radiators and oil cooler, but in order to try to keep the height of the engine deck down it used a slanted rear hull and angled fan to pull air through the radiators and extract hot air out of the rear of the hull with a large vent on the left side of the hull. This avoided having a bulge like that used on the T-62 but still gave the tank sufficient air flow.

The new prototype, now dubbed Obiekt-172 using the UVZ designation system, underwent trials and was found to have reliable performance but also retained the 'baked-in' flaws of the T-64A. In one of the great uses of indirect euphemism, Venediktov initially asked Kartsev if he could take measures to strengthen the running gear of the prototype (i.e. substituting the UVZ running gear set-up first envisaged on the Obiekt-167). Kartsev duly asked Moscow if he could make changes to the design of the tank, with the implied goal of simplifying production as requested in his original tasking for a mobilization variant of the Kharkov-designed T-64. He was granted permission and under the direction of Venediktov the engineers went to work.

But on 15 December 1968, things changed at UVZ. Since 1948, Ivan Okunev had been the director of the factory and had backed every move made by Kartsev in regard to tank development. However, on that date he was replaced by Ivan F. Krutyakov due to failing health on the order of Zhosef Kotin, who had become Deputy Minister for Defence Production for Tanks on 9 January 1968. Kotin personally disliked Okunev and wanted one of 'his' men in charge of the plant. Krutyakov, as new plant director – but also a highly experienced military engineer – was not inclined to accept having the chief designer dictate what the factory did instead of the director dictating policy. He was also beholden to many bureaucrats in Moscow, so things did not get off on the right foot.

When Krutyakov examined where Kartsev was going with his Obiekt-172 project, he immediately found fault with Kartsev's newly developed concepts and variations from their initial guidance to simply install a V-45 engine into the T-64A tank. His summary judgment was that the work was a 'mistake'.

While the UVZ rolled out its first Obiekt-172 prototype, serial number 808V172-1, on 11 September 1968 and began testing, Kharkov had meantime pushed to do its own work on developing the wartime mobilization tank and worked on their Obiekt-439, which was developed in December 1968.

In February 1968 the MOP tested the first two Obiekt-172 tank prototypes; at the same time Popov at LKZ in Leningrad was told to build 20 pre-production Obiekt-219 tanks for testing. Trials were duly carried out in March 1968 with the usual 'findings' or noted problems and failings of the tanks requiring factory corrections.

Meanwhile, internal tensions continued to boil over at UVZ in Nizhny Tagil, resulting in Kartsev sending a letter to the SM SSSR in March 1969 requesting he be reassigned, as he could not work with Krutyakov. Krutyakov in turn was irritated that instead of just following his orders to create a V-45-engined T-64A, Kartsev had 'green-lighted' Venediktov to redesign a tank using components from the Obiekt-167M tank – the stillborn T-62B – in the Kharkov-supplied tank to rectify what the UZV designers saw as its flaws. Venediktov and the designers from Department 520 went to town, and the new tank – designated Obiekt-172M – was quite different externally and internally from its predecessor.

The Obiekt-172M only resembled the T-64A at first glance. The UVZ design changed nearly everything the UVZ KB disliked about the Kharkov tank design. Externally, while it retained the new UVZ rear end, the tank was now fitted with a complete UVZ suspension and the running gear originally designed for the Obiekt-167. This had large-diameter wide wheels with rubber tyres, three lever-action shock absorbers versus the hydraulic-spring assisted type from Kharkov, three return rollers, and a broader RMSh live track with rubber bushed hinges that had proven to last for up to 5,000km.

The Obiekt-172M initially inherited the T-64A turret. The distinctive cross-turret coincidence rangefinder secondary port of the TPD1-49 sight (TPD2-49 as mounted on the early series production T-72 tanks) is clearly seen in this view.

Internally the biggest change was that the UVZ KB had fitted their own 'Zhelud' autoloader in place of the hated mechanical autoloader from Kharkov. Now carrying 22 rounds in the new tank hull, this had previously been demonstrated to Minister of Defence Production (MOP) Zverev. Zverev had initially been angry this did not copy the Kharkov design, but was soon won over by its speed, accuracy and safety and even recommended that Kharkov adopt it for the T-64A. As with engineers worldwide, including all Soviet factories, the 'not invented here' mentality was strong, and in keeping with that fine tradition Kharkov duly ignored his request.

The Obiekt-172M also now featured a built-in OPVT system that permitted the crew to easily prepare the tank for submergence during deep river wading. Covers flipped over the main radiator air intakes and exhausts, a port cover fitted over the engine exhaust outlet with one-way valves, and the single three-section snorkel was carried on the rear of the turret and mounted on the gunner's hatch cover when in use. The T-64A needed twin snorkels, one for air intake and one that bolted to the exhaust port with a large plenum, in order to keep the cooling system operating.

The Obiekt-172M also adopted a superior fire suppression system developed in Chelyabinsk that had been turned down by Kharkov, so the tank was now also safer from internal fires. A second prototype, Obiekt-173, was built on the T-64A chassis and also fitted with the 'Zhelud' autoloader.

While Kartsev was 'promoted' to the Scientific Technical Council of the Main Armoured Vehicle Directorate (NTK GBTU) on 18 August 1968, the Obiekt-172M and Obiekt-173 tanks went for testing. The dam broke on this on 18 October 1969 when the MOP condemned the idea of rebuilding the T-64A to a completely different tank (bearing in mind the original intent was to have UVZ as a 'doubler' facility to produce the T-64 series with a ChTZ-built V-2-45 series engine). MOP filed a list of some 126 'findings' on the tank as well as sneeringly commenting that it was 'not worthwhile'.

However, the view of the MO and General Staff of the Soviet Army was completely different. They had been dealing with the ecentricities of the Obiekt-430, 432 and 434 tanks for 15 years and were fed up with a tank design claiming great promise but only delivering headaches. In the mind of Minister of Defence and Marshal of the Soviet Union A. A. Grechko, the Obiekt-172M was the first alternative design that showed the promise of a new tank that was a significant leap ahead but still showed the essential required traits of reliability and durability. They pushed the MOP to 're-evaluate their position' and carry out further trials. The stance of Grechko was key, as he was the only one who could stand up to Ustinov, as he had similar status in the SM SSSR and the TsK (Politburo). Subsequent comparative testing reported on 31 December 1969 showed that with all the tanks having lists of 'findings' applied and none actually failing during trials, the Obiekt-172M was considered superior to the T-64A in many areas, most of them centring on reliability.

Venediktov was invited before the MOP on 7 January 1970 and was – unsurprisingly – grilled over his attempts to 'reinvent' the T-64 tank. Krutyakov as UVZ plant director apologized on his behalf, but Venediktov stood his ground. Krutyakov came away stunned that in spite of the pressure from Ustinov and his entourage most of the attendees were more pleased with the Obiekt-172M than with the T-64A.

Undeterred, some months later Ustinov wrote a Resolution for the SM SSSR issued on 11 May 1970 that ordered the organization for production of T-64A tanks at all MOP factories – Kharkov, Leningrad, Nizhny Tagil, Omsk and Chelyabinsk – with no mention made of the Obiekt-172M tank anywhere in the document. But when Ustinov was not apparently paying attention, on 12 May (i.e. the very following day) the TsK KPSS i SM SSSR somewhat unexpectedly released Resolution No. 326-113 'about undertaking work to further improve the Obiekt-172 tank' which authorized further development of the UVZ Obiekt-172M tank in its own right rather than UVZ acting as a 'doubler plant' for T-64A assembly. The latter Resolution emphatically stated the only tank UVZ would produce would be the Obiekt-172M. Glavtank* chief Nikolay Kucherenko was apoplectic as he knew that this meant that UVZ in Nizhny Tagil would build 'their' tank and not 'our' tank, as he considered the Kharkov-designed T-64A. On the same day Krutyakov was derided for the poor quality and performance of the Obiekt-172M prototypes. Krutyakov reviewed the claims related to the UVZ modifications, which for the most part were actually focused on the inherent problems with the T-64A parent of that tank rather than the Obiekt-172M.

Three Obiekt-172M prototypes were readied by 11 July 1970, and on 11 September the NIIBT test polygon at Kubinka published their assessment that the Obiekt-172M tanks were superior to the T-64A in nearly all areas save durability; the early Transmash-designed and ChTZ-built V-45K engines had some reliability issues or, as per the previously noted Russian description for such early problems, 'children's diseases'.

On 15 December 1970 the pro-Kharkov backers once again launched tirades about the Obiekt-172M tank recently tested at Kubinka and demanded it be seen as 'not worthwhile for continued development'. Despite this, testing continued and on 10 February 1971, Krutyakov was ordered to personally make sure that ten Obiekt-172M tanks were assembled with maximum attention to quality control for comparative testing purposes before they were shipped from the factory. A further evaluation by the MOP on 26 April, with the tests dubbed 'Star Runs' (but sarcastically known as 'cockroach races' by the participants!), again found the corrected Obiekt-172M prototypes to be superior to the T-64A in all areas except overall combat weight.

Ustinov did not appreciate the challenge to his largely personal decision that the T-64A was the only tank the Soviet Army needed – even though the Soviet Army had some operational reservations about the tank. On 7 May UVZ was

---

* Glavtank – 1st Main Directorate of the Ministry of Transport Machine Building, i.e. tank production, which post-war replaced the NKTP.

ordered to build another 15 Obiekt-172Ms for comparative testing against 15 T-64A tanks and 15 Obiekt-219 tanks, and to prepare to build another 150 for testing within military units. Testing began in June even though Kucherenko now complained widely that nobody liked 'our tank' and all of them sided with 'their tank' – Obiekt-172M was clearly preferred by the military over the T-64A. As testing proceeded, Defence Minister Grechko visited Kharkov and declared that even though things were now going well for their tank, he still had reservations about it.

The comparative test report summary provided on 20 October 1971 after several months and 10,000–11,000km travelled in Belorussia, Ukraine, Turkmenistan and the mountains of the Caucasus did little to change that view. The 15 Obiekt-172M tanks performed well,* but seven of the 15 T-64A tanks encountered significant technical failures under testing. Ustinov was furious and demanded even more testing in an attempt to prove the superiority of the T-64A. But when some reports were apparently re-written, three days later Grechko intervened, reprimanding 'a representative' from the MOP for skewing results in favour of the T-64A, which the military clearly disbelieved. He made the point of assigning Marshal of Tank Troops Babazhanyan to oversee the testing.

In December, more improvements were authorized. UVZ received permission to build another new prototype, Obiekt-172-2M, under the project name of 'Buyvol' (buffalo). Kharkov meantime received permission to develop the 1EhTs29 'Agat' combination remote control 12.7mm machine gun and commander's cupola and sighting system for the T-64A, as well as the 'Kadr-2' laser rangefinder. On 1 June 1972 all armoured vehicles would be considered for fitting the Type 902 series 'Tucha' remote smoke screen creation system (i.e. smoke grenade launchers).

Undeterred, Ustinov decided to put the upstart tank through the wringer. He ordered the T-64A to undergo a massive series of tests across the USSR along with the Obiekt-172M and the new Obiekt-219, the Leningrad LKZ plant's turbine-powered alternative to the T-64A. Popov and his designers were also not enamoured with the Kharkov suspension and created two new versions, Obiekt-219sp1 and Obiekt-219sp2. The latter had six medium-diameter road wheels with rubber tyres like those used by Nizhny Tagil, as well as a better designed track than the one from Kharkov. A total of 15 Obiekt-172M, ten T-64A and six Obiekt-219sp2 tanks, all of which had been modified based on the findings of

---

* The benchmarks during 10,000–11,000km of tank testing were against an expected factory guarantee of 3,000km and engine life of 350 working hours before rebuild. Track life was noted as inadequate during trials, being 4,500–5,000km vs an expectation of 6,500–7,000km. (Source: MO Report on the Results of Military Testing of 15 '172M' tanks manufactured by UVZ in 1972.)

the earlier trials, were chosen to participate in the additional competitive trials.

The new trials began on 19 June 1972 and were completed on 11 October, being closely monitored by MO and MOP representatives. Interim reports were not favourable to the T-64A, and in an attempt to pre-empt the final report Kucherenko wrote an impassioned plea to Soviet Premier Leonid Brezhnev to cancel planned production of the Obiekt-172M tank. His plea fell on deaf ears, and in his diary Kucherenko noted that he felt that all of his allies had given up on the Kharkov tank. At the time of these 1972 competitive trials, the T-64 had been in series production for five years, and the modified T-64A for three years, with many changes based on operational use and experience, while the Obiekt-172M and turbine powered Obiekt-219 prototypes were vying for the 'next generation' MBT title, with the latter also having the backing of D. F. Ustinov.

The results of the 'Star Runs' were discussed at a meeting of the MOP on 25 January 1973 and the testers had high praise for both the Obiekt-172M tanks and the new Obiekt-219sp2 tanks. There were no catastrophic failures with any of the three rival tank types tested, however. Kharkov personnel still proclaimed their tank as the best (as did the other two factions) and Kucherenko claimed the UVZ reports were pure fiction. Still not satisfied, Ustinov ordered yet another series of tests with the Obiekt-172M and sent ten of them to the 5th Guards Tank Army in the Urals MD (UVO) for additional running testing. The tanks completed this bout of testing on 7 April with high marks for all.

V. I. Podrezov, who directly participated in the described trials and tribulations, later noted that the MOP 'employed many Doctors and Candidates of Technical Science' who were not always objective. The '*mozgovaya*' (i.e. key – or literally 'brains' – group) for instance wrote a summary that after 3,000km of testing, two T-72 (Obiekt-172M) tanks had 'worked their resource' (i.e. were mechanically worn out) and should be pulled from the trials. The effect of downward pressure from D. F. Ustinov and General Yu. M. Potapov was not insignificant.

On 13 June Marshal Yakubovskiy (Commander of Ground Forces) and Marshal Babazhanyan (Commander of Tank Troops) held a symposium on all three tank types and found the Obiekt-172M and Obiekt-219sp2 as best meeting requirements. The former was cheaper and simpler than the T-64 (which would become a major factor in its longevity and export success), but the Obiekt-219sp2 received high marks for reliability and overall speed even though it was extremely fuel inefficient. After this, even with Ustinov's resistance, Zverev caved in to the Soviet Army's demands and ordered the Obiekt-172M tank into production at the UVZ.

On 7 August 1973, Obiekt-172M was accepted for series production and service with the Soviet Army as the T-72 main battle tank in accordance with

LEFT The Obiekt-172M glacis now incorporated four splash strips ahead of the driver-mechanic's vision device and the distinctive 'V' water deflector of the series production T-72.

Resolution No. 554-172 of the TsK KPSS i SM SSSR 'about taking into the armed forces a new medium tank'. The order was confirmed by Soviet Ministry of Defence Order No. 0148 dated 13 August 1973. The factory decided to honour its birthplace and affectionately named the tank the 'Ural'.

The early development of the T-72 tank had been traumatic, its detractors many, and its very existence born of some bureaucratic subterfuge. The tank would, however, in its own right become one of the most successful and best-known Soviet-era tanks in history, both at home and abroad, with its greatest ever combat engagements being undertaken at the time of writing, more than half a century after the tank entered service with the Soviet Army.

LEFT The development of the T-72 was not in isolation, as the rival design bureaus in Kharkov (T-64), Leningrad (T-80) and Nizhny Tagil (T-72) were all developing their respective MBT designs based on a common set of specifications (TTTs). Some design features common to the T-72 series can be seen on this early Obiekt-219 (T-80) built in 1975–76.

CHAPTER 2
DEVELOPMENT OF THE T-72 MAIN BATTLE TANK

ONLY THE FIRST BATTLE IS OVER...

While the T-72 was now a fact and given life by the MOP, Ustinov still remained vehemently against the tank and a good number of personnel in the MOP, Glavtank and Kharkov still considered it a 'counterfeit' and 'stolen design'. But since all three tanks – the T-64, the T-72 and later the T-80 series production version of the Obiekt-219 – were all based on the exact same TTTs (design parameters) and ordered to use the same basic hull and turret arrangement, the argument is not entirely valid.

Externally all three tanks looked similar, but they had different running gear layouts and hull rear arrangements. Each used a different engine – the T-64A used the 5TDF two-cycle diesel developing 700hp, the T-72 used the four-cycle V-46 diesel of 780hp, and the T-80 was powered by the GTD-1000T turbine of 1,000shp. All of the tanks were armed with the 125mm 2A26 variant of the D-81 gun, used cross-turret rangefinders, and initially had the same Kharkov-developed twin 7-speed transmissions. LKZ in Leningrad soon developed a 4-speed transmission using a fluid coupling clutch similar to the Chrysler 'Dynaflow' transmissions used in American cars. This needed a clutch to change gears, but could be stopped in any gear without stalling the engine.

The biggest difference among the three designs was the fact that both the Kharkov and Leningrad tanks used the 28-round mechanical loader and the UVZ machine used the 22-round 'Zhelud' cassette-type automatic loader. While both devices used a carousel principle and fit under the turret floor, the propellant casings on the former stuck up like a fence post around the turret floor and were exposed to any damage that entered the fighting compartment such as the jet from a High Explosive Anti-Tank (HEAT) projectile. While all of them stowed additional ammunition – up to 17 rounds of two-part ammunition – around the inside of the fighting compartment, 22 of those rounds were safely under the floor and away from flash damage in the T-72.

The main difference between the Kharkov and Nizhny Tagil tanks and the Leningrad-built turbine powered tank was range.

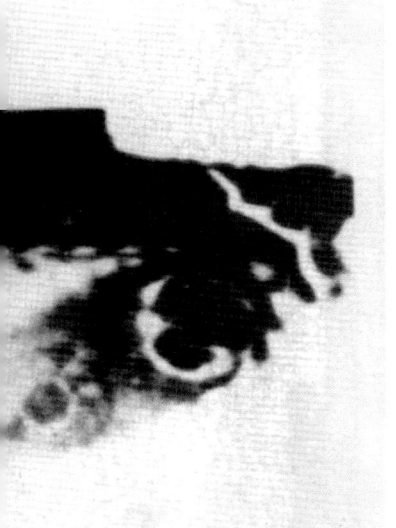

An early intelligence-release photograph of the 'T-64/72'. With the benefit of 50 years of hindsight, the distinct development histories of the T-64 and T-72 are well known, as are the origins of the Obiekt-432/434, and the later Obiekt-166M/167 origins of the T-72. But in the mid 1970s this was all unknown and photographs such as this were the staple of NATO recognition manuals in the period. The tank shown is an early T-64.

Both the T-64A and T-72 could achieve ranges of up to 650–700km on highways with twin 200-litre auxiliary fuel tanks, but even with those same additional tanks (and often a third one) the best the thirsty T-80 could do at the time was around 385km. Marshal Babazhanyan among others noted that Soviet Army units equipped with T-80s would need double the number of fuel tanker trucks to feed their appetites.

The main problem facing the T-72 was not technical, however, but rather the ongoing enmity of Dmitriy Ustinov. He was still irate that the upstart tank had beaten his 'chosen one' and even now was still preferred by the military over his other favoured competitor, the T-80. Behind the scenes, Ustinov worked with the MOP to ensure that the T-72 would not be receiving the same upgrades that would be lavished on the T-64 and T-80 tanks.

Ustinov, a former design and mechanical engineer, had been Minister of Armaments from 1941 to 1953. He had during the war directed the evacuation of military plants in the autumn of 1941, including the evacuation of T-34 production tooling from Plant No. 183 in Kharkov to the very plant in Nizhny Tagil now developing the future T-72. Though not a military man, he knew tanks, artillery, manufacturing and logistics. He was also concurrently a member of the Politburo of the TsK KPSS (and Party Secretary from 1965 to 1976) and

The public debut of the T-72 (Obiekt-172M) MBT on Red Square, Moscow, 7 November 1977. (ITAR-TASS)

a formidable character in the Soviet Union. For the purposes of 'sneaking a new tank past the system', Ustinov was not a man to be crossed lightly.

In the meantime, on 12 August 1973, the MOP issued Order 339 which was the go-ahead to fit the new 9K112 'Kobra' through-the-bore ATGM system to the T-64A via its adoption of the improved 2A46 version of the 125mm D-81 gun. This was not planned for the T-72, but options were later included to install it in the T-80. The new 2A46 smoothbore gun was ordered to replace the 2A26 in production on 18 March 1974.

These images show T-72 (Obiekt-172M) tanks returning from the debut 7 November 1977 Red Square parade.

Meanwhile, UVZ worked on two more versions of the T-72: the Obiekt-172-2M 'Buyvol' was refined and ready for testing and approval, and in line with requests by the Soviet Army another variant was undergoing testing. This was the Obiekt-175, a T-72 fitted with the prototype 130mm D-85 rifled gun which was a favourite calibre of many backers in the military. The factory dubbed this variant the 'Ural-1' and built ten tanks for trials purposes.

At some point in the production run of the T-72 a change was made to the fuel system that permitted the two 200-litre auxiliary fuel tanks to be plumbed into the main fuel system of the tank. This was now adopted and retrofitted to all T-72s. Soviet tank crews had previously had to pump the fuel out from the auxiliary tanks into the main fuel tanks using either a hand pump or small electric pump.

Both tanks and the prototype Obiekt-447A tank from Kharkov – a T-64 variant fitted with a new fire control system as well as the 9K112 'Kobra' ATGM system – underwent trials for an acceptance decision by Defence Minister Marshal Grechko starting on 14 October 1975. Marshal Grechko recommended that they all continue in development.

In early 1976 the ten Obiekt-175 tanks were forwarded for state testing, but things changed for the worse for UVZ on 26 April of that year when Marshal Grechko died. Premier Brezhnev immediately promoted his old friend Dmitriy Ustinov to Marshal of the Soviet Union and made him Defence Minister.

Now having both the MO and MOP under his control, Ustinov wasted no time and on 6 May launched an attack on the T-72 over its 'poor quality and low standards'. So he once again ordered the tank to undergo high stress testing. On 11 May 1976 Kucherenko wrote another passionate letter to Brezhnev to stop series production of the T-72 in favour of the more advanced T-64 and T-80. But too many members of the General Staff and Soviet Army leadership were now endeared with the rugged, reliable and crew-training friendly T-72, and protested accordingly.

What also again came into play was what is referred to by some authors as the network of 'Clans'. Each geographic region of the USSR had its own politicians who defended the work of the industries in that area, and three of the biggest 'Clans' were those from Ukraine, Leningrad and the Urals. Their members in the Politburo and Council of Ministers (SM SSSR) as well as the Duma (parliament) all fought for 'their' people. The Urals 'Clan' definitely stuck up for the beleaguered T-72 tank from its very inception.

While the factory had been found remiss under Krutyakov (and fined 200,000 roubles for sloppy work and delays, most likely due to Krutyakov's indifference over the T-72), the T-72 tank still excelled during testing. Meantime, on 4 June 1976 in Kharkov Aleksandr Morozov asked to retire due to poor

LEFT The Obiekt-172M and early T-72 Ural tanks had distinctly sloped turret frontal armour which would in later variants change shape more than once. Note the early 8-bolt road wheels and lack of side skirts, which appeared on the T-72A. (Sergei Popsueivich)

BELOW An early T-72 Ural tank in Soviet Army service. Note the early sighting arrangement, 8-bolt road wheels and lack of side skirts or radiation protection, which appeared almost a decade after the T-72 tank entered service.

health and in his place Nikolay A. Shomin was named as new chief designer at KhKBM (as it was known from 1 January 1966 when KB-60M and Experimental Workshop No. 190 were combined under the direction of Morozov). With the revered Morozov out of the picture, much of the high-echelon support for the T-64 tank began to wane.

The second coincidence rangefinder port for the TPD2-49 rangefinder and L2AG searchlight (now moved to the right of the gun barrel) are features of the early production Obiekt-172M and T-72 'Ural' tanks. This later tank with increased turret frontal armour is located at the T-34 Museum at Sholokovo near Moscow.

The rival tanks to the original T-64A would nevertheless both come into service. Following the service acceptance of the Obiekt-172M on 7 August 1973 as the T-72 MBT, the first version of the Obiekt-219sp2 production model was also accepted for service on 6 June 1976 as the T-80 MBT. Three months later, on 3 September per Resolution 733-244 of the SM SSSR, Obiekt-447A was also accepted for service as the T-64B, with a version of this tank without the 'Kobra' system being concurrently accepted as the T-64B1. The Soviet Union now had three 'rival' tank designs in service, all based on the same TTTs originally outlined at the end of the previous decade.

Under pressure from T-72 backers in both the MO and MOP, Ustinov relented slightly from his previous hard-line stance, and on 16 December 1976 per Resolution 1043-361 of the SM SSSR, UVZ was ordered to work on an improved model of the T-72 tank.

Venediktov used what he was permitted to exploit in his reworking of the T-72. While he was able to carry out trials with the 1A33 fire control system from the T-64B, he was not permitted to adopt it nor use it in the new version of the tank, which was ultimately provided with the 1A40 system. Venediktov did use a more modern TPK-41 electro-optical sight with a built-in laser rangefinder, which permitted him to remove the 'hump' for the right optic of the rangefinder from the turret, as well as a TPN-3-49* passive night sight and L-4A (Luna-4) infrared searchlight with a range of 1,300m. The tank also featured a new composite type of armour in the front lobes of the turret using ceramic rodding in the armour. This created two large bumps that clearly differentiate the new tank from the old one. A 16mm appliqué armour plate was also added

---

*   The TPN-3-49 sight was developed specifically for the D-81TM (2A46) gun series.

to the glacis, and starting on 1 January 1979, the UVZ also began installing full-length rubber skirts (10mm thick rubber with embedded steel mesh) on the sides above the level of the road wheels.

The new tank, developed as Obiekt-176, was adopted for service in June 1979 as the T-72A. Shortly after it appeared in numbers, American satellite photo interpreters spotted the changes and due to their bulged shape dubbed it the 'Dolly Parton' turret after the buxom Tennessee country and western singer. In 1981 they briefed this to then-Secretary of Defense Caspar Weinberger, who did not see the humour and ordered that it never be referred to in that manner again; so of course all American and NATO intelligence and military personnel called it the 'Dolly Parton'…

Concurrently with domestic production changes, Soviet client states were complaining of the obsolescence of their T-54, T-55 and T-62 tanks relative to potential Western options, especially after the Yom Kippur War with Israel in 1973. All of them – as well as the Warsaw Pact states – wanted more modern tanks. Defence Minister Ustinov knew the Soviet Union would need to offer an improved export tank, but refused to consider at that time selling either the T-64 or T-80 tank to any of them. But the 'despised' and mechanically less complex T-72 fitted the bill, and Ustinov felt he could placate the Ural backers while at the same time ensuring they would not be building as many T-72 tanks for the Soviet Army. He subsequently ordered UVZ to make an export version of the tank.

The decision to export the T-72 was taken in 1975, with Warsaw Pact countries being the first priority as per standard Soviet policy, and with licence production of the tank being organized in Czechoslovakia and Poland. The decision to export the earlier T-62 had in part been as a result of the Chinese recovering a T-62 after a border clash on Damansky Island in the Ussuri River in 1969, with the secrets of the T-62's then revolutionary armament and 115mm Armour-Piercing Fin-Stabilized Discarding Sabot (AFPSDS) ammunition being duly compromised. The reasoning for the export of the T-72 was less dramatic. As noted, Soviet client states were in need of a more modern tank. The T-72 was the most mainstream and perhaps even mundane of the T-64, T-72 and newly minted T-80 design options that the Soviet Union had for equipping their own arsenal. The T-72 was thereby an obvious utilitarian choice for general distribution. The memoirs of Krutyakov, who as UVZ Plant Director from 1969 to 1979 oversaw the development and production of the T-72, make reference to a visit made by Ustinov to India when the T-72 was in early series production, which resulted in a commitment to build a tank plant in India and sell up to 5,000 tanks to the country. In 1974, as UVZ began series production of the T-72, it produced precisely 220 tanks, with the production plan for 1976 being

This Soviet T-72 training stand clearly shows the compactness of the T-72 turret and the autoloader system used on the tank, which was in other forms also central to the T-64 and T-80 MBTs, in all cases allowing the crew of concurrent Soviet MBTs to be reduced to three.

500 tanks. The substantial contract was not fulfilled due to changes in the Indian government, but had it been signed, UVZ would have had no option but to concentrate on the T-72 as the Soviet Union's export tank of choice, while Kharkov and Leningrad continued to produce tanks primarily for the Soviet Army. Whether Ustinov was a sales genius or perhaps arranging some payback with UVZ is not recorded for posterity, but the T-72 was by far the best option as an export tank when compared with the T-64A and T-80.

Venediktov meantime did not want to expend any of the actual high-tech and classified items on an export tank, and the State would in any event clearly not allow it, so the plant substituted homogenous armour protection in the export tanks. The first version, simply dubbed the T-72 (Obiekt-172M-Eh), was offered for sale starting in 1978. These tanks were based on the technology of the original T-72 and were all coded as variations on the Obiekt-172M. Seven models of this tank were produced with Э (Eh – Export) suffixes differentiating them; however, there were two versions of each model, one for the Warsaw Pact and one for so-called Third World customers. The Warsaw Pact models were better equipped and in the case of the later tanks had improved armour protection with similar composite armour to the T-72A. Countries outside the Soviet Union and the Warsaw Pact received monolithic steel armour only. The final export model, the T-72S (Obiekt-172M-Eh8), was an export version of the later T-72B, the majority of which were sold to Iran, with others being re-absorbed into the Russian Army post-1995 under the original domestic T-72B designation.

In the mid 1970s, at a time when the T-64 and T-72 development paths remained somewhat opaque abroad, and the T-80 was emerging as the new enigmatic Soviet tank of choice, the T-72 was made public very early in its service life. In 1977, foreign military delegations were invited to inspect Soviet armour at a military base in the Moscow suburbs, with the visit of a French delegation being particularly well publicized, while on 7 November 1977 the T-72 'Ural' series, in the form of the early Obiekt-172M, made its public debut on Red Square for the 60th Anniversary of the October Revolution parade, at a time when the T-64 had still never been paraded in public despite nearly a decade in service. The T-72 series would subsequently be regularly seen on Red Square over the next decade or so, and would also be displayed during the last ever Soviet-era military parade, held on Red Square on 7 November 1990. The T-72 would as it transpired long outlive the Soviet Union where it had been created.

By 1977, the T-72 was a very much known entity, the standard Soviet Army 'low risk development' workhorse MBT, as had been the T-55 and the T-54 in previous years, while the T-64 and T-80 retained their 'mystery' status abroad for some years to come. Operating three rather than two concurrent generation MBT types with similar design and characteristics but different engine and fuel types would meanwhile provide the Soviet Army with additional logistics challenges in addition to the perennial inter-design bureau rivalry. In the meantime, on the domestic front, on 13 September 1979, Nikolay Kucherenko died, and with him went the last of the opponents of the T-72 bar Ustinov outside of the control of either the MO or MOP.

A T-72A M-1983 during a public exhibition at Kubinka. Note the distinctive 902 series smoke dischargers and external turret radiation lining.

RIGHT An early T-72 (Obiekt-172) towing a T-72A during a winter exercise.

BELOW A T-72A with KMT-6M2 mine clearing plough attachments during a Soviet exercise.

Later that month, competitive testing was carried out in the Carpathian MD with the T-62, T-64A, T-64B, T-72 and T-80. Overall, the T-72 was perhaps the all-around winner, but the 1A33 'Ob' fire control system in the T-64B (which Ustinov had denied to the T-72) was judged to be the best such system installed on any of the tanks present.

As with all Soviet tanks, no sooner was the T-72A approved for production than the MOP ordered the UVZ to begin work on a new model; this was per Resolution 635-188 of the SM SSSR dated 5 July 1981. This tank was once more to only incrementally be improved over the T-72A as Ustinov did not want its abilities to exceed those of the T-64B or the newer models of the T-80 in development. Ustinov, the most consistent detractor of the T-72, would however also die on 20 December 1984 after a long illness. With Ustinov out of the picture, most human obstacles in the way of making the T-72 the premier Soviet tank were now gone. While the T-80 was popular with its crews and had many good qualities, its fuel requirements still kept it from being considered the most practical tank overall by the Soviet Army.

The MOP had tasked the UVZ with designing an improved version of the T-72A on 1 January 1981, which had proceeded apace as development was already no longer being deliberately retarded by Ustinov, who was in increasing ill health. A week after Ustinov's death in 1984, the new variant, the T-72B, was on 27 December accepted for service. This had the new 1A40 fire control system, which proved simple and reliable in service, as well as the new 9K120 'Svir' (named after a river) laser-guided through-the-bore ATGM. The new 1G13 sight of the 1A40 system provided both laser ranging and missile guidance in a combined unit.

The tank also had a totally new turret using a new system of armour protection which was easier to install, maintain and upgrade than the one used in the T-64B and T-80B models. Dubbed 'Otrazheniye' (reflection), it used the concept of non-explosive reactive armour or 'bulge' armour. This would bulge when struck by kinetic projectiles and absorb their velocity.

ABOVE A T-72AV in post-Soviet Kharkiv in 1997. (Viktor Maskovsky)

LEFT A T-72AV without the 'Kontakt-1' ERA blocks demounted in storage in the 1990s.

The T-64B and T-80B used a hollow section in the bottom of the cast steel turret that was filled with aluminium cast over a matrix of ceramic balls – called 'Ultrafarfor' – to provide for increased protection from both HEAT and APFSDS rounds. While very effective, it was difficult to get the casting just right and not melt the wires holding the balls in a matrix; when that happened, they all wound up jammed together in the middle of the armour array and offered little protection. But the T-72B had its hollow cheeks filled with slanted stacked arrays of materials (rubber, aluminium, steel) spaced about 30mm apart and covering the frontal 60-degree arc of the turret. Very effective in use, this not only made it easier for repairing and returning tanks to combat, but also to upgrade as newer materials were developed.

As with the T-64B, a version of the tank without the 9K120 ATGM system was also built at the same time as the T-72B1. Approximately one in three tanks was fitted with the external 'nadboy' radiation shielding appliqué, as at the time it was still felt that tactical nuclear warfare was a viable concept for major wars and the lead tanks would need the protection.

In 1981, ChTZ in Chelyabinsk also began assembly of the T-72 tank, initially in moderate numbers, with 25 tanks being built in 1981, doubling to 50 in 1982 as full series production ensued. Production output doubled again in 1983 to 100 tanks, with production continuing at ChTZ until 1990, by which time 1,874 T-72A, T-72B and T-72B1 tanks had been built at the plant.

The further development and production of Soviet main battle tanks changed due to two events that took place during their production run. The first one occurred in 1982 when the Israel Defence Forces invaded Lebanon under Operation *Peace for Galilee* to shut down Syrian forces and their Hezbollah allies in that country. It marked the first time that the export T-72M tanks were used in combat, with mixed results, mostly due to Syrian mistakes, but the conflict also revealed the use of explosive reactive armour (ERA) protection on tanks in action. The IDF used M48 tanks fitted with 'Blazer' ERA and these proved nearly invulnerable to both RPGs and ATGMs fitted with HEAT warheads.

Soviet scientists from VNII-100 and VNII Stali had actually started working on this concept at the end of the Great Patriotic War to prevent damage from German *Panzerfaust* weapons. They eventually found the method of using two steel plates with a thin layer of explosives between them that would detonate when struck by a HEAT projectile and the jet stream from the warhead struck the explosives. The plates would then fly off in different directions, thereby deflecting the molten metal stream and preventing it from penetrating the main armour beneath. But when demonstrated to the General Staff and Soviet Army commanders, all of them to a man had stated that they did not want to mount explosives on the outsides of their tanks and add to any damage to the tank when it detonated!

An early Soviet T-72B1 during Soviet winter exercises in the 1980s.

When the IDF's 'Blazer' ERA was demonstrated for the General Staff and Soviet Army commanders in late 1982 (using a tank captured by the Syrians and shipped to Kubinka for evaluation) they were crestfallen at how 'safe' and effective it really was in reality. Orders were quickly drafted and in a very short period of time the 4A20 'Kontakt-1' ERA system went into production under the term 'dynamic protection' (DZ), or 'complex of dynamic protection' (KDZ).

By the mid 1980s the T-72 was meanwhile becoming more of a known entity than the still enigmatic T-64 and newer T-80, having seen combat in Lebanon and on a far greater scale during the Iran–Iraq War. On 9 May 1985 the Soviet Union commemorated the 40th Anniversary of Victory in Europe in World War II with a major military parade on Moscow's Red Square for foreign military attaché and public consumption. The parade included several new weapons systems, including the public debut of the new T-72B (T-72B1) tank, alongside the sole public appearance on Red Square of the T-64, in the form of the T-64B1, the only time the T-64 was ever displayed at the public event.

Starting in late 1985, the T-72B and T-72B1 began being fitted with the 'Kontakt-1' 'DZ' (ERA) system. The base tank designations were maintained in service in the Soviet Union (all subsequent T-72 models up to the T-72B3 being simply described as 'B' or by model year), but the models were for many years known as the T-72BV and T-72B1V by foreign military intelligence (V being 'vrzyvatelniy' or explosive armour fitted).*

Most other Soviet tanks were either retrofitted with the new system or like the T-64BV, T-64B1V, T-80BV and T-80B1V arrived from the factory fitted with it.

Based on demands from foreign clients, in 1987 a stripped-down version of the T-72B was offered for export as the T-72S 'Shilden'. The main differences

---

* In Soviet Army service the T-72BV was referred to only as the T-72B, the 'BV' designation widely applied in the West being an assumption on the basis that the earlier T-72A when fitted with ERA had been designated T-72AV.

Soviet T-72B1 tanks modified for fitment of 'Kontakt-1' ERA blocks during summer exercises in the 1980s.

were that it had none of the Nuclear, Biological, Chemical (NBC) protection or radiation liner components; it did use a V-84 engine and was offered with the option of an air conditioning system for hot weather operators. This placed the condenser unit in one of the former 'ZIP' stowage bins on the turret and had a compressor unit driven by the engine; however, at the time there were no foreign orders for this option.

An incident in 1986 unrelated to the Soviet Army and its tank operations would have an effect on Soviet NBC warfare tactics and also the future development of Soviet tanks, including the T-72, and armoured vehicles mounted on tank chassis. On 26 April 1986 Reactor No. 4 of the Chernobyl nuclear power station violently exploded when an emergency shutdown drill went horribly wrong. Once the immediate situation was stabilized, the Soviet Army was ordered to send in NBC personnel and radiation-lined vehicles including the T-55 based IMR-1 combat engineer vehicle to work on repairing the damage. But in short order the Soviets found to their horror that neither the 'nadboy' appliqué nor the 'podboy' radiation lining of the IMR vehicles was sufficient to shield the crews at such a highly radioactive ground zero site, and the tanks also suffered from gaps due to openings for their viewers and weapons system mounts as well as normal functioning items. Air cleaners proved dangerous as they pulled in massive amounts of radioactive dust, while engine cooling systems also sucked it into the engine bay and radiators where it represented a lingering danger for tank crews and service personnel alike.

MOP trouble-shooter Yuriy Kostenko was one of the men assigned to solve the problem, but it took time. Their final result was sealing as much of the IMR vehicles as was possible, removing all viewports and replacing them with remote control cameras, and adding massive amounts of lead shielding to the vehicles. Crews were also limited to no more than 30 minutes in the area of the reactor. As the vehicles could not be effectively decontaminated, once they became too 'hot' to use further they were moved out to a vehicle 'cemetery' and abandoned, where they remain to this day.

In view of this unexpected operational experience, enthusiasm for fitting tanks with not only the 'podboy' internal liner but the 'nadboy' external liners waned. The 'nadboy' liners were found to trap more radiation particles on the tank exterior than was desirable; the concept that a tank could easily cross a contaminated area and protect the crew was found to be flawed, although the nuclear reactor incident involved significantly more radiation exposure than theoretically moving quickly though a contaminated area. The whole subject of radiation protection was nevertheless revisited. The result was that few new production T-72B tanks were eventually fitted with the external liner and the entire concept of 'safe' tactical nuclear warfare was deemed unworkable. However, further testing showed that the 'podboy' liner did provide an additional advantage in that it stopped internal armour spalling when hit by kinetic projectiles, and thus was a useful retention.

But by the late 1980s the West had now fielded much improved tanks such as the M1A1 Abrams, the FV4030 Challenger 1 and the Leopard 2A4 series tanks. All of them were modern and, while heavy, were very mobile tanks with thermal sights – something the Soviets were having massive problems with in development – and with guns that could penetrate most early model Soviet tanks at ranges of 1,500m or more.* On 19 June 1986, UVZ was tasked per Resolution 741-208 of the SM SSSR with developing a new version of the T-72B that could compete with these tanks on the battlefield.

But for once UVZ decided to try something different: simultaneously developing a revolutionary design and an evolutionary design and competitively testing them. The former became Obiekt-187 and the latter Obiekt-188.

Obiekt-187 was a completely different animal for the UVZ designers. It used a new hull design with a longer bow and no weak spots in the glacis: all of the three main battle tanks – T-64, T-72, T80 – had what the designers called a 'décolletage' in front of the driver-mechanic that was the weakest spot of the

---

* When the Soviet Union received detailed intelligence on the first generation of thermal vision systems being fielded abroad, Kartsev had been at the time against such systems, and had offered a new generation of infrared projectors as an alternative.

glacis due to his viewers and hatch projection. Obiekt-187 moved the driver back and made the glacis a solid piece.

The turret was no longer a casting with additional protection built into it, but now a welded structure with internal arrays that increased its kinetic armour protection from 650mm rolled homogenous armour (RHA) equivalent to 900mm RHA equivalent. It was fitted with the new 1A45T fire control system and mounted a 125mm 2A66 gun, an interim model between the 2A46 line and the proposed 2A82 gun. As there was more room in the new turret, it was designed to handle newer rounds like the 'Svinets-2' APFSDS round of increased penetration capability.

With six different prototypes fitted with different engines for testing, the top choice was a new design of engine, an X-type engine developed by Transmash in Barnaul in collaboration with ChTZ in Chelyabinsk as manufacturer and other enterprises that could produce 1,200 to 1,500hp based on its stage of development. Six tanks were built for trials evaluation, but after testing were not considered viable at the time and dropped. One reason is that the tanks required a lot of electronics and computer controls that were not readily available or considered financially viable at the time.

On the other hand, Obiekt-188 was an improved model of the T-72, intended to bring the T-72 tank close to the operational characteristics of the T-80U/UD derived from the Obiekt-219 prototypes. The design offered significant improvements, but did have some new wrinkles added in. First, it used built-in ERA in the form of the new 'Kontakt-5' system that was also partially effective against APFSDS ammunition. It added the new 1A45T modification of the 1A45 'Irtish' fire control system, which in some prototypes was fitted with a thermal sight system, partially linked to the fire control system. The commander and gunner had a small thermal viewer that was separate from the sight and located on the level of their laps, so it was difficult to view in operation.

The tank now used the V-84S version of the V-2 engine design with more power (840hp), and also added a new feature: exhaust cooling. The Soviet military well understood that the West used thermal sights and could easily spot the exhaust emissions from their tanks in the dark, so an attempt was made to cool the exhaust by what was dubbed a 'Silfon' or duct that pulled in cold air from the air intake and mixed it with the exhaust gases to cool them down upon exiting the tank.

The tank also added the first integrated electro-optical defence system of any tank in the world. Dubbed the KOEhP or 'Shtora-1', the system was designed to automatically detect threats from laser rangefinders and laser ATGM guidance systems and either jam them or block the tank from view. It consisted of four 'fine grain' sensors and four 'coarse grain' sensors, each with a 50-degree field of view, mounted on the turret with aspect views of roughly 45, 135, 225 and 315 degrees to cover the entire tank. One set reacted to laser rangefinders and the other to laser target designators. When struck by a laser beam, they automatically swivelled the turret in the direction of the threat while warning the crew; if a rangefinder, it fired Type 902 'Tucha' smoke grenades to cover the tank's retreat. If a targeting laser, the two TShU-11 projector lights on either side of the hull started blinking strobe-fashion with IR light to disrupt the missile guidance tracker. The twin projectors glowed orange when working, giving the tank a particularly eerie appearance when operating. They could also work as either IR or white searchlights.

The first two prototypes of the Obiekt-188 began state trials in January 1989, which proved particularly successful. However, several seminal events took place which would delay both the tank's eventual acceptance for service – and also its ultimate service designation.

Starting on 9 November 1989 the Warsaw Pact began to disintegrate with the literal fall of the Berlin Wall. Shortly thereafter, the rest of the Warsaw Pact nations withdrew, changed governments, and the Soviet groups of forces left East Germany, Poland, Czechoslovakia and Hungary. Concurrently, Romania, Bulgaria and the Soviet Baltic Republics starting with Lithuania began to break away and declare independence. While diehard Soviet *apparatchiks* tried to prevent total disintegration starting in December 1990, it was obvious that Premier Mikhail Gorbachev agreed with the independence movements. On 19 August 1991, a coup was staged against him by hardcore Party members including Minister of Defence Yazov, but Armed Forces Commander Pavel Grachev refused to participate and the coup quickly collapsed with Chairman of the Supreme Soviet Union Boris Yeltsin backing Gorbachev. Four months later the Soviet Union would be dissolved into its constituent republics, with the Russian Federation retaining the largest landmass but only about 40 per cent of the Soviet population.

Meanwhile, in the Middle East, events were brewing that would also have a bearing on the future development of the T-72 tank. On 2 August 1990, Saddam Hussein of Iraq invaded neighbouring Kuwait to both take back Iraq's '19th Province' as defined by Iraq and to wipe out the large debt Iraq owed to the rulers of that country that had helped finance Iraq's war with Iran from 1980 to 1988. The US, backed by a UN resolution, formed a coalition of nations to force Saddam Hussein to leave Kuwait. On 17 January 1991 Operation *Desert Shield* became *Desert Storm*, with war between the Coalition and Iraq. The ground phase of the war began on 19 February 1991, and by 28 February the war was over, with Iraq soundly defeated.

A T-72B1 with 'Kontakt-1' ERA armour fitment, Dagestan, August–September 1999.

According to Coalition sources, Iraq lost more than 1,860 tanks in that war, with significant losses of T-72 tanks. Consisting of a combination of Soviet-built T-72M and T-72M1 tanks as well as others from Poland and Czechoslovakia, all that were encountered by Coalition forces were destroyed, captured or abandoned, with no losses to Coalition tanks. While Soviet analysts knew they were not equivalent to the Soviet domestic tanks, the reports of how easily they were defeated did not greatly help Soviet tank sales on the international arms market.

As events leading to the First Gulf War were unfolding in the Middle East in 1990, another event closer to home in the Soviet Union had a major impact on the development of the T-72 tank, and Soviet and future Russian Federation tank development in general. This was the signing on 19 November 1990 of the Treaty on Conventional Forces in Europe (the CFE Treaty), which came into force in July 1992, by which time the entire geopolitical landscape between the Soviet Union and NATO nations had changed. As part of the agreement, the Soviet Union committed to the verifiable reduction of most classes of weapons, with tank numbers on the European landmass west of the Ural Mountains to be a total of 20,000, to be mirrored by NATO countries. In order to comply, all excess tank inventory was to be scrapped within three years (i.e. by 1995). In June 1991, the Soviet Union pledged to destroy the first 6,000 tanks. While many tanks had been moved to strategic storage east of the Ural Mountains long before the Treaty was signed, and large numbers of ageing T-54, T-55 and T-62s were consigned to being cut up for scrap, many almost new T-72 and T-80 tanks were also so consigned, the fields of such abandoned tanks being regularly shown in the press around the world in the early 1990s. In 1990, the Soviet Union had 5,086 T-72 tanks of all modifications in the European part of the USSR as defined in the Treaty. As regards individual Soviet republics, 246 T-72 tanks were located in Armenia, 314 in Azerbaijan, 1,607 in Belorussia, 251 in Georgia and 1,045 in Ukraine. In 1992, the now post-Soviet Russian Federation retained 1,980 T-72 tanks in European Russia west of the Ural Mountains. The overall tank scrappage target originally agreed in 1990 was not achieved by 1995, at which time a five-year extension to the year 2000 was granted. To the surprise of many analysts, General-Lieutenant Dmitriy Volkogonov later declared that prior to the break-up the USSR had a total of 77,000 tanks under its control, going back as far as World War II vintage T-34-85 and IS-2 tanks held in long-term strategic storage.

In 1990, the T-72B with the 1K13-49 combination sight and 9K120 'Svir' ATGM launch capability was meanwhile paraded on Moscow's Red Square, such that foreign observers could maintain currency on the tank's development progress versus the T-72B1. Twenty-five T-72B tanks of the 2nd Guards Tamanskaya Motorized Rifle Division were paraded alongside 25 T-80UD tanks of the 4th Guards Kantemirovskaya Tank Division during the 9 May Victory Parade and the 7 November October Revolution anniversary parade the same year. Though it was unimaginable at the time, the November 1990 parade was to be the final Soviet-era Red Square military parade, and also the final Soviet-era public appearance of the T-72 tank. The T-72 tank would reappear on Moscow's streets the following year – but on this occasion integral to putting down a failed coup attempt.

At the beginning of what would prove a historic year in Soviet and Russian history, the Obiekt-188 tank was after the aforementioned prolonged trials recommended for production and service by a joint decision of the MO and MOP on 27 March 1991 as the T-72BM, subject to state approval. Further geopolitical events would however overtake these plans. Feedback on the performance of Iraqi-crewed T-72s in the First Gulf War was also taken on board by the designers at UVZ, the MO and the MOP, such that a final decision was again delayed pending further review. The overwhelming majority of armour losses in the war were due to air-power and artillery. Nevertheless, UVZ made the decision that the armour and protection elements of the Obiekt-188 required further upgrading which was undertaken in the following months as the Soviet

Union endured rapid change. On 30 September 1992 a small Establishment Lot of the latest modification of the Obiekt-188 underwent state acceptance trials, repeating the process that the previous prototypes had undergone at the beginning of 1991, but now for acceptance approval for the Russian rather than the Soviet Army.

The final 'Soviet-era' production version of the T-72 was as noted evaluated for service acceptance at a time of massive geopolitical change, as the Soviet Union was dissolved into constituent former Soviet and now independent republics during the final months of the tank's development. The delay in introducing the improved T-72BM and its formal acceptance as a new tank design was during the momentous end-game period in Soviet history. There were armed clashes and military interventions in several Soviet republics, an attempted coup in Moscow followed by the dissolution of the Soviet Union and related resignation of its President, Mikhail Gorbachev, with the Soviet Union formally ceasing to exist as a legal entity on 26 December 1991. T-72 tanks of the 2nd Guards Tamanskaya MRD had been deployed in Moscow during the earlier failed coup attempt there in August 1991, and it was from the top of a T-72 tank parked outside the Russian 'Beliy Dom' (White House) parliament building that Boris Yeltsin made his famous speech regarding the aspirations and hopes of the Russian and Soviet people in a rapidly deteriorating internal political situation.

After the dissolution of the Soviet Union, military purchases in the Russian Federation and in all of the former republics were cut down to nearly zero, with money spent on shoring up civil infrastructure. Tanks were no longer a priority in the new post-Cold War era, and production of the T-80 was halted at LKZ in Leningrad, as was T-80 production at Kharkov, now Kharkiv in independent Ukraine. In the meantime, the Obiekt-188 prototypes underwent extensive testing on the UVZ test polygon in Nizhny Tagil, at Kubinka in the Moscow oblast, in Central Asia and in Siberia, covering a total distance travelled of 14,000km without serious defects or requiring capital repair.

One year later, following the final proving trials conducted in the first week of October 1992, the same Boris Yeltsin, now the first President of the Russian Federation, signed Resolution No. 759-58 of the Russian Government on 5 October 1992, accepting the Obiekt-188 (technically the T-72BM) into service with the Russian Army as the T-90 main battle tank, with a related decision to sell the T-90S export variant abroad concurrently with deliveries of the domestic T-90 to the Russian Army. At the time service acceptance was approved, the new tank was actually referred to in official documents as the T-72BU (U-Usovershenstvovanniy – T-72B improved), and the intent had as noted been to take it into service as the T-72BU (BM). The decision to change

The fate of many T-72 tanks in the 1990s. A subsequently upgraded Obiekt-172M (T-72) at the Strelnya strategic storage facility near St Petersburg.

the designation to T-90 – 'the first tank of the Russian Federation' – was made by President Boris Yeltsin, making a clean 'marketing' break from its Soviet lineage. From this point onward the T-90 lineage for several years diverged from that of the preceding T-72, albeit with an interesting turn in events with regard to the earlier T-72 being reinvigorated in later years.

At another point in history, the T-72 would have gradually been replaced in service by the newer T-90, and over time been relegated to secondary roles, or further offered for export. The development of the T-72 tank series was far from complete, however, and in later years the T-72 would, uniquely in Soviet and Russian tank design history, hold its own 'coup' by re-entering series production (actually capital rebuild as a new tank model) at what would in other circumstances have been near the end of its service life. The new T-72 modifications brought the tank up to a similar level of combat capability as the T-90 that had replaced it in production, effectively replacing the later T-90 tank designed to replace the original T-72, and at much reduced unit cost.

This dramatic change in fortune for the Soviet-era T-72 tank was very much due to the changed environment since 1991, with less need (as it seemed at the time) for tanks in domestic service, and consequently fewer orders, drastically reduced budgets, and basic interest. The T-72 would, however, three decades later, in what would in other circumstances be typically the end of a tank's operational service life, be operationally deployed in large numbers in a major war ostensibly between two former Soviet states.

Back in 1992, with the T-90 formally taking over the mantle of 'main production tank type' from the T-72, the thought that the older T-72 that had effectively already 'served its time' would still be in service, including in Russian Army service combat operations, three decades hence was hard to imagine, either in the Russian Federation or abroad. In 1992, the T-72B, which had just been technically replaced in production by the new T-90, was still a new tank and not yet ready for capital rebuilding; however, the ongoing lessons learned from combat in Afghanistan and by foreign client states and other technical advances indicated that improvements had to be made for improved firing accuracy and not least crew safety. As a result, some of the modifications made for the T-55 and T-62 due to experiences in Afghanistan and more recently with the T-72 and T-80 in Chechnya were later adapted to the T-72B, including a mine resistant floor plate and a suspended driver-mechanic's seat. The tank also was given a new environmental sensor system which used a mast mounting to determine wind direction and speed and air density, which fed into the sighting system. Finally, the tank began to be fitted with the V-84MS engine installation with the 'Silfon' exhaust cooling system.

The revised tank was designated during development as the Obiekt-184A for T-72Bs and Obiekt-184A1 for T-72B1s. Approximately 30 to 60 tanks a year were put through the upgrade system, with other incremental upgrades undertaken concurrently. Tanks began to be fitted with the new UMSh universal twin-pin tracks based on the T-80 tank track design, and those tanks fitted with ERA were upgraded to the newer 'Kontakt-5' ERA suite. However, it was not until 1998 that Western intelligence agencies spotted the differences in the tanks. Approximately 750 tanks were estimated as having gone through rebuilding, with the previous T-72B designation being retained in operational service despite the changes.

In the new realities of the post-Soviet Russian Federation, the export version of the T-72B with ERA – designated at the time T-72S – was paraded in 1995 at the 50th Anniversary of the Victory in Europe in 1945 held in Moscow.* In the early to mid 1990s, the Russian Federation and Ukraine competed for international export sales, both countries at the time having the same domestic problem of tank production capability but a lack of defence ministry orders, hence looking abroad to maintain sales, and with that to retain experienced staff for the future. The T-72S tanks demonstrated in Moscow in 1995 were ultimately absorbed into the Russian Army as standard T-72B tanks rather than being exported to Iran, to where the majority of T-72S tanks were sold.

With the advent of the T-90, customers (and the Russian Army) meantime also wanted an improved version of the T-72B. Under what was designated Project 'Rogatka' (slingshot) the UVZ developed what was felt to be the ultimate variant of the T-72, the T-72B2. First publicly displayed in 2006, this tank incorporated the latest developments to include:

---

* Although officially described at the time as T-72S, the tanks were effectively Russian T-72B tanks with the 1K13-49 combination sight but reduced side 'Kontakt-1' armour.

In the second decade of the 21st century, the T-72 underwent a major rebuild and modernization programme, with the earlier T-72BA/BM/B1/B2 modifications merging via the T-72B M-1989 into the T-72B3 (Obiekt-184-3) series, as seen here at the Army 2015 exhibition near Moscow. (Andrey Aksenov)

- Built-in 'Relikt' third generation ERA protection on the glacis and attached protection on the turret and forward skirt sections, now made of light steel plates and rubber;
- 'Reshotka' slat armour grilles on the rear sides and rear of the tank;
- V-92S engine of 1,000hp fitted with the 'Silfon' cooling device;
- T-90 style wide wheels with UMSh tracks;
- 2A46M-5 improved gun with more rigidity in the barrel;
- An integrated fire control system based around the Belarusian 'Sosna-U' thermal sight (using the licence-built French CATHARINE thermal imager) and laser rangefinder and missile guidance system, the TIUS tank information and control system, the DVE-BS meteorological sensor mast, and coupled to a UUI-2 muzzle reference system and a thermal jacketed barrel;
- R-168 digital radio sets replacing the older R-173 and R-163 series radio sets;
- All of the previous T-72BA upgrades;
- The 'Nakidka' thermal blanketing system to suppress the tank's infrared heat signature.

The tank was offered in two options: major warfare, with more 'Relikt' coverage and the 'Nakidka' blankets, and urban warfare, with more 'Reshotka' sections and no blankets.

An export rebuilding version using most of the same components was offered for the T-72M1 as the T-72M1M, which fitted most of these components to that tank but left its basic armour and hull protection as it was.

A T-72B3 at the Alabino polygon near Moscow in 2019. (Esa Muikku)

The upgrades proved relatively expensive, however, and as a result the Duma vetoed spending the money. So, the factory and MOP decided to see if they could produce a 'reduced cost' version of the improved T-72B with as many T-72B2 improvements incorporated as possible. Somewhat ironically, it was also determined that the T-72B2 was a better tank than the then in-production flagship T-90 Model 1992.

The Russian Army had meanwhile since 1991 continued to operate its ageing Soviet-era tank inventory without substantial investment in upgrades or replacement models, and by the middle of the first decade of the 21st century, much of the Soviet-era military inventory still in use was in urgent need of replacement. There began a gradual revamp of all manner of military equipment development, with an associated increase in design bureau activity and defence procurement budgets and a gradual recovery from the fiscal and military capability doldrums of the 1990s.

On 9 May 2008, the Russian Federation held the first full-scale military parade on Red Square since the closing days of the Soviet Union in 1990, now ostensibly commemorating 'Victory Day' as opposed to the Russian Revolution or May Day as was the case in the Soviet era. At the time, the reasoning was generally accepted as a mix of factors: the focus of the population on the sacrifices of the generation that had fought in World War II, national unity in general, and to showcase the emerging new generation of 'tekhnika' or military equipment. It was also the beginning of a re-armament programme that signalled a change in the trust factor that had been so very prevalent in the Russian Federation of the 1990s. In 2008, NATO announced that Ukraine was eligible to become a NATO member state, which the Russian government made clear was considered an existential threat for the Russian Federation. On 12 December 2007, a few months before the inaugural post-Soviet Red Square parade, just as rehearsals were beginning in the Moscow suburbs, the Russian Federation had also suspended its CFE treaty implementation. Geopolitics had changed, though the general public in the Russian Federation and in the US and Europe would remain oblivious to the subtle changes for many years to come. The Russian Army was gradually modernized technically and operationally, and military production expanded and reorganized. On 10 May 2023, the Russian Federation would formally withdraw from the Soviet-era CFE Treaty altogether.

In August 2008, there was a short five-day war between the Russian Federation and Georgia, as described in Chapter 5. The significance for the T-72 was that Russian T-72 tanks were engaged in combat against Georgian T-72AV and B1 tanks of similar vintage, some of the latter having been upgraded by foreign states. In a situation that had occurred in Chechnya and would later repeat on a much larger scale in the former Ukrainian Donetsk and Lugansk regions, in Ukraine and the Kursk oblast of the Russian Federation, Soviet-era designed T-72 tanks were being used in combat between two former Soviet states.

Meanwhile, the T-72B upgrade development programme continued, resulting in 2010 in the T-72B3 version, which would soon thereafter become a series production model. This tank uses the basic T-72BA upgrades but with the addition of the 'Sosna-U' sight complex, the 2A46M-5 gun, the V-92S2 engine in place of the V-84MS as available, and also the UMSh tracks. It also added another new development: a camming version of the autoloader that now permits the tank to use ammunition up to 10cm longer (APFSDS rounds like 'Svinets-2') with greater armour penetration. While slightly cheaper in most respects than the T-72B2 variant, it provides most of the advantages of that tank. The T-72B3, now as the T-72B3M, was first seen in public on Moscow's Red Square during the 9 May 2017 Victory Parade, somewhat ironically replacing the later developed T-90A at that annual memorial event.

Returning a few years to when the T-72 was initially deployed abroad, Ustinov had prevented the T-72 tank from going into the premier Soviet force groupings – the Group of Soviet Forces Germany or GSFG (DDR/GDR: East Germany) and the Southern Group of Forces (Hungary) – and only permitted them in the Northern Group of Forces (Poland), the Central Group of Forces (Czechoslovakia) and some of the Western Military District armies. GSFG was equipped with two armies of T-64s and three armies of T-80s by 1985, but there were no T-72s other than those in the Nationale Volksarmee (NVA) of East Germany.

The Soviet Union as noted had also begun to export the T-72 abroad since as early as 1975 at a time when the T-72 was a current tank in Soviet Army inventory. The T-72Э1 (T-72Eh-1) was the export version of the T-72, the T-72Э2, Э3 and Э4 were export versions of the T-72A, known abroad as the T-72M, with modifications to the turret armour, ammunition complement and

A T-72B3M on Tverskaya Ulitsa, Moscow on 6 May 2018 pending a Victory Parade rehearsal on Red Square.

'KZ' tank protection systems. The T-72Э5 and T-72Э6 were based on the late production model T-72A and known abroad from the end of the 1970s as the T-72M1. The 1987 developed T-72S (only formally designated as such in the post-Soviet era) was based on the T-72B with similar armour, ammunition and KZ protection adjustments as for earlier export models. The first export clients beyond Soviet states were Czechoslovakia, the DDR/GDR (East Germany) and Poland. Beyond the Warsaw Pact, tanks were exported relatively early in their production life to Algeria, Libya, Syria and Iraq. At the very end of the 1970s, the Soviet Union also provided Czechoslovakia with the production drawings to assemble the T-72 locally for domestic and export purposes, with the T-72 being produced there from 1981, with subsequent versions being designated T-72M and T-72M1. Poland began T-72 production under the same arrangement from 1982. In the decade from 1981 to 1991, Czechoslovakia produced 897 T-72, T-72M and T-72M1 tanks, with Poland in the same time period assembling 757 T-72 tanks. Yugoslavia at the beginning of the 1980s received a licence to locally produce the T-72, with India also receiving such a licence during the decade.

In the immediate post-Soviet era, the Russian Federation continued exports at a time when domestic 'sales' were practically non-existent due to an assumed peace having been established in international politics, with the resultant lack of interest and demand for tanks domestically. In the post-Soviet era, several former Soviet republics, particularly Ukraine, developed their own upgrades of the T-72 tank, as did Poland, the Czech and Slovakian republics and Yugoslavia, while China, India, Iran and Pakistan all developed indigenous versions of the original Soviet tank. As such the full story of the T-72 is, as might be expected, immense, hence the concentration in this book on Soviet and post-Soviet state T-72 tanks. These provide the core of a much more extensive subject, as would be expected considering the extremely long production and service history at home and abroad. To this day, the T-72 in its various iterations can be found in many foreign armies, often in not so small quantities.

The modern Russian Army today in the third decade of the 21st century is primarily equipped with modernized late model T-72s, T-80s and the later T-90/T-90M tanks. In response to a changing geopolitical situation, Russia postponed the development of the high-technology but high-risk T-14 tank design in favour of major rebuild modifications to the tried and proven T-72 and T-80 tanks more suited to mass conventional warfare – and mass production. As has been shown on the battlefield in the present time, all tanks, whether the latest or long-serving and proven models, have been destroyed by new generations of weapons, not least drones. At the time of writing, Russian new-build tanks are now being provided with additional drone protection 'Reshotka', while the T-90M is being redesigned to incorporate its own reconnaissance drone as part of its defensive systems.

With regard to the T-64, to which the T-72 was the proverbial troublesome black sheep in the early 1970s when the tanks (or rather their respective design bureaus) were vying for position, all T-64s were taken out of Russian inventory in the 1990s, as, having been built in Kharkov (today Kharkiv in independent Ukraine), they were more difficult to service and maintain after 1991. The T-64 and its later modifications have meantime served the Ukrainian Army well in recent combat. A small number of T-64 tanks also continue to serve in the Donets and Lugansk autonomous republics (DNR and LNR respectively).

The T-72 was in full series production at Uralvagonzavod (UVZ) in Nizhny Tagil from 1974 until 1990, and also at ChTZ from 1981 to 1990, with 20,544 tanks having been delivered during that time, with the total number of T-72 tanks and foreign derivatives built being over 30,000 according to Russian sources. The tank was built in several major series, with innumerable upgrades also being undertaken in batches during 'capremont' (capital rebuild), such that few tanks over time retained their original specification – or appearance. The T-72 tank is also as previously noted unique in Soviet and now Russian tank development history, in that the B3 and most recent B3M versions have been upgraded to such an extent that they effectively rendered their original replacement – the T-90 – as being less cost effective than the tank it replaced, the rebuilding of existing tanks being more efficient for mass production, which is a major consideration in defence planning in the 21st century.

With thousands of T-72 tanks still in active combat service today more than half a century after the tank entered series production, the T-72 in its many upgraded models is destined to remain front and centre of modern conflicts for many years to come.

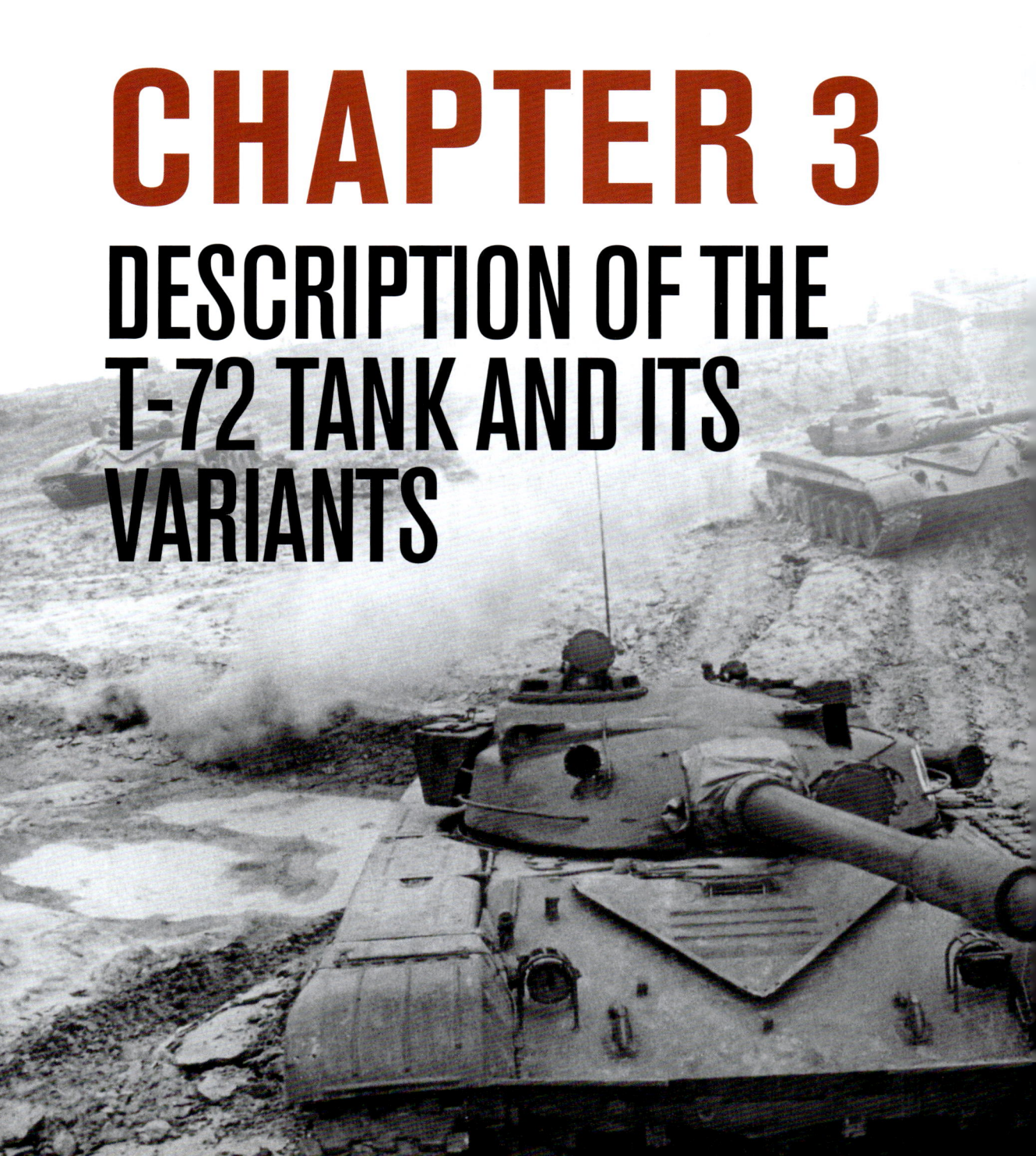

CHAPTER 3
DESCRIPTION OF THE T-72 TANK AND ITS VARIANTS

Obiekt-172M tanks during Soviet manoeuvres. Note the early turret with the original L2 series searchlight to the left of the barrel. (Sergei Popsuevich)

OVERVIEW

Soviet tanks tended to follow rather linear development plans, but readers should note that since the beginning of the Soviet tank industry tanks were often modified mid production run without any changes being noted in their designators. An early production tank and a late production tank of the same type may have the same designator but have a large number of parts and components changed or modified, such that a T-72A or T-72B may completely change external appearance and yet still be labelled simply as 'A' or 'B' in service. While for example the US Army does this via Modification Work Orders or MWOs, the Soviet Union did not use such a system. Chronological tank production model year 'M-xxxx' designations were used by the production plant, but can thereafter be somewhat arbitrary due to later modifications, with 'capremont' (capital repair/rebuild) work being carried out on relatively small batches of tanks at a time after 14,000km/12,000km (first/second capital rebuilds), which results in few tanks looking identical despite their initial designators. The T-72 series of tanks reflects this Soviet-era norm.

OBIEKT-172 (1968)

Per directions from the MOP dated 5 January 1968, Kharkov shipped two early production T-64A tanks to Nizhny Tagil for conversion to use the new V-45 diesel engine. This engine was higher, longer and heavier than the 5TDF engine used by Kharkov, and it was not designed to provide power off both ends of the crankshaft. The installation of the Transmash (Barnaul)-developed and ChTZ (Chelyabinsk)-built V-45 engine at UVZ would thereby need some rework in order to accommodate the new engine and attach the twin 7-speed gearboxes of the T-64A.

The rework required the rear of the hull to be sectioned and a new rear assembly welded onto the existing T-64A hull. UVZ used their classical installation of the V-45 with the initially 730hp engine sitting transversely at the front of the engine bay, offset to the left, and the air cleaner and air intake

A later production Obiekt-172M (i.e. series production T-72 Ural) crossing a river on a GSP ferry. Note the new L2 IR projector location.

on the right. For power take-off, the normal UVZ 'guitara' transfer case was used, but due to the restrictions on using as much of the donor T-64A as possible a new power transfer and splitter assembly was designed to deliver the engine power to the transmissions.

As Kartsev and his team did not like the 'extraction' cooling system of the T-64A – one that uses the pressure from the engine exhaust to create a vacuum and draw cool air through the radiators – they installed traditional UVZ radiators in the middle of the engine compartment over the power transmission components. This needed an extractor fan to draw the air through the radiators, and so a mechanism was added to drive the fan from the transfer and splitter box. The fan was however larger than the ones in the T-55 and T-62, so the designers leaned it backwards (with the hull rear angled to the same degree) and placed it offset to the left side of the hull. The oil cooler was mounted to the left of the fan but was cooled by the airflow it created inside the engine bay. As with all previous UVZ designs, airflow could be regulated by 'zhaluzi' (louvres) below the external grilles.

All other elements of the T-64A were kept intact. These included its complete running gear – thin cast aluminium road wheels with internal buffering and no rubber tyres, lightweight twin-pin cast track links, three piston-type shock absorbers (on road wheel positions 1, 2 and 6) and three return rollers. The turret was also maintained intact, with its TPN-1-49 sight and cross-turret coincidence rangefinder, an L-2 searchlight mounted to the left of the gun, and its 28-round mechanical loader inside the turret.

This used a rotating carousel with each complete round stowed in an articulated frame. The projectile was stowed flat on the floor and the propellant charge (combustible casing and steel stub casing or 'poddon') stuck up at a 90-degree angle. Loading was accomplished by elevating the frame and straightening it out as it approached the breech. When the 'fork' with the projectile was opposite the breech, both projectile and charge were rammed into it at the same time.

When the two prototypes underwent testing, the engine and power transmission worked reasonably well even with the normal problems with the new V-45 engine. But the running gear had numerous problems and proved fragile, and the mechanical loader was capricious and often would not operate correctly if the hull was canted right or left. Valeriy Venediktov asked Leonid Kartsev if he could make changes to the tank to improve its functionality; Kartsev passed the request on to the MOP and received permission to make any changes that they saw fit to use on the tank, resulting in the Obiekt-172M. A total of 17 Obiekt-172 prototypes with the original T-64A running gear were built in 1968–69.

OBIEKT-172M (1968)

Having received the go-ahead via Kartsev, V. N. Venediktov at TsKBTM completely reworked the design of the tank, making significant changes. Venediktov's design team used the entire suspension from the Obiekt-167 chassis; this consisted of six twin 780mm by 90mm road wheels, cast aluminium with rubber tyres, on each side of the hull in place of the thin Kharkov road wheels. One innovation by the UVZ designers in using these wheels was that they were actually two separate disks held together by eight large bolts. Previously the wheels for the T-55 and T-62 (and late T-54s) were one unit cast together, with separate tyres fitted to both disks.

The piston-action shock absorbers were replaced by the UZV-preferred lever-action type that used a rotary motion with a lever connected to the road wheel arm to provide damping. Only three return rollers were used on this tank and the drive sprockets were changed over to initially use the standard T-54/55/62 OMSh open-hinged track links, but after one prototype was fitted with them the rest of the prototypes changed over to use the more durable RMSh tracks. These had a rubber bushing in the hinges and a life span of 5,000–7,000km.

The mechanical changes to the power plant and driveline made for the Obiekt-172 were retained with minor modifications and improvements. The

TOP An early production Obiekt-172M with the L2 IR illuminator to the left of the gun barrel.

RIGHT An Obiekt-172M belonging to the UVZ museum on display in Nizhny Tagil in 1998. Note the searchlight position. (Alexandr Koshchavtsev)

engine was the improved V-45K now developing 780hp.* The powerplant used the 'guitara' transfer case and power splitter case to the twin 7-speed transmissions. These had a synchronized shift mechanism that changed both transmission gears simultaneously. Steering was by skid braking of each side, as standard.

The composite glacis of the T-64A was retained – a sandwich of two layers of steel armour with a centre section of fibreglass, 80mm steel plus 105mm

---

* The 'K' was rumoured to stand for Kartsev as it was the engine for 'his' tank. (However, as it was built at ChTZ, renamed ChKZ in 1941 after the evacuation of KV heavy tank production tooling from the LKZ 'Kirov' plant in Leningrad, 'Kirov' is a more likely explanation, or perhaps 'Kompressor'.)

Obiekt-172M tanks of the 44th Tank Training Regiment, Vladimir, 1988.

fibreglass plus 20mm steel, all set at 68 degrees from the vertical. Equivalent RHA protection was 550–600mm against known threats in the late 1960s. The tank also used the cast homogenous armour turret of the T-64A with all of the T-64A components intact, to include the L-2 searchlight mounted on the left side of the gun. It used the TPD-2-49 sight/rangefinder with a cross-turret coincidence rangefinder and TPN-1-49 night sight; the commander was provided with a TKN-3 sight. The gunner sat on the left, but unlike previous tanks the commander now sat on the right.

The main gun was the 2A26 version of the 125mm D-81T gun using separate loading ammunition stowed in cassettes under the turret floor. This used the very slick 'Zhelud' (acorn) autoloader system consisting of an elevator, a rammer and a stub casing ejector. Once an indexed projectile was selected, doors in the floor opened up and the elevator, mounted angled to the rear, pulled the cassette up to the top. The projectile was loaded into the lower compartment of the cassette, and the propellant charge in the upper compartment. It stopped with the lower compartment opposite the open breech, with the gun at a slight upward angle (around 2 degrees 30 minutes of arc). The rammer would then ram the projectile, retract, drop the cassette down, ram the propellant charge, and then drop the cassette into the floor. When the gun fired, a small fork would grab the expended stub casing, open a hatch in the rear of the turret roof, and forcibly eject the casing to a distance of up to 7m behind the tank. This feature caused the only modification to the T-64A turret: a bump-out in the centre rear of the turret to accommodate the loader elevator and also the hatch for stub casing ejection.

An Obiekt-172M in strategic storage in Ukraine during the 1990s. With independence, Ukraine inherited a large number of Soviet-era T-72 tanks of different modifications.

Ammunition consisted of a variety of High Explosive – Fragmentation (HE-FRAG), APFSDS and HEAT rounds stowed inside the fighting compartment. Twenty-two rounds were loaded into the autoloader cassettes, and another 17 were stowed around the inside of the fighting compartment. Projectiles were around 700 to 900mm in length, and propellant casings around 400mm. Three charges and four projectiles were stowed forward in a 'stellazh' combination fuel tank and ammunition rack to the right of the driver;* nine propellant charges were stowed in the larger rear 'stellazh' tank behind the autoloader, with six projectiles stowed on the firewall; five more charges were stowed around the available spaces next to the turret or on the turret floor, as were three projectiles; three more projectiles were stowed on the left wall of the hull above the autoloader. The tank used a coaxial 7.62mm PKT machine gun and its ammunition, some 2,000 rounds in eight 250-round canisters, was also stowed around the inside of the fighting compartment. The T-72 and its 125mm main armament was designed for a typical direct-fire engagement range of 960–1,000m, and could penetrate 290–340mm of vertical RHA armour at ranges of up to 2,000m.

The tank was fitted with the new OPVT underwater driving system based on the one developed in 1966 for the T-62 medium tank. Unlike the T-64A, which needed a snorkel for air intake as well as one for the exhaust system to provide

* The Russian term 'stellazh' literally refers to a fuel tank with stowage internal to it rather than simply a stowage rack.

A surviving early 'hybrid' Obiekt-172M tank located in Ekaterinburg. Early prototypes were fitted with modified T-64A turrets. Note the commander's cupola. (Esa Muikku)

extraction cooling, the Obiekt-172M only need a single snorkel. This was the current three-section type as used on the T-55 and T-62 and compacted down to around 1.25m in length, making a 3.8m-long tube when assembled. Due to the fact that the tank did not have an MK-4 viewer to replace with the snorkel as on the other tanks, a small hatch was fitted to the gunner's hatch and the snorkel attached to that opening. It retained the same concept of inflatable seals on the turret race, a bilge pump in the front of the engine bay, and permanently attached covers for the radiator air intakes on the engine deck under a reinforced steel cover. On this tank, the covers for the two sections of the radiator air exhaust were hinged at the rear of the hull to cover the openings when preparing for wading. A four-port 'flapper' was bolted to the engine exhaust port to prevent water entrance. The tank was also fitted with an automatic opening device to pop the engine hatches open when the tank emerged from the water.

The tank also now fitted the 'Soda' anti-napalm and fire suppression system developed by Chelyabinsk and first fitted to the T-62 tank. This used a number of heat sensors and two fixed bottles of suppressant to extinguish fires in the engine bay.

Communications were provided by an R-123 VHF FM radio of 10 to 20 watts power output, connected to an R-124 tank intercom system with a TPU-A1 (commander) or TPU-A2 (driver and gunner) at each crew position.

The first three Obiekt-172M prototypes were developed in 1968 and 1969, with three prototypes and a mock-up for component testing being built in 1970. In 1971 a further three prototypes were built, plus 15 Obiekt-172M tanks for military trials. In 1972 nine 'pre-series' tanks were built based on the findings of the 1971 trials plus another ten tanks for further military trials. In 1973 the first 30 tanks destined for Soviet Army service were completed.

These views show a column of T-72 M-1978 tanks, with modified sighting and IR searchlight locations. These are in fact T-72M export models in domestic service. Note the fire extinguisher container where the original TPD2-49 sight port has been deleted.

OBIEKT-173 (1968-70)

As the UVZ soon received additional T-64A tanks for developmental purposes, an attempt was made to see if the UVZ designed OKR 'Zhelud' autoloader could be fitted to the T-64A as a matter of course. Three tanks were converted, but even though testing appears to have been successful no further efforts were made in this area. Kharkov refused to use this design due to two reasons: first, it only held 22 rounds versus their own design with 28, and second, they had not invented it.

T-72 'URAL' MAIN BATTLE TANK (1970-75)

There were three Obiekt-172M prototypes built in 1970 and a further 15 built for initial service evaluation trials (rebuilt prototypes conflate the figures slightly) plus 30 tanks built in 1973 for prolonged operational service evaluation. After the tank was formally adopted for service as the T-72 'Ural' some additional changes were introduced to the full series production models of the tank.

The tank received existing production versions of most of its initial equipment, such as the 2A26M version of the 125mm D-81T gun. This had some refinements, but the main differences were that it was now designed to operate with the 'Zhelud' autoloader and was fitted with a thermal shroud to reduce the effect of heat changes on the barrel reducing accuracy. Fire control was now by the improved TPD-2-49 gunner's sight, which also retained the optical coincidence rangefinder. The tank was also fitted with the 2Eh28M 'Siren' two-axis hydro-electric armament stabilizer.

In 1974, during series production, the tank was fitted with an integral tourelle mount for the new 12.7mm NST machine gun for use against helicopters and light vehicles. This was now mounted on the commander's cupola instead of the previous mounting on the loader's cupola. Six 50-round ammunition canisters were carried (300 rounds total) inside the turret and fighting compartment. The mount rotated separately from the commander's cupola, and when 'buttoned up' the gun was normally locked to the rear of the tank to not interfere with the commander's forward view of the battlefield.

The engine was upgraded to the series production version of the V-45K, now the V-46, that now produced 780hp. Minor changes were made to stowage and fuel capacity but the tank was still capable of 650-700km range on roads.

Externally, the biggest change was the movement of the L-2AG searchlight from the left side of the gun to its 'proper' (by UVZ standards) place above the coaxial machine gun port on the right side of the turret.

Some early production T-72 tanks were fitted with 'povorotny' (literally rotating) spring-out armour plates, but they were susceptible to damage and were replaced by skirts on the T-72A. These plates are fitted to a later production tank now located at the Tank Museum in Great Britain.

Two stowage (ZIP) bins were fitted to the turret, one on the right rear of the turret and one behind the turret. These stowed covers and fittings for the OPVT equipment and other components. Four ZIP bins along the left fender carried the necessary tools, cleaning rod for the main gun, spare parts and fittings for other components of the tank.

While most of the Obiekt-172M tanks were not fitted with a self-entrenching blade, the full series production T-72 was fitted with one from 1974. This was now a UVZ design and not a simple replication of the Kharkov design. In use a good crew could dig a hull-down scrape using the blade in about 20 minutes.

The tank retained things which had been 'rationalized' with the T-55 and T-72 such as the 'Soda' fire suppression system and the overpressure NBC protection system. It retained the new OPVT system introduced in the Obiekt-172M tanks and stowed the three-section snorkel on the rear of the turret, usually with one of the ZIP bins.

The communications system consisted of the R-123 VHF FM radio set and amplifier and the R-124 tank intercom system, with each crewmember having a TPU access port and the option to control the system. A variable height whip antenna was used with sections permitting antenna heights of 1, 3 or 4m, based on terrain and necessary range requirements.

One carryover from the T-64A 'parent' design was the use of the Kharkov-designed 'povorotnye ekrani' (turning screens) or 'flipper' armour panels, as described by NATO analysts, carried on the fenders. These were spring loaded plates made of 3mm aluminium sheet metal which swung out when placed in the operational position, opening to approximately a 60-degree angle. They covered the area to the side from the top of the road wheels to the turret race and were designed to provide overlapping protection for the frontal 60-degree arc of the tank from HEAT projectiles such as RPGs, ATGMs and tank gun rounds. They were found to be somewhat fragile as they tended to catch on brushwood when travelling cross country, and while not all of the tanks were so fitted they were soon replaced when the T-72A was introduced. The tank entered full series production in 1974 as the T-72 'Ural'. Two hundred and twenty T-72 series production tanks and three command tanks were built in 1974, effectively being the 'ustannovochnaya partiya' or establishment lot that determined the actual effectiveness of the T-72 in Soviet military service.

An early production T-72 with T-72A upgrades and a T-62 tank driving through an NBC decontamination station.

RIGHT An original Obiekt-172M (T-72) tank with later T-72A upgrades, including the reinforced fabric side skirts, located at Nevsky Pyatachok in 2019.

BOTH BELOW This T-72 tank, located at the T-34 Museum at Sholokovo, is described as a T-72 M-1978. It is an early production tank which has undergone capital rebuild during its service life, with later features such as the addition of radiation lining while retaining early features such as the housing for the TPD2-49 coincidence rangefinder-sight.

OBIEKT-175 (1975–76)

The Obiekt-175 (subsequently the T-72 'Ural-1') was a series of prototypes built and tested from 1975. Three prototypes were converted from series production T-72 tank chassis in 1975 and a further five in 1976, with another five tanks converted for long-term endurance testing of individual components for improving the series production T-72 MBT.

T-72 'URAL-1' TANK (1975–79)

During its production run the T-72 did receive a few incremental upgrades, with the biggest visible one being the replacement of the NII 'Staly' 'povorotnye ekrani' or rotating 'flipper' aluminium armour screens with steel reinforced rubber side skirts. Later changes included a 125mm D-81TM (2A26M2) gun and an improved V-46-4 engine. This tank was produced from 1975 to 1979.

T-72 WITH AIR CONDITIONING

Due to prospective sales to foreign clients with operations in desert conditions, in 1972 testing was carried out with a T-72 (Obiekt-172M) tank fitted with either the M-13 or M-13A 'Freon' air conditioners. While the tank completed testing, no further work was carried out with this project.

OBIEKT-172-2M 'BUYVOL' (1972–74)

While the early T-72s were undergoing testing, a second prototype of an improved T-72 was built by UVZ under the internal designator 'Buyvol' (buffalo)* designed to protect against 125mm equivalent sub-calibre ammunition. The first prototype was built in 1972, with seven subsequent prototypes with differing configurations built in total from 1971 to 1974, all in turn based on early pre-production Obiekt-172M tanks. The 'Buyvol' had improved armour protection, a 2A26M2 gun, a 'Zhasmin-2' armament stabilizer, a V-67 diesel engine developing 840hp, and an automatic air pre-heating device for starting the engine in cold weather. The first prototype (Obrazets No. 1) was tested concurrently with the 15 Obiekt-172M tanks subjected to prolonged trials under the direction of General Yu. M. Potapov in 1972. While it was an improvement on the T-72, due to what were seen as only incremental changes from the base tank (and not inconsequentially complete indifference on the part of Ustinov), the tank was not adopted for service. Some of its features, such as the steel skirting (16mm steel along the hull reducing to 5mm by the MTO (engine compartment) were however later added (in modified steel reinforced rubber form) to the T-72. A prototype 'Buyvol', based on an Obiekt-172M, Serial Number N10VT9678 (Н10ВТ9678) and rebuilt as an Obiekt-172-2M, survived the cutting torch for many years, being located in the Kubinka Yard.

---

* Although the buffalo is not native to Russia, the animal was well known throughout Russian history, with even ships having carried the name.

T-72K COMMANDER'S TANK (1974)

The traditional commander's version of the T-72 followed in 1974, with the usual changes made to accommodate a higher-level commander. The primary change was the addition of a second radio set: either the R-123 for commanders at company and initially battalion level or a new and superior R-130M HF AM radio set in place of the older R-112 radio; this could provide a range of up to 350km at the halt with either voice or Morse transmissions using the single sideband or SSB option.

Commanders also received additional items such as an artillery planning sheet that permitted the commander to call in artillery fire as needed. The tank also carried the TNA-3 land navigation system for the commander's use. The GNK-48 gyrocompass was replaced by the GKN-59.

Power when sitting at a fixed site was provided by one of several models of 24-volt AB-1 DC generators that were situated inside the fighting compartment to the right of the driver. This necessitated removing six rounds from the model's stowage and also two canisters of 250 rounds each of 7.62mm ammunition.

Other than tactical markings, command tanks essentially had nothing externally to differentiate them from line tanks except for the tube to stow the collapsible antenna, usually mounted under the auxiliary fuel tanks and above the unditching log.

OBIEKT-172MN (1972–75)

A certain coterie in the Soviet Army still placed great faith in heavy rifled guns, so a prototype of a T-72 armed with a 130mm LP-36Ye (2A50) rifled gun designed by SKB Perm and using separate loading ammunition was developed. Development took three years, but in 1975 it was decided it was a dead end and the project was terminated.

T-72A M-1979 tanks cross Red Square on 7 November 1982. These are M models destined for export. Note the early pattern road wheels.

A T-72A M-1979 tank from the same 1982 parade turning under the Krymsky Val bridge onto Sadovaya Koltso (the Moscow Garden Ring). Note the early wheels and the barely noticeable second fire extinguisher container in front of the rear turret basket.

OBIEKT-172MD (1975)

Another derivative T-72 tank, armed with a 125mm D-89T (2A49) high-power smoothbore gun, was developed, but the gun was not accepted for service and the project was terminated.

OBIEKT-172-3M (1974–76)

Another developmental model, this tank combined the 130mm 2A50 gun along with a 12-tube set of the Type 902A 'Tucha' smoke grenade launchers and the TPD-K1 rangefinder. But, as noted with the Object 172MD, the gun was not accepted for service and the project was terminated. A single prototype, or per some sources two, was built.

OBIEKT-175 (1976)

This was another incremental improvement in the T-72 that included new protection and technical characteristics as well as a new 130mm D-85 gun. Ten tanks were built for testing, but the design was not approved for production.

T-72 MODEL 1976 (1976)

This was a rationalized version of the T-72 that moved the L2G searchlight to the right of the main gun (per UVZ format), featured changes in the aspect of the turret's shape, and was fitted with a new Freon 114V2 fire suppression system. The tank was produced from 1976 to 1979.

OBIEKT-172MP (1977)

Another milestone in the life of the T-72, this tank was the test bed for the improved 2A46M gun. When accepted for service, the new gun was installed in the T-72A model tanks in 1981.

T-72 MODEL 1978 (1978)

Essentially this tank was the pre-production version of what became the T-72A, as it was fitted with the new 'Kvarts' turret from June 1978 onwards, as well as the TPN-3-49 gunner's sight and modified L-4A searchlight and other changes to include skirts and the Type 902A 'Tucha' system. This tank was briefly dubbed the 'Ural-1' tank before receiving the new designator.

OBIEKT-172M WITH R-23 AUTOMATIC AIR-DEFENCE CANNON (1979)

In an attempt to increase firepower against helicopters and light targets, experiments were conducted with a single-barrelled 23mm cannon mounted on the commander's cupola. The system was not adopted for service with the Soviet Army.

T-72A M-1979 (T-72M export) tanks on parade in Moscow on 7 November 1983. Note the turret fire extinguisher container fitted to M export models at this time.

A T-72A transiting on a low-loader rail wagon, standard procedure for long distance moves.

OBIEKT-172M WITH AG-17T AND 'STRELA-3' AIR DEFENCE MISSILE SYSTEM (1979)

Another interim test model, this variant of the T-72 was fitted with an AG-17T 30mm automatic grenade launcher and a 'Strela-3' (SA-14) surface-to-air missile system on the commander's hatch. While tested in the first half of 1979 at the test polygon at Kubinka, this arrangement was not accepted for use in the Soviet Army. (The Korean People's Army has however adopted very similar weapons mounts on their 'Chon'ma' tanks.)

EARLY T-72 PROTOTYPE AND PRE-PRODUCTION TANKS WITH KHARKOV AND MODIFIED TURRETS

The standard 'series production' turret installed on later Obiekt-172M and subsequent series production tanks was cast at the ZSO plant in Chelyabinsk (Plant No. 200, today Stankomash). The T-72 prototypes and the pre-series 'Establishment Lot' tanks were however fitted with turret castings designed in Kharkov, with the standard Obiekt-434 turret roof also having turret rear modifications on some tanks.

A small number of Kharkov-origin or Obiekt-434 turret roof section turrets were further modified with a distinctive 'bump' in the turret rear. The seven surviving early turrets with the distinctive rear turret 'bump' are today not fitted to their original hulls, but nevertheless represent a window into the many developments, experiments and nuances common to all Soviet tank development.

The T-72 now located at the Victory Garden memorial complex in Chelyabinsk is one such surviving example of the small number of tanks so produced. The base T-72 was built in March 1975, fitted with an original T-64 turret (plant drawing 434.10.001SB) assembled in August 1973. The turret rear has been modified with a distinctive 'bump' on the turret rear (part drawing V172.10.031) and was for many years used for training officer cadets at the Chelyabinsk Tank Academy. Another similar example is located at the NTIIM (Nizhny Tagil Metal Testing Institute), mounted on a T-72A M-1989 production hull. Another example, a pre-series production T-72 built in 1973 with a Kharkov-built and further modified turret, was located at the Kamenets-Podolsk Military Engineering Institute, but was destroyed in 2015 after being relocated to the Yaroslavsky polygon as a range target. Turrets with these rear 'bumps' were installed on some tanks until February or March 1974.

T-72A TANK (1979–84)

As with all Soviet tanks, when progress was made in the area of technology and enough changes were necessary, a new model of tank was introduced. In the case of the T-72, this was the T-72A. Beginning life in 1975 as the Obiekt-176, most of the original T-72 design was retained intact, but it received three major changes.

First was a new main gun and fire control system. The latter was the new TPD-K1 laser rangefinder sight, which was assessed as accurate to +/-10m. Early production tanks used the early T-72 turret shell and a modified mount on the left side for the gunner's sight that had a large hood and the new sight installed there; the TPD-2-49 tube housing was either left in place or in some cases cut out and replaced, and if left in place it was blanked off with an armoured panel welded in place. This was married to the improved 2A46 gun (as of 1981 the 2A46M) that had a strengthened barrel and increased barrel life (most of the early guns had a barrel life of 150 APFSDS rounds before condemnation).

The tank was also fitted with the TPN-3-49 gunner's night sight and a new L-4A 'Luna-4' searchlight that had a white light range of 1,300m and an infrared range of 500m. The sights were later integrated into the new 1A40 fire control system. This included a UVBU target tracking device and indicator module with ballistic correction device including a cant sensor. The ammunition stowage was increased by five rounds to 44.

Second, it now had improved armour protection via a new turret and redesigned glacis. The new design of turret gave it increased ballistic protection against both APFSDS and HEAT ammunition. The turret was bulged forward and a combination filler element referred to as 'Kvarts' (quartz) was inserted into pockets inside the turret composed of silicon rods. This boosted protection to around 500mm equivalent rolled homogenous armour (RHA) levels against APFSDS and 560mm against HEAT. As previously noted, US imagery

ABOVE A T-72A produced in 1979 during a Soviet military exercise.

LEFT This view of a T-72A M-1983 during an open day at the Kubinka polygon shows clearly the 'nadboy' external radiation liner and L-4 IR illuminator searchlight.

A T-72A M-1983 on the Naberezhny embankment returning from a Red Square parade.

T-72A M-1983 tanks and BMP-1 MICVs during Soviet combined arms summer manoeuvres.

interpreters felt the bulges made it look like looking down the front of a buxom woman's dress, and given the most obvious American personality with that specific 'design feature', country singer Dolly Parton, they nicknamed it the 'Dolly Parton' turret.

The hull glacis was originally a repeat of the T-72, but a new design was also accompanied by a 30mm appliqué plate welded to the base glacis. This now changed it from 80mm armour/105mm fibreglass/20mm armour plate to 60mm armour/100mm fibreglass/50mm armour. This did not make a material change to its HEAT resistance but gave it better performance against APFSDS.

Third, the early 'flipper' panels were fully replaced by full-length rubber skirts. The skirts were 10mm thick and were filled with a steel mesh to assist in providing a measure of protection against HEAT rounds, specifically RPGs and ATGMs. Also included for protection was the new 'Tucha' (little black cloud) Type 902A smoke grenade system with 12 grenade launchers on the front sides of the turret (seven on the left, five on the right), which could be used to selectively generate smoke curtains 50–200m in front of the tank. The tank also retained the traditional Soviet TDA smoke generator system that injected fuel into the hot exhaust to create a smokescreen.

The tank also had some modifications to its running gear, with new torsion bars increasing dynamic travel to 285mm, and an improved engine, the V-46-6. Just as the next variant, the T-72B, was about to enter production, the T-72A engine was in late 1984 once again upgraded to the V-84, developing 840hp. As well as the 'Soda' fire suppression system, the tank also sported the 'Sota' (honeycomb) anti-napalm system in the engine bay to protect against the jellied flame fuel.

Some of the T-72A tanks were also (officially as the T-72 M-1983) fitted with the 'nadboy' external radiation cladding for protection from nuclear radiation after a nuclear burst and when operating in a contaminated area. This complemented the 'podboy' liner inside the tank.

The new tank was accepted for service by the Soviet Ministry of Defence on 22 July 1979 as the T-72A. During the production run, a change was made to the wheel disks, henceforth being now slightly wider with only six locating bolts instead of the original eight bolt pattern to hold them together.

T-72AK COMMAND TANK (1979)

As with the T-72, the T-72A was also accompanied by an equivalent command variant. This was virtually identical to the T-72K model except for the new platform, but as before carried a reduced main gun capacity of only 36 rounds.

OBIEKT-172M FITTED WITH A TKN-5U PKN (1980)

An experimental TKN-5U commander's panoramic combination day/night-sighting complex was tested on a T-72. While the concept was good, Soviet technology was at the time not capable of achieving the desired results, and the project was terminated.

OBIEKT-172M-1 WITH KD-45-3 ENGINE (1981)

This was an attempt to increase the engine performance and power in the T-72A by installing a new diesel engine design producing 880hp. It was not successful and the tank was not accepted for service.

T-72A MODEL 1981 (1981)

This was an improved version of the T-72A and as well as all other incremental changes it now adopted the 2A46M 125mm gun and the 1A40 fire control system as well as mine-proofed seat mounting for the driver-mechanic.

OBIEKT-179 (1981)

An attempt was made to fit the 1A33 'Ob' fire control system used in the T-64B tank into T-72A series tanks. This required the installation of a 2A46M-3 gun and related systems to handle the revised 9K122 'Kobra-U' through-the-bore guided missile system based on the one used by the T-64A. After testing in 1983

ABOVE This overhead view of a T-72A M-1983 clearly shows the 'nadboy' external turret radiation lining.

RIGHT A T-72A M-1983 at a Ukrainian base in the 1990s.

T-72A tanks of different origin during Soviet summer exercises.

the system appears to have been accepted for service, but as Ustinov was adamant that the T-72 tank must play second fiddle to the T-64 tank series, the Obiekt-179 project was dropped.

OBIEKT-177 (1981)

In parallel with the Obiekt-179 programme, the UVZ and UKBTM designers refitted a T-72A with the new 1A40-1 sighting complex that could fire and control the 9K120 'Svir' through-the-bore guided missile. Unlike the 1A33 'Ob' system which used radio waves, the 'Svir' used laser beam guidance. While testing was very successful, once again Ustinov denied the use of the system on the T-72A. However, after his death in 1984, the system was approved for use in the T-72B in 1985.

OBIEKT-172M-1 WITH 'AYNET' COMPLEX (1982)

One Soviet weapon system perfected over time was a projectile that could be set to detonate overhead enemy troops in order to inflict damage even when dug in. The brainchild of Professor Odintsev from the Bauman Institute, the concept was to either programme the shell in the tank's autoloader, or alternatively to cue it to be detonated from the tank when it reached the correct range from the firing tank. While the technology was not quite up to the task in 1983 when tested, consistent developments now have this system being provided for some T-72B3 and T-90 tanks. The Obiekt-172M-1 was designated as 'Izdeliye' (article) rather than 'Obiekt' in some technical documents.

T-72A MODEL 1981 (1983)

Another incremental improvement in the T-72A, this model mounted 'nadboy' external radiation lining on the outside of the tank and also added a second ZIP storage bin on the left side of the turret.

T-72AV WITH 'KONTAKT-1' ERA (1982–85)

In the early to mid-1980s, T-72A tanks began to be fitted with first-generation 'Kontakt-1' 'Dynamicheskaya Zaschita' (DZ) or dynamic protection as a package also referred to as KDZ – additional ERA armour protection – to the glacis and turret and also attached to the armoured side skirts. The T-72A 'Kontakt-1' ERA modernization package was developed at UVZ from 1982 in order that T-72 tanks in service could be retrofitted with the ERA armour blocks at BTRZ tank repair depots as they came in for capital overhaul. The 902B 'Tucha' smoke grenade launchers were moved to a single block mounted further to the rear on the left side of the turret, as on the T-72A M-1983 production model. The reasoning for the ERA fitment is detailed in the later description of the modifications introduced on factory production T-72B tanks.

As the time period involved in upgrading the tanks in small batches was literally years, there are variations in the layout of the ERA armour, and on the base tank models being upgraded. The generic description of the widely undertaken upgrades was to T-72AV standard, a term used by the Soviet Defence Ministry (MO) and the Soviet Army. The later T-72B when fitted with the same 'Kontakt-1' ERA was by contrast not designated T-72BV in the Soviet Union, though generally designated as such abroad following the (false) logic of linear

A T-72A M-1983 at the Partizanskaya Polyanna museum near Bryansk.

LEFT AND BELOW This T-72A M-1983 is one of many T-72 tanks that Ukraine inherited after the break-up of the Soviet Union.

continuity in terminology. The ERA layout on later T-72B-based tanks differed from that used on the earlier T-72AV tanks, particularly on the turret. The 'DZ' ERA was also fitted to export T-72M1 tanks from 1985.

OBIEKT-172M/M-1 FOR OKR 'OTRYAZAYEMOST-2' (1983)

This testing was based on Syrian experience in Lebanon the previous year, where the IDF 105mm M111 APDS rounds had penetrated T-72 tanks in Syrian service. It attached an appliqué armour plate to the glacis of the tanks to increase protection against these projectiles. It was adopted and many early production tanks received this 16mm armour plate appliqué.

ABOVE A T-72A M-1983 at the Partizanskaya Polyanna memorial complex near Bryansk.

RIGHT A T-72A produced in 1983 or later at Patriot Park, near Moscow, with the standard configuration TPDK-1 gunner's sight/rangefinder and TPN-3-49 night sight. (Esa Muikku)

OBIEKT-172M-1 WITH THE TSHU-1 COMPLEX (1984)

This was the first effort by the Soviet Union to develop an electro-optical suppression system, transliterated in English as KOEhP. It used integrated sensors and high-power infrared searchlights to blind trackers for anti-tank guided missiles as well as automatically fire smoke grenades when sensing an enemy laser beam striking the sensors. While this first variant was not successful, later systems were fielded as the 'Shtora' system on T-90 tanks.

OBIEKT-785 (1974)

An interesting aside to the mainstream T-72 development history is the Obiekt-785 developed by GSKB-2 at Chelyabinsk over more than a decade from the mid 1970s to the mid 1980s. Design and development work on the Obiekt-785 'next generation' prototype had started several years before the Chelyabinsk tank plant began to be used as a 'doubler' plant from 1982, assembling the UVZ-designed T-72 tank, with 1,894 T-72A, T-72B and T-72B1 tanks built at Chelyabinsk from 1982 to 1990.

The Obiekt-785 was designed by a team led by GSKB-2 chief designer Valeriy Vershinsky who had assumed the role in 1974, and also participated in the organization of T-72 series production at ChTZ. Vershinsky had worked in the GSKB-2 design group at Chelyabinsk since 1956, and had participated in developing the T-10 heavy tank and later its modernization, and on experimental heavy and missile tanks and potential BMP designs. From 1981 until his retirement in 1996 he would head the bureau.

Work on Obiekt-785 started around 1974, being formally presented at a 'Perspektiva' (perspectives) discussion during a regular meeting of tank KB head designers and MOP department heads held in MOP on 24 February 1975. Each head designer described the work of his KB on future tank developments, and Vershinsky presented the Obiekt-785.

The Obiekt-785 developed at Chelyabinsk was at the time a revolutionary concept with more powerful armament and ammunition types, an improved autoloading mechanism and a new engine type, but was in fact a proposed tank testbed vehicle, based on available parts. The T-72 hull was used but with T-80 running gear (the same concept as later also applied to other vehicles such as the 2S19 'Msta-S'). The hull was lengthened behind the turret ring with an additional wheel station (i.e. seven wheels per side) with the provision of steel protective side screens. The hull glacis was a new design but similar to Morozov's ideas for Obiekt-480. The driver-mechanic's semi-reclined seat position was on the front left side of the hull. All his viewing devices were placed on the hull roof, increasing the armour integrity of the frontal armour plate. This construction was later 'borrowed' for the Obiekt-187, 195 and 477 experimental tanks.

The new tank was to have a combat weight of 43 tonnes, 700mm of hull front and 600mm turret front RHA equivalent armour protection, and a maximum road speed of 75km/h.

Armament was to consist either of the smoothbore 125mm 2A82, an improvement on the 2A46, or a rifled 130mm M-65 gun, in each case with an ammunition complement of 50 unitary rounds with 30 (32) rounds located in an 'MZ' carousel. This carousel was called overcomplicated at the February 1975 meeting, but it allowed a significantly higher rate of fire.

The new turret design was based on the T-72 turret construction but had a distinctive turret bustle. The tank was to be fitted with the 'Drozd' KAZ (active defence system) (as also planned for the KhKBM Obiekt-480 and other perspective designs), with in the case of the Obiekt-785 a total of 18 launch tubes, but it was never installed.

The engine compartment was completely new, as well as the engine itself, namely a 2V-16 (A-53-2) 16-cylinder X-type diesel with hydromechanical transmission mounted in an MTU-2 monobloc which occupied an internal volume of about 3.60m. Design of the 2V family of unified X-type engines for

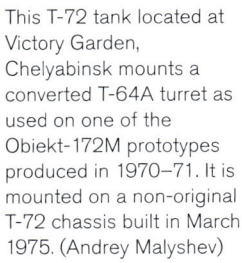

This T-72 tank located at Victory Garden, Chelyabinsk mounts a converted T-64A turret as used on one of the Obiekt-172M prototypes produced in 1970–71. It is mounted on a non-original T-72 chassis built in March 1975. (Andrey Malyshev)

ABOVE This turret roof view clearly shows the modified T-64A turret rear. The series production UVZ turret casting was modified to better accomodate the autoloader, hence the more bulbous turret rear casting, usually hidden by the rear turret stowage box. (Andrey Malyshev)

LEFT The modified prototype T-64A turret on this tank, one of only seven known surviving examples of the early T-64A turret conversion mounted on early Obiekt-172M prototypes, extended at the rear to accommodate the UVZ designed autoloader. (Alexander Morzhitsky)

future tanks and BMPs was started in 1970 by the the TsK KPSU and the SM SSSR. Work started at SKB-75, Chelyabinsk, under chief designer Vladimir Butov. Future variants of the Chelyabinsk engine, the 2V-16-1 and 2V-16-2, would be tested in the later Obiekt-186. The driver-mechanic controlled the engine via an electro-hydraulic servo control system. Engine power output was 1,200hp but the ejector type cooling system (as used on the IS/T-10 heavy tanks) consumed around 200hp, for a useful power output of 1,000hp. The tank was fitted with a Planetary type gearbox with 3F and 1R gears.

A prototype was built and tested for service, being planned to be ready for production in 1981, but the prototype then faded into obscurity as ChTZ geared up for series production of the T-72. The Chelyabinsk-created 'next generation' prototype is not mentioned in the official UVZ history. Why the Chelyabinsk design faded into obscurity is not known, but internal rivalries between design groups and production plants will doubtless have been a factor, or the tank may not have been considered a viable concept with UVZ at the centre of T-72 MBT design and production. Almost a decade later, UVZ developed the Obiekt-187, which incorporated some of the improvements tested on the Chelyabinsk Obiekt-785 prototype.

T-72B MAIN BATTLE TANK – OBIEKT-184 (1985)

While the T-64B had introduced through-the-bore anti-tank guided missile capability to Soviet main battle tanks in 1979, it took until 1985 before the Soviet hierarchy permitted the T-72 to receive equivalent capability. It also received more modern fire controls and a newly designed turret using a new style of increased armour protection.

The new system used the 1K13 primary gunner's sight, which included both a laser rangefinder as well as an improved laser guidance system to work with the new ATGM projectile. The complete weapons system was called the 9K120

The ChTZ-designed and -built Obiekt-785 during trials.

'Svir' with its core armament being the 9M119 ATGM. Also called the 3UBK14 in its complete form, it was a two-piece projectile that was assembled in the breech and embodied an ejector charge, a control module, a warhead and a motor assembly. When launched the ejector propelled it out of the barrel at low speed, and about 15m in front of the tank the motor would then kick in. Maximum range was 5,000m and it was given an 80 per cent hit probability. Penetration was assessed as able to defeat any modern tank but it would take later modifications to defeat both ERA and base armour.

The projectile was compatible with the 2A46M gun so no major changes were necessary. Unlike the older 9M112 'Kobra' used in the T-64B (and T-80B) the projectile could be hand-loaded; the other required mechanical loading and indexing for assembly.

But while the T-64B and T-80B went on to newer integrated fire control systems, the T-72B used the older 1A40-1 system. While not a bad system, it was still inferior to the 1A33 and 1A42 systems in the other tanks – once again a lingering drawback from Ustinov's decrees.

Ammunition capacity was increased to 46 rounds as follows:

- Five rounds stowed on the turret floor and under the gunner's seat (not above the turret ring);
- 18 in the hull with three full rounds in the forward 'stellazh' rack, four on the right side of the firewall, four on the left side of the firewall, three on the left side beneath the gunner's seat, one projectile behind the battery rack, and three rounds to the left of the battery rack;
- Four in the turret with one in front of the commander's seat, two behind his seat, and one in front of the gunner's seat;
- 19 rounds with one in the right forward 'stellazh' rack, three in the right main 'stellazh' rack, 12 in the midships 'stellazh' rack, and three behind the battery rack.

The tank carried 2,000 rounds of 7.62mm ammunition in eight canisters of 250 rounds and 300 rounds of 12.7mm ammunition in six 50-round canisters. Full armament also included AKMS-74 5.45mm assault rifles with 300 rounds and ten F-1 hand grenades, which had also been standard on all other variants of the T-72.

The turret was however a totally new design of protection. While the T-64B and T-80B used the 'Ultrafarfor' ceramic balls held in a wire matrix and cast inside of an aluminium core, the UVZ designers used a new multi-plate array similar to those used on Western main battle tanks.

Beginning with a new design in 1981, the turret (Part 172.10.100sb) had two large cheek pockets cast into it, and inside each one were 21 sandwiches composed of 21mm steel, 6mm rubber and 3mm aluminium that were mounted vertically and spaced 22mm apart. A 45mm-thick armoured plate was also part of the array. A thin armoured cover was welded to the top of the pocket, which meant in combat the arrays could be removed and replaced if need be or repaired in the field.

This gave the tank a 20 per cent increase in turret protection compared with the T-72A. Later production tanks used plates of 2mm aluminium, 15mm steel and 4mm rubber; the first configuration was apparently dubbed 'Otrazheniye-1' and

These images show a T-72AV used in trials located at the Kubinka Tank Museum in 2009. The T-72AV was fitted with first-generation 'Kontakt-1' ERA blocks on the hull and turret, with the turret front blocks mounted in a 'V' configuration on frames, providing additional stand-off protection.

An ex-Georgian Army T-72AV showing the turret roof ERA installation.

the second 'Otrazehniye-2' (reflection). As might be expected, foreign military intelligence analysts dubbed the appearance of the increased turret frontal armour the 'Super Dolly Parton' to be consistent with earlier easy to remember designations.

The glacis armour was internally redesigned to use a new spaced array involving the fibreglass layers. While originally the glacis had used 105mm (actually two plates of 60mm and 45mm sandwiched together) it now changed to thin spaced plates with 60mm armour, three 15mm fibreglass plates spaced about 20mm apart, and 50mm armour base. This increased its armour protection from 360mm to 490mm. The radio sets were also upgraded, with the tank now mounting the R-173 'Abzats' (indent) VHF FM radio with a broader frequency range of 30–79.95 MHz and the R-174 intercom system. Minor changes were made to the running gear and power plant, with the engine installation now becoming first the V-84-1 and then the V-84M, both still developing 840hp. Some T-72B tanks were also fitted with the 'nadboy' external nuclear radiation cladding system for possible use in contaminated areas, but after the Chernobyl disaster in August 1986 this seems to have been discontinued.

Despite myriad changes in specification and external appearance, the base designation 'T-72B' continued to be used until 1992 when the planned service T-72BM debut of Obiekt-188 development was redesignated T-90. During these many years, the construction and appearance of the tank underwent many changes, with for instance the 'DZ' ERA armour layout being modified and the 'Kontakt-1' ERA being replaced by 'Kontakt-5', and the turret ultimately being

ABOVE LEFT This overhead view of a T-72AV at a tank training school clearly shows the turret roof and engine deck layouts. (Sergei Popsuevich)

BOTH ABOVE RIGHT A T-72AV captured in Georgia in 2008. Note the turret front mounting of the 'Kontakt-1' ERA blocks, forming additional stand-off protection.

LEFT AND BELOW A T-72AV located in a Ukrainian base in the 1990s, with the frame mountings for the dismounted 'Kontakt-1' ERA blocks clearly visible.

changed from cast to welded, with the tank gradually morphing via the T-72BA (BM) to the current T-72B3 models. Each modification had a specific model year designation, T-72B M-1985, M-1987, M-1989, etc., but all were generally known in Soviet Army service simply as T-72B.

T-72B1 MAIN BATTLE TANK (1985)

As with the T-64B and T-80B, a version of the T-72 was produced without the 9K120 'Svir' system as the T-72B1. Its primary difference was the retention of the TPD-K1 sight in place of the 1K13.

T-72BK AND T-72B1K COMMANDER'S TANKS (1985)

As with the previous T-72 models there were also command models of both tanks, again differing in whether or not the 'Svir' ATGM system was fitted. Now the tank carried the R-173 radio set and in some cases the R-173P receiver; this permitted the commander to have ten pre-set channels for transmission and ten pre-set channels for monitoring. The R-130M was now replaced by the R-134 HF AM transceiver as well and all additional command equipment used in previous tanks was retained.

T-72B/B1 (T-72 'BV' AND 'B1V') MAIN BATTLE TANKS (1985)

The 'Kontakt-1' ERA packaging, introduced as a retrofit on service operational T-72 tanks as the T-72AV (as previously detailed), was also introduced on series production T-72B tanks. The introduction of 'DZ' ERA armour was however based on events far from the Soviet Union, leading to both the T-72AV regional BTRZ (tank repair workshop) upgrades and later T-72B factory installations.

A T-72B1 traverses Red Square, 7 November 1986. (ITAR-TASS)

This overhead view of a T-72B1 returning from a Red Square parade on 7 November 1987 shows the additional turret frontal armour of the original T-72B series.

As the T-72B and T-72B1 tanks were in early series production, the aforementioned major change was made to Soviet tanks across the board. In 1982 the Israel Defence Forces had invaded Lebanon to deal with both Hezbollah and their Syrian backers, and a number of armour clashes had taken place. The IDF managed to destroy a number of export T-72 tanks but also had tank losses, namely M48 tanks fitted with their 'Blazer' explosive reactive armour (ERA) panels. One was shipped back to the USSR for evaluation, and the results rocked the General Staff and Soviet Army command.

Soviet scientists had put forth the aforementioned concept of 'DZ' – 'Dynamicheskaya Zaschita' or explosive reactive armour (ERA) as early as 1945, basically to defeat the then common threat of German 'Panzerfaust' RPG weapons. But when briefed to the higher commanders, they were dismissed as no commander wanted any sort of explosives on the outside of their tanks at a time when 'desantniki' or tank-borne infantry was the norm. Demonstrations of the probable advantages of the new discovery were for a time discredited and ignored in the Soviet Union.

With the discovery that another country had researched and developed the same concept, and fielded it, the generals were faced with a dilemma. This now foreign development of a system the Soviet Union had considered and rejected nearly four decades prior would negate the results of all current RPG and ATGM weapons in the Soviet inventory, as well as leave their own tanks vulnerable to attack by foreign ATGM and HEAT weapons. A crash programme was thereby carried out and in 1985 NII Stali produced the first viable Soviet ERA system called 'Kontakt-1' (DZ element index 4S20).

The system concept was simple. Studs were welded onto the armour of a tank and a weatherproof steel cover was bolted to them. Inside the cover were two plates made of thin layers of steel with explosives set in between them and mounted at an angle to each other inside the cover. When struck by a HEAT projectile or warhead, when the molten stream penetrated the cover it would detonate the two plates, with them flying off in different directions and dissipating the stream, causing it to be relatively ineffective by the time it struck the base armour. The containers came in several different shapes but nearly all were the same relative size.

The initial fit for new factory-built T-72B and T-72B1 tanks (retrofit on existing T-72A tanks was undertaken as tanks came in for rebuild) amounted to 61 containers on the upper and lower glacis, 70 on the turret, and 96 in two groups of 48 on the side skirts and upper skirts of the sides. Variations did appear, with the most bizarre one being a unit that, pending a visit by foreign military delegations, stacked three containers on top of each other at each mounting point, perhaps for deliberate 'public' consumption. While some Western observers now felt this particular layout surely made the tank 'invincible' against HEAT projectiles, more studious types noted that it also blocked off the tank's sights and vision devices from any sort of view of the battlefield …

The turret ERA layout as fitted to the T-72B and T-72B1 differed significantly from that of the earlier T-72AV retrofit package, the distinctive forward-facing V-angled upper and lower container mounting frames over the

A T-72B returning from the 7 November 1990 Victory Parade in Moscow, with the tank in three-colour camouflage. (Mikhail Baryatinsky)

The complexities of T-72 identification. The tank resembles a T-72A as manufactured in 1983–84, but it retains the housing for the original rangefinder of the Obiekt-172M. The L-2AG IR illuminator is still located on the left side of the gun barrel, but the tank also has the later roadwheels and 'T-72A' side skirts, and T-72 M-1983 turret radiation lining. The appearance of a T-72 could alter dramatically as a result of one or more rebuilds during its service life, this possibly being a testbed tank based on a repaired hull from one tank and the turret from another.

front surface of the turret on the former being replaced by the ERA blocks being mounted more or less flush with the turret contours on the series production version of the latter.

OBIEKT-186 (1985)

Obiekt-186 was an effort to upgrade the T-72B, with improved firepower and a new fire control system, and powered by the SKB-75 (Chelyabinsk)-designed 2V-16-1 1,000hp or 2V-16-2 1,200hp experimental diesel engines coupled to a new mechanical transmission, fitted in two UVZ-built Obiekt-186 tanks.

The Obiekt-186 was armed with a 125mm smoothbore 2A66 (D-91T) gun, a new design of welded turret, a new fire control system and other improvements. The Obiekt-186 had the same six wheels per side as the T-72 but with modified wheel spacing and the hull slightly lengthened. This work took place within the framework of the 'Sovershenstvovaniye-72A' (Improvement-72A) development theme between 1983 and 1987. The alternative engines were fitted on the two Obiekt-186 prototypes, air filtering system throughput volumes doubled, and the two cooling system radiators were enlarged so that now each had its own fan. The radiator size was so large that the engine compartment effectively became non-armoured from above. The exhaust now pointed to the rear, not to the side.

The first Obiekt-186 was assembled in autumn–winter 1983, with main tests beginning in December 1985. The second test stage was from 4 June 1986 to 29 February 1987 and the third stage from 5 March to 1 June 1987. The tank became 15 per cent faster than the T-72B but fuel consumption increased accordingly. Both engines worked about 200 hours during tests. The project was terminated in 1987 and the tank was not accepted for service.

T-72B1 tanks fitted with ERA during operations in Dagestan in August–September 1983. Note the heavily damaged track guards on the lead tank.

OBIEKT-185 (1986)

This was a second attempt to improve the T-72B, armed with the same 2A66 (D-91T) gun but with the OKR 'Anker' autoloader system. While not accepted, the efforts made on this tank became part of the OKR 'Sovershenstvovaniye-72B' programme and also were used in the Obiekt-187 tank programme.

OBIEKT-184 WITH V-86 ENGINE (1986)

This was another attempt to increase the performance of the T-72B with the use of a V-86 engine developing 865hp. Two tanks were modified, but the engine was not judged a success and it was not adopted for the T-72B.

OBIEKT-184 WITH KD-34 ENGINE (1986)

This was yet another engine modification effort for the T-72B, but this time the new engine was the Barnaul-developed KD-34 of 1,000hp. Testing did continue into the 1990s but the engine was not adopted.

OBIEKT-172M AS PART OF OKR 'VELIZH' (1987)

As the GO-27 NBC protection system was getting long in the tooth, Soviet tank designers tried to develop newer systems under this prototype design work programme. Two variants, 'Velizh-1' and 'Velizh-2', were tested and appeared to have passed all trials so were recommended for acceptance. While this was turned down, the system continued testing in the Obiekt-187 tank programme and eventually led to the acceptance of the PKUZ-1 NBC protection complex used in rebuilt T-72s and in the T-90 tank.

OBIEKT-184K WITH AP-18EH APU (1987)

One problem faced by command tanks was the small AB-1 series auxiliary power unit (APU) 'donkey engine' generator sets contained within the tank hull, as they were limited in their power output. It was also seen as undesirable to keep a small engine running inside the tank's interior. As the tanks needed more and more power, and it was felt to be detrimental to run the APU for long periods of time at rest, an effort was made to adapt the AP-18Eh gas-turbine generator to the T-72 series of tanks. However, it was felt that the smaller generator was still sufficient for most needs and the project was not approved for adoption.

A T-72B1 at the Kubinka test polygon in 1996. The tank, fitted with an OPVT snorkel, is being prepared for deep wading.

OBIEKT-188 (T-72BM) (T-90) (1987–92)

The Obiekt-188, which was ultimately accepted into service with the post-Soviet Russian Army in accordance with Resolution No. 759-58 of the Russian government on 5 October 1992 as the T-90 MBT, was originally intended as a further upgrade of the T-72B. The prototypes were developed in parallel with the Obiekt-188-1, with the prototypes being competitively developed for intended service as the T-72BM MBT, with the renaming of the tank design as the T-90 being detailed in the previous chapter.

The Obiekt-188 was developed and tested as a series of prototypes, to be armed with the 125mm 2A46M-2 smoothbore gun with the 1A42 fire control system linked to the 2Eh42-4 'Zhasmin' gun stabilizer linked to the DVE-BS wind sensor. The 9K119 'Refleks' ATGM system was integral to the design, as was the 12.7mm 'Utes' turret machine gun. The engine was the V-84MS developing 840hp.

A T-72B1 (Obiekt-184-1) tank of the 336th Separate Guards Naval Infantry Brigade of the Baltic Fleet, Baltiysk, Kaliningrad. The T-72B/B1 with DZ (Obiekt-184/184-1 per factory drawings, with and without the 9K120 'Svir' ATGM capability) was never designated T-72BV in Soviet service, which was a foreign assumption that the designation would follow the logic of the similarly modified T-72AV.

OBIEKT-188-1 (T-72BM) (1987–92)

The Obiekt-188-1 (T-72BM) was a deep modernization of the T-72B tank described as such (Usovershenstvovanniy T-72B) (T-72BU) in factory documentation and developed in parallel with the Obiekt-188 which would become the future T-90 MBT. The Obiekt-188-1 included the following new systems: built-in dynamic protection (ERA), the 1A40-1 fire control system, the TShU-1 'Shtora' electro-optical suppression system, and a V-84-1 engine developing 840hp. The tank successfully completed all testing including trials with 125mm 2A66 main armament, but with the decision that the series production tank should be fitted with the 125mm 2A46M weapon. The Obiekt-188-1 was belatedly accepted for service by a Russian Government Resolution dated 5 October 1992 confirmed by the Ministry of Defence of the Russian Federation (MO RF) on 28 August 1993. The tank was not however placed into series production as the T-72BM as it was close to the specification of the Obiekt-188 already accepted for production as the T-90 the previous year, though elements were incorporated into the series production T-90 M-1992. The nomenclature and development chronology of the Obiekt-188 and Obiekt-188-1 may seem somewhat opaque, but this is a reflection of the times of great national change in which the prototypes were developed.

OBIEKT-187 (1988)

With the Obiekt-187 programme, the UKBTM designers decided to try a radical approach to improving the T-72 family. Six different prototypes were built, all with different engines, but they all shared common features to include:

- A new glacis design that eliminated the 'décolletage' weakness of the T-64, T-72 and T-80 tanks in front of the driver-mechanic's position;
- A new turret design that sat the turret crew members on the floor of the tanks to both reduce the height of the turret and provide them increased protection;
- A new autoloader that was isolated from the crew members.

But the design appeared as the Soviet Union began to collapse, and while testing continued for several years the Obiekt-188 was ultimately accepted into service as the T-90 tank.

T-72BA AND T-72B1A, T-72BKA AND T-72BK1A MAIN BATTLE TANKS (1989)

Things changed rapidly in the four years following the introduction of the B models, with the most important from the viewpoint of history and development of the tank being the death of vehement opponent Dmitriy Ustinov. As a result of the changes, the T-72B series was now considered worthwhile for major upgrades to both firepower and protection. This was carried out under project OKR 'Motobol' and while changes began in 1989, due to the assumed 'peace dividend' resulting from the break-up of the Soviet Union and the years of financial doldrum for defence spending that followed, it was not until 2005 that the T-72BA series was formally accepted for service under a Resolution of the President of the Russian Federation dated 16 April 2005.

With more than 16 years having elapsed between early incremental upgrades being developed and final approval for major 'capremont' (capital rebuild) of the T-72B series on a cross-platform basis, combined with sporadic financing for tank developments over those years, no two years of T-72BA tank modification in consequence have the same equipment or fittings. The biggest problem was that while the idea was first put forth in 1989, the fall of the Berlin Wall in that

T-72B1 tanks during a training exercise at the Alabino garrison in 2017. (Esa Muikku)

year and the collapse of the USSR less than two years later meant that funding for the post-Soviet Russian military was reduced to minimum levels due to a reorientation toward more civilian spending and introspection over how much had been lavished on the military over the years. Production numbers were miniscule by prior Soviet standards, varying from ten to 30 tanks a year until 1998, when batches of up to 60 were rebuilt. The total number of upgraded B models produced by 2005 was around 750 tanks.*

One of the first changes was an incremental upgrade to the fire control system, with a new computer and the most visible element of the change, the DVE-BS integrated sensor mast, at the rear of the turret. This mast provided both weather data (temperature, humidity, and wind direction and speed) as well as laser warning protection provided by sensors on the mast. In 2000 this was again modified with integration into the 1A40-1M fire control system with a new digital ballistic computer.

The ATGM system was upgraded with the 1K13-19 sight and the use of the newer 9M119M 'Refleks' projectile. Also added was the 2Eh42-4 stabilizer system for increased accuracy when firing on the move. Finally, the tanks received the 1A40-M2 fire control system.

Another change introduced during upgrading was the installation of a new autoloader elevator that cams the cassette to permit a longer projectile to be carried and inserted into the breech. As the cassette is elevated from the carousel, the autoloader tilts the front of the cassette upward until the projectile is aligned with the breech and then levels out, inserting the tip of the projectile into the chamber. Ramming is then carried out in the conventional manner, and the empty cassette reverses direction back into the carousel. The result is that projectiles up to 10cm longer like the new 'Svinets' (lead) and 'Vakuum' (vacuum) series can now be carried and used.

Mobility upgrades could include the use of the more modern T-90 road wheels, which were given bigger disks but wider and thinner rubber tyres. They also began to switch over from the tried and true RMSh tracks to the new UMSh twin-pin universal tracks. Based on the design of T-80 tracks but wider and broader, these tracks also could from 1999 be fitted with 'asfaltnyy' (asphalt) rubber pads (drawing 188.91.009sb) for use on paved roads to reduce damage to asphalt surfaces. The engine could be replaced with the new V-84MS model;

ABOVE A T-72B being loaded onto an Antonov-124 transport aircraft. (Sergei Popsuevich)

NEXT PAGES The war in Ukraine resulted in improvisations against new threats, particularly drones. The field-fabricated grille armour, as seen on these T-72B1s, was quickly incorporated into factory delivered modifications.

---

* The T-72B 'Usovershenstvovanniy' (improved/upgraded) was ultimately better known as the T-72BA in several modifications. The tank was also however sometimes referred to as the T-72BU based on the 'U' improvements, in the same manner as the 'U' in T-80U/T-80UD.

TOP LEFT T-72S tanks awaiting start-up orders on Kutuzovsky Prospekt, Moscow, for the 9 May 1995 Victory Parade.

TOP RIGHT The T-72S was an export version of the T-72B, built for India, with most features of the T-72B, including the sighting for the 9K120 'Svir' ATGM system, but reduced ERA.

RIGHT A T-72 with a Guards Tank Division banner awaiting starting instructions.

BELOW An overhead view of a T-72S moving in Moscow on 9 May 1995. (Mikhail Baryatinsky)

this was identical in most respects to the earlier V-84 models but was now fitted with the 'Silfon' cold air exhaust induction system to lower the thermal heat signature of the tank. Tanks rebuilt from 1998 to 2002 were fitted with the V-84MS engine developing 840hp rather than the V-92S2. Only from 2003 were T-72BA tanks fitted with the V-92S2 engine developing 1,000hp, borrowed from the T-90S version originally developed for export to India. As can be seen, the specifics of domestic and export production variants are in themselves labyrinthine, to which the later T-72B3 (M1M) modernizations, ostensibly for export, and generically labelled as 'M' for 'modernized', can be added.

The T-72BA specification tank rebuilds also received some of the older BDD package upgrades from the T-55 and T-62 in the form of the standoff floor plate to reduce vulnerability to mines together with the insertion of braces and a suspended driver's seat to protect him from mine blasts. The driver-mechanic also received an improved TVN-5 night-driving viewer.

TOP LEFT AND RIGHT A T-72S (T-72B) of the Kantemirovskaya Tank Division in 1996. Note the hull side ERA arrangement compared with the standard T-72B. Some T-72S tanks were in the mid 1990s absorbed into the Russian Army as T-72Bs.

CENTRE AND LEFT A T-72S (T-72B) on display during an open day at the Kantemirovskaya Tank Division in 1996.

A T-72S (T-72B) belonging to the Kubinka Tank Museum at the 70th anniversary of the NIII-38 Institute at Kubinka on 14 July 2001.

The tanks also gradually received the newer 'Kontakt-5' (called 'Generation 1.5') ERA fit with newer insert plates (DZ element index 4S22) that provided two-way deflection and a claimed 100 per cent more protection from APFSDS than the earlier 'Kontakt-1' series using significantly less explosive. Originally these were mounted in the same containers as the 'Kontakt-1' but a later modification changed the array layout, and also the installation method.

Firstly, the glacis was modified, with the appliqué plates being removed and a new system that partially embedded the ERA modules in the glacis installed. The containers on the sides were removed, and in some cases new skirts with steel panels were fitted instead. These had a small gap in the plates which turned out to be right where the track run under the skirts was located (the philosophy was that if the projectiles hit the tracks edge on they would surely be stopped). Three rectangular steel plates with ERA fitted were mounted in staggered fashion on the front of the skirts. Finally, new containers with a wedge shape were fitted around the circumference of the front of the turret; older style containers were left in place on the turret roof. Due to the subtlety of the changes the Western intelligence organizations missed the upgrades for several years. The T-72BA is as with most T-72 models not a single modification, but a series of incremental changes spanning the initial development of a capital rebuild plan begun in 1988 based on the Obiekt-184A through to as late as 2005, when final approval for the upgrades already undertaken was

These views show T-72B (M-1989) tanks, also referred to as T-72BA, consigned to storage and awaiting the cutting torch at Strelnya, near St Petersburg, in 1997. The T-72BM (Obiekt-188-1) modification had meanwhile been accepted for service but did not enter series production. This abandoned tank retains the sighting of the earlier T-72B with 'Svir' ATGM capability, and in service would have had an L4 IR illuminator to the right of the barrel.

The somewhat amorphous T-72B (M-1989) tank model, with numerous modifications including a new 'Kontakt-5' armour layout, would due to changing geopolitics be subsequently developed from 2010 as the T-72B3 series, and modified for export as the M1M.

Views of a further modified T-72B tracing its lineage to the T-72B (M-1989) was the T-72M1M (specifically Obiekt-172M1M) developed in 2009 as an export model, with the second variant seen here first demonstrated in public at MVSV-2010. The M1M is fitted with the 'Sosna-U' gunner's combination sight, PNK-4M commander's sight, DVE-BS wind/combination sensor mast, 'Relikt' glacis KDZ armour, 'Kontakt-5' turret and hull side armour, and T-90 derived components, including the distinctive armour panels on the front sections of the side skirts. The tank is powered by the V-92S2 developing 1,000hp. (All photographs Andrey Aksenov)

TOP A T-72B3 (M-2013) in standard configuration, as demonstrated at the RAE-2013 exhibition in Nizhny Tagil. The tank, generically described at the time as T-72B 'Modernization', has the UVZ camouflage pattern used only for exhibitions. (Alexander Koshchavtsev)

CENTRE A T-72B3 (Obiekt-184-3) on display at Patriot Park in 2014. The T-72B3 was adopted for service in 2012. This tank does not have the T-90 type additional armour panels fitted on the side skirts.

LEFT The distinctive turret armour and sighting layout of the T-72B3, with 'Sosna-U' combination sight and distinctive DVE-BS combination wind sensor mast. (Andrey Aksenov)

Views of a further modified T-72B tracing its lineage to the T-72B (M-1989) was the T-72M1M (specifically Obiekt-172M1M) developed in 2009 as an export model, with the second variant seen here first demonstrated in public at MVSV-2010. The M1M is fitted with the 'Sosna-U' gunner's combination sight, PNK-4M commander's sight, DVE-BS wind/combination sensor mast, 'Relikt' glacis KDZ armour, 'Kontakt-5' turret and hull side armour, and T-90 derived components including the distinctive armour panels or the front sections of the side skirts. The tank is powered by the V-92S2 developing 1,000hp. (All photographs Andrey Aksenov)

formally signed off. Due to the ambiguous geopolitics of the time, some T-72BA tanks were driven to storage yards awaiting the cutting torch while further changes only a few years ahead would result in a factory-based reinvigoration of the T-72 series as the T-72B3 series.

ABOVE The engine deck of the T-72B3. Note the external fuel tanks and feed hose arrangements.

LEFT A T-72B3 tank on display at the Army 2017 exhibition. (Andrey Aksenov)

TOP LEFT T-72B3 (unofficially T-72B3 M-2012) tanks on parade in Samara on 9 May 2017. The side skirt armour plates are inherited from the T-90. (Aleksey Kostin)

TOP RIGHT A T-72B3 tank in standard configuration, Patriot Park, 2018. (Esa Muikku)

OBIEKT-184 WITH AN A-68 ENGINE (1989)

This was yet another effort to upgrade the engine of the T-72B, this time with an A-68 diesel of from 920 to 880hp based on options and state of tuning. It also was not accepted for service.

T-72A AND T-72B FITTED WITH 'RESHOTKA' ARMOUR (1995)

The early weeks of combat in Chechnya proved to be a disaster, particularly during December 1994 in the lead up to the storming of Grozny, and many of the tanks were found to suffer badly from RPG-7, SPG-9 and 9M111 weapons used in close combat in urban areas. As a result, a number of T-72A and T-72B tanks in use there were fitted with 'Reshotka' (grille) slat armour protection for the sides and rear of the turret and the hull. This concept has been further developed with the T-72B 'Rogatka' and also current T-72B3 tanks, and is now widely applied more generally on tanks and other armoured vehicles.

RIGHT A T-72B3 at the Alabino polygon in 2018. (Esa Muikku)

OBIEKT-184 WITH V-92S1 ENGINE (1995)

This effort to improve the performance of the T-72B proved more successful. This time the tank was fitted with a V-92S1 engine developing 1,000hp. This engine also was fitted with the 'Silfon' ducted exhaust system using cool air from the engine air intake to reduce exhaust temperature and lower the infrared signature of the tank. It began to be fitted to new project tanks as well as capital rebuilding of tanks into the T-72B3 variant with the V-92S2 variant after 1998.

TOP A T-72B3 during a demonstration, Alabino polygon, 2018. (Esa Muikku)

CENTRE LEFT A T-72B3 (left) and T-90A (right) at the Alabino polygon in 2018. When viewed together, the subtle differences in equipment such as the 'Shtora-1' system, DZ armour layout and even the 902 'Tucha' launcher layout are evident. (Esa Muikku)

CENTRE RIGHT A T-72B3 at the Alabino polygon in 2019. Note the turret frontal 'Kontakt-5' KDZ layout compared with the later T-72B3M, the 'Sosna-U' combination sight, and side skirts with additional panels not mounted. (Esa Muikku)

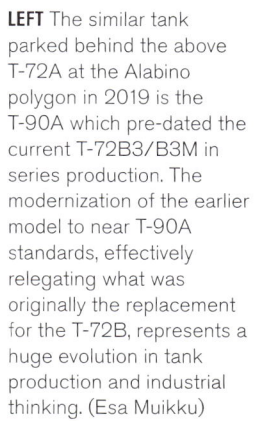

LEFT The similar tank parked behind the above T-72A at the Alabino polygon in 2019 is the T-90A which pre-dated the current T-72B3/B3M in series production. The modernization of the earlier model to near T-90A standards, effectively relegating what was originally the replacement for the T-72B, represents a huge evolution in tank production and industrial thinking. (Esa Muikku)

Two T-72B3 tanks at the Alabino polygon in 2018. (Esa Muikku)

OBIEKT-184 FITTED WITH THE 'SANOYET-2' FIRE CONTROL SYSTEM (1996)

One area where Russian tanks lagged behind their Western counterparts was development of an integrated fire control system using a thermal imaging sight. Such a system, 'Sanoyet-2', was jointly developed by UKBTM, TsKB 'Peleng' (Minsk, Belarus), and SAT of France. It was not however accepted for service and not offered for export sales. Later the Russians would use the Belorussian/French 'Sosna-U' sighting complex instead for this function.

OBIEKT-184 FITTED WITH 'ARENA-Eh' ACTIVE PROTECTION COMPLEX (2002)

Since World War II, Soviet and now Russian designers have worked on active measures to defeat first rocket propelled grenades such as the Panzerfaust and bazooka and later anti-tank guided missiles. The 'Arena-Eh' system was developed for first the T-80B MBT and later adapted for testing on the T-72B.

This system uses a radar sensor set to detect incoming projectiles. When they come into the range of the system, it automatically fires off a munition that detonates about 7 metres from the tank, spraying shrapnel down on the incoming projectile and shredding it.

While the system works very well from the perspective of the tank crew, thus far the motorized rifle troops that would be accompanying the tank do not want it used around them. Which is logical enough, in that few soldiers would want to have what amounts to an anti-personnel mine detonated over their heads. The system is slowly working its way into approval, doubtless with some accompanying HSE guidelines for operational deployment.

OBIEKT-184 FITTED WITH 4S23 'RELIKT' DYNAMIC PROTECTION (2002–05)

As experience and design work continued with dynamic protection, a new generation was developed by NII Staly as the 4S23 'Relikt' ERA system for 'built-in dynamic protection' or VDZ. The previous 'Kontakt-1' and 'Kontakt-5' systems were considered 'attached' systems or NDZ, as they were fitted to studs welded to the armour of the tank. The 'Relikt' (relic) system as later known is embedded in the armour protection itself, especially on the glacis of the tank. The system was designed for fitment to the T-72B3 and T-90MS tanks and tank support vehicles such as the BMPT. It provides a claimed 100 per cent better protection against cumulative rounds than the 4S20 elements of the earlier 'Kontakt-1' system, with less explosive content in the VDZ boxes.

T-72B2 'ROGATKA' MAIN BATTLE TANK (2005)

When the Soviet Union collapsed, the tanks it possessed were dispersed throughout all of the former republics. There followed an adjustment period whereby each republic absorbed its tank fleet under domestic control, and made local provisions with regard to standardization, maintenance and not least the matter of spare parts. In the 1990s, the initial post-Cold War period was also one

BOTTOM LEFT A T-72B (M) with additional soft KDZ armour at the Army 2017 exhibition at Patriot Park near Moscow. (Andrey Aksenov)

BOTTOM RIGHT The turret on the T-72B (M) with soft KDZ has a standard T-72B3 configuration. The 'soft' armour is simply designated 'cased' or 'bagged' DZ. (Andrey Aksenov)

RIGHT The hull glacis of the T-72B3 with integrated 'Relikt' DZ armour.

ABOVE The views in these three images show how the side skirts are castellated on this T-72B3 variant and fitted with soft KDZ packs, with standard 'Reshotka' grille armour at the rear.

whereby the need to maintain large tank fleets was now considered unnecessary in light of the new era of peace and cooperation, with budgets for new military equipment projects also being significantly restricted in the Russian Federation and all former Soviet states. The number of tanks in service dropped from a Soviet peak of nearly 77,000 total tanks including strategic storage reserves down to around 24,000 dispersed throughout the former Soviet Union, of which 38 per cent or just over 9,000 were T-72 models. Of these, only the T-72B series tanks were felt worth counting as first-line weapons in the post-1991 Russian Army. Large numbers of relatively new tank types, including T-64, T-72 and T-80 models, were put into long-term strategic storage, with many such tanks simply scrapped.

TOP LEFT The same T-72B3 (M) with 'soft' DZ armour on the hull side skirts. (Esa Muikku)

TOP RIGHT The standard commander's observation mask has changed little in many years.

LEFT A T-72B3M on display at the Army 2018 exhibition at Patriot Park. Note the turret side and hull side armour on this tank. The modification is, not for the first time at an exhibition, generically labelled as 'T-72 modernization'.

RIGHT A T-72B3M (T-72B3 M-2016) moving towards the Victory Parade on Red Square, 9 May 2017. Note the additional 'Relikt' armour modules on the turret and side skirts.

In 1992 the Russian Federation adopted the new T-90 tank, which was a heavily reworked T-72 model, but one that would be considered as its own tank in the manner of the T-54 as opposed to the T-55. When that occurred, even the modernized T-72BA series tanks were felt to be inferior to the T-90 and some upgrades and changes to the T-72 series were now considered worthwhile. The result emerged in 2006 as a modification of the T-72B tank as the Obiekt-184M, with the project name 'Rogatka-1' (slingshot).

In this case the T-72B was stripped down completely and totally rebuilt from the ground up. Firstly, the tank was fitted with much of the running gear and power plant from the T-90 with the new wheels, suspension, UMSh tracks and V-92S2 engine with the 'Silfon' device and new exhaust outlet. This engine boosted the power output to 1,000hp – nearly three times that of the original BD-2 engine from 1937 that subsequent V-2 series tank engines were based on.

The complete fire control and missile control systems were replaced with new components such as the 2A46M-5 gun with associated VVS-2 muzzle reference system for increased accuracy. This has a chromed bore and is 20 per cent more

BOTTOM LEFT The modified 'Sosna-U' thermal combination sight on the T-72B3M now provides increased target engagement and rate of fire.

BOTTOM RIGHT A T-72B3M moving towards the 9 May 2017 Victory Parade in Moscow.

LEFT A column of T-72B3M tanks from the rear. The additional 'Relikt' DZ modules and rear 'Reshotka' grilles add additional rear protection, almost prescient in their design.

BELOW A T-72B3M returning from the 9 May 2017 Victory Parade. The new side skirts with 'Relikt' armour are evident in this view.

rigid than the earlier 2A46M. The fire control system was replaced with digital equipment centred on the 'Sosna-U' (pine tree) integrated thermal sight and laser rangefinder and missile guidance system developed in Belarus and using the French Thomson-CSF 'Catherine' thermal matrix. All of this fed into the tank information control system or TIUS and included a newer version of the DVE-BS multipurpose sensor system. The tank did keep the older TPD-K1 sight as a backup in case of failure.

The TIUS system also integrated a GLONASS/GPS dual receiver positioning system for use in battlefield command and control systems. This was also fed into an R-168-25-U2 'Akvedukt' (aqueduct) twin VHF FM transceiver system which linked the tank to the 'Manevr' battlefield command and control system, with one part of the dual transceiver used for digital traffic and one for voice communications. In some cases, the tank commander can reportedly send an image of what he and the gunner see with the 'Sosna-U' sight to their higher commander.

These images show a T-72B3M on Tverskaya Ulitsa awaiting the 6 May 2018 Victory Parade rehearsal. The T-72B3M has significantly increased 'Relikt' DZ and 'Reshotka' grille armour protection compared with the earlier T-72B3. The T-72B3M is armed with the 125mm 2A46-5 gun with improved 'Sosna-U' sighting, firing accuracy and rate of fire.

The tank also received a number of most significant upgrades in protection. The major one is the use of the new 4S23 'Relikt' DZ (ERA) system which is combined with the armour of the tank on the glacis and several newly designed wedge-shaped modules on the turret. These contain 394 individual elements in 28 large glacis, skirt and turret modules and 19 smaller containers on the turret roof that are able to provide protection against both HEAT and APFSDS.

The tank was to be offered with two different fitting out options based on planned operations. For large-scale warfare against sophisticated peer opponents, it was to be fitted with the 'Nakidka' (cloak) thermal suppression blanket system that covered the entire tank. This was reported to be both capable of thermal suppression and radar absorbent to reduce detection on the battlefield.

The other option was intended for local warfare, which dispensed with the 'Nakidka' blankets but added 11 modules of 'Reshotka' (grille) armour around the rear of the sides and the rear of the tank to protect against RPG and ATGM fire as the Russian Army had encountered in Chechnya. UVZ representatives noted that both options could not be used at the same time as they each defeated the other's good qualities.

Somewhat ironically, the combined options applied to the T-72B tanks now made for a tank superior to the flagship T-90 and T-90A tanks being produced by UVZ! But in the end, although the modifications did make for a very effective and viable tank, it was felt to be far too expensive at a time of limited defence budgets in Russia and was not at that time adopted for service.

T-72 WITH 1K713 FIRING AND DESTRUCTION SIMULATOR COMPLEX (2009)

This effort was focused on combat simulation in a manner similar to the US Army MILES programme for interactive field training of units. Carried out under OKR 'Kotlas-KZ', it was developed by the UKBTM, 'Tochpribor' (Novosibirsk), and OAO 'Peleng' in Minsk. While it underwent testing in the Siberian Military District, it was not accepted for service.

T-72B3 MAIN BATTLE TANK (2011)

In 2011 the Russian Federation decided to cease production of the T-90 series as gun-tanks (other variants have continued in production as they replaced T-72 based models). The idea at the time was that design work would then concentrate on the proposed T-95 tank then in development, but this was quickly considered non-viable, and work began on the T-14 'Armata' follow-on tank. But with the rejection of the T-72B2 there was still a need to increase the combat capability

TOP The engine deck for the V-92S2F engine developing 1,130hp as installed in the T-72B3M. (Andrey Aksenov)

CENTRE A T-72B3M followed by a BMPT 'Terminator' moving towards the 6 May 2018 Victory Parade daytime rehearsal.

BOTTOM The frontal DZ armour array layout is retained from the T-72B3. Moscow, 6 May 2018.

of the long-serving 'low risk' T-72 tank design to maintain its modernity. A solution had to be found, with the result being a compromise design.

The redesign work, intended to modernize the armament, armour and fire control capability of the T-72B to the level of the current service T-90A, resulted in the Obiekt-184-2, or T-72B3, a tank which used many of the components of the T-72B2 but that would be much cheaper to mass produce (rebuild). The tank got much of the 'good stuff' to include the 2A46M-5 gun, the 'Sosna-U' fire control system and sighting complex with thermal imaging and a 1A40-4 gunner's back-up sight, commander's TKN-3MK combined day/night sight, the R-168-25-U2 radio installation, GLONASS/GPS receiver, and some of the 'Reshotka' grille armour fittings. But the tank was provided with a V-84-1 (V-84M) engine developing 840hp instead of the newer V-92S2 type, though still providing a claimed 60km/h road speed and 550km road range, and kept the older 'Kontakt-5' ERA system. Even so, the unit price of upgrading the tank was around 52 million roubles; at the same time a new-build T-90A tank was 70 million roubles.

The T-72B3 tank was formally accepted for service on 19 October 2012, with the Russian Army receiving its first tanks the same year. From 2014, the B3 was again modernized, with improvements including a new engine installation developing 1,130hp, with the T-72B3 being incrementally modified on an ongoing basis thereafter. By 2019, 558 T-72B tanks had been through the upgrade process. Upgrading was carried out by both UVZ in Nizhny Tagil and OZTM (Omsktransmash) in Omsk. They continued to be upgraded for the Russian Army, with more undergoing the process in 2021. It should be noted that the generic T-72B3 designation, as with the T-72B before, encompasses a wide range of modifications undertaken over several years.

T-72B3M tanks parade through Red Square during the 9 May 2019 Victory Parade.

T-72B URBAN COMBAT VARIANT (2013)

In 2013 UVZ offered a suite of additional fittings for the T-72B to make the tank more suitable for combat in urban fighting. Based on experience in Chechnya, and more recent observation of urban combat in Syria, the new 'Gorodskoi' (urban) model featured the following modifications:

- A TBS-86 dozer blade assembly for obstacle clearing;
- 'Reshotka' grille armour sections;
- Modified ERA on the side skirts with additional protection for the MTO;
- A 'pulpit' with glass panels for the commander to permit him to use the 12.7mm machine gun without exposure to small arms fire;
- An RP-377UVM1L radio signal jamming system against command detonated mines;
- Additional floor armour panels.

The 'Gorodskoi' variant was first demonstrated by UKBTM at the RAE-2013 arms show in Nizhny Tagil in 2013, the prototype being based on a T-72M1M tank. In 2016 it was demonstrated abroad for the first time, at the KADEX-2016 exhibition in Astana, Kazakhstan. While this variant has not been series produced or sold abroad, there is significant interest in this type of urban warfare package as urban warfare – and now protection from drones – has become an increasing reality for tank forces in recent years.

T-72B3M tanks return from the 75th Anniversary Victory Parade on 9 May 2020. (Andrey Aksenov)

LEFT A T-72B3 Urban prototype at the RAE-2013 exhibition at Nizhny Tagil. The tank has a TBS-86 dozer for clearing rubble, secondary KDZ on the side skirts, rear 'reshotka' grille armour, and an armoured turret cupola. (Alexander Koshchavtsev)

BELOW The camouflage scheme as used on this T-72B3 Urban is used by UVZ for exhibitions and is not adopted by the Russian Army. Export tanks have alternative colour schemes.

T-72B3M/T-72B4 MAIN BATTLE TANK

The new 'Armata' universal tank platform appeared in the early to mid 2010s, with the T-14 'Armata' making its formal public debut on Moscow's Red Square on 9 May 2015. At the time, the Russian Ministry of Defence announced that it was going to buy 2,200 machines of the 'Armata' platform, including the T-14 (main battle tank), T-15 (heavy infantry combat vehicle) and T-16 (armoured repair and recovery vehicle). For reasons that remain opaque, perhaps related to complexity for its assigned main battle tank role, ongoing internal debate, funding allocation, or simply the high risk that such a technology leap represents, series production has not commenced, with only around 20 total tanks built. As a result of this apparently stalled programme, a contingency plan was introduced to upgrade T-72B3 tanks to T-72B3M standard, the prototype being developed as the Obiekt-184-4, with the production tank being referred to variously as the T-72B3M, T-72BM3, T-72B4, or T-72B UBKh.

Major features of the T-72B3M upgrade are a switch to the 'Relikt' ERA system first shown on the T-72B2 and also a new V-92S2F engine developing 1,130hp. Reportedly 150 to 170 tanks were initially forecast for this upgrade. The commander also received an independent commander's thermal viewer on the rear of the turret for his use. It also is equipped with a new thermal sight produced in Belarus as well as an automatic target tracking system. The T-72B3M also has upgraded communications via R-168 'Akvedukt' series radio sets. Lastly, the driver-mechanic has a 'glass cockpit' display that provides him with information on all tank systems.

The T-72B3M was revealed to the public far quicker than previous upgrades, participating in military parades in Moscow and in some other Russian cities, and it has also participated in one of the first new 'Tank Biathlon' challenges conducted in Russia on an annual basis whereby participating standard line tanks in service with a number of operational units are competitively tested. The T-72B4 is a sub-variant that was initially developed specifically for use in this international competition. This also provides a panoramic thermal imager for the commander plus a new automatic shifting system for the transmission, but so far is not projected to be a combat upgrade for wide scale modification.

T-72B3M tank awaiting an evening parade rehearsal in May 2020. (Andrey Aksenov)

The extensive additional 'Relikt' DZ modules and 'Reshotka' turret on the turret rear of the T-72B3M. (Andrey Aksenov)

T-72B3 WITH IMPROVED OVERHEAD PROTECTION (2019)

A new variant with additional overhead protection on the turret roof appeared in 2019 intended to provide additional protection against top-attack ATGMs and drones. The latter were at the time not given any emphasis in the public domain, but the development of drones in an anti-tank role was already well advanced in several nations. The subject of overhead protection returned to prominence with the launch of the Russian-termed Special Military Operation in February 2022, with the subsequent widespread use of new generation ATGMs and in particular drones. Additional protection to guard against such threats extended far beyond the welding of roof armour on tanks as noted further below. Russian T-72 and other tanks were initially provided with field modifications against the latest threat to tanks on the battlefield, with factory-built modifications also being quickly developed.

T-72B3 M-2016 WITH ADDITIONAL 'SOFT' KDZ ARMOUR (2016)

A further modification of the T-72B3 developed by UVZ in 2016 was displayed at the Army 2017 exhibition at Patriot Park near Kubinka alongside the standard T-72B3. The most obvious difference was the fitment of 'soft' DZ armour packages with 4S24 inserts on the existing side skirts. The prototype was also armed with 125mm 2A46M-5-01 armament and powered by a V-92S2F engine developing 1,130hp. The additional armour packages are currently in combat service with the Russian Army on tanks, BMPT vehicles and other tracked armour.

T-72B3 MODEL 2022 TANKS (2022)

With the fighting in eastern Ukraine, Russian (and also Ukrainian and NATO) tanks have been subjected to new threats that were for obvious reasons not taken into consideration when designing the T-72 series. The biggest threats to tanks on both sides of the conflict have as noted above come from top attack weapons and drones, and as a result the T-72B3 and T-72B3M have been modified, sometimes drastically in appearance, to meet these weapons.

The tanks now have new side skirts with a deeper profile, additional 'soft' KDZ armour as first seen in public in 2017, improved smoke grenade launcher systems with protection from weapons fragmentation, a cover for the thermal sight operated from inside the turret, and a steel frame with grille armour placed over the turret roof. The tanks are also fitted with additional modules of ERA and 'Reshotka' grille armour panels on the rear sides, rear panel and turret rear of the vehicle. Combat weight with these modifications is now 50 metric tonnes.

Further field improvisations, followed soon thereafter by factory modifications of the T-72B3/T-72B3M tanks, were shown in 2022–23, now with ERA blocks fitted to turret roof racking and netting on the sides and rear to stop fly-in drone attacks. The tanks were also fitted with a four-band electronic suppression system to defeat guided weapons and command detonated mines. The tank modification also can use 'Nakidka' thermal suppression blankets.

T-72 CONTINGENCY ARMOUR IN UKRAINE AND KURSK OBLAST 2022–25

As noted above, the fighting in eastern Ukraine since February 2022, and in the Kursk Oblast of Russia from August 2024, has seen the operational deployment of various anti-tank weapons not previously used in combined arms operations against similarly armed peer or near peer opponents, and the game-changing mass deployment of aerial drones in an anti-tank role. This has resulted in ad-hoc field modifications and later factory options for providing additional screening to interfere with incoming munitions. This screening includes overhead turret and hull mesh screens mounted on fabricated frames as noted above (reminiscent of the screen armour applied to some tanks on the streets of Berlin in 1945 to protect from Panzerfaust weapons fired at short range) and even entire canopies surrounding the tank, generically named 'cherepakha' or 'turtle tanks' for obvious reasons. Though somewhat ungainly looking, the simple screening is highly effective in its intended role. As in all wars, the additional armour is a case of tank combat crews in the field doing what they need to do to in order to protect themselves due to a sudden change

This rear view of a T-72B3M column in Moscow for the 75th Anniversary Victory Parade in 2020 clearly shows the additional armour arrays protecting the turret and hull rear sections. (Andrey Aksenov)

in battlefield technology. The rapid evolution of a rudimentary response followed by factory modifications is a case of Russian adaptation and learning as in Soviet times past, based on combat experience. Ukrainian-operated T-72 and T-64 tanks and those supplied by NATO countries have also had similar modifications during the conflict for exactly the same reason, the use of drones being the latest challenge to the tank as a weapon on the battlefield rather than to tanks of any specific country.

FURTHER T-72 DEVELOPMENTS

The debate as to whether or not to fit the T-72 series tanks with the trialled and proven 'Arena-M' active countermeasures system remains open. In development for more than 20 years, this system uses radar to locate incoming ballistic threats to the tank (projectiles, RPGs, ATGMs) and fire an explosive puck containing steel balls to shred or destroy the incoming threat before it hits the tank. The main argument against its use has been the presence of friendly infantry in front of the tank when a puck is launched, who have no desire to be hit by what amounts to shotgun sized pellets from behind. The technical 'findings' from full-scale combined arms combat on disputed Ukrainian and on Russian soil still ongoing at the time of writing will without doubt lead to further modifications and redesigns of the T-72 tank as it is used in major combat engagements not seen in Europe since World War II.

CHAPTER 4
DERIVATIVE VEHICLES

The IMR-3 is a further development of the IMR-2M, based on a combination of T-72 and T-90 components. (Alexander Koshchavstev)

INTRODUCTION

Unlike either the technically more complex T-64 or T-80, the T-72 proved to be an optimum platform for related derivative vehicles, which for T-72 equipped units also reduced the number of parts and spares needed to keep the entire tank park in operation. The main reason behind this decision was the fact that the V-2 series engines were solid, reliable four-cycle diesels that were easily adapted to lug, pull or tow other vehicles and systems. The T-64's two-cycle diesel was too 'peaky' in terms of output revs/torque and not well suited to those functions; the turbine engine in the T-80 was even worse. Efforts were made to produce recovery vehicles, engineer vehicles and command and control vehicles on those chassis, but as of writing none of them have made it into series production.

ENGINEER VEHICLES

As early as 1933, the Soviet Union developed the concept of a 'column route' ('kolonniy put' – колонный путь) whereby off-road routes were prepared for use by the mechanized elements of combined-arms units. Specialist vehicles to fulfil the clearance aspect of this concept on existing blocked roads and cross country were developed in the immediate post-war Cold War period, initially tracked tractors such as the BAT and BAT-M, later followed by far more specialized vehicles.

The Soviets generally broke engineer vehicles into specific task classifications such as obstacle removal and clearing vehicles, bulldozers, terrain reconnaissance vehicles, bridge-layers, and obstacle creating vehicles. Where feasible, vehicles for specific functions used the same chassis as the vehicle they were supporting, e.g. medium tank chassis for medium tank combat units, BMP chassis for BMP units, etc. In the case of the T-72 tank chassis, they were successful in many of those items, including:

- The IMR-2 (Inzhenermaya Mashina Razgrazheniya) armoured obstacle clearing vehicle series;
- A BTU bulldozer blade for general use;

- The MTU-72 armoured bridge-layer vehicle;
- The BMR-3 armoured mine clearing vehicle.

IMR-2 (ИМР-2) COMBAT ENGINEER VEHICLES

The T-72A-based IMR-2 was designed as a replacement for the successful T-55-based IMR and IMR-1 obstacle clearing vehicles, which were designed for operation in conventional and potential NBC environments. Nearly all of the earlier IMR-1 components and mechanisms were updated to fit on the new chassis. The original design work was undertaken at the SKB-200 bureau in Chelyabinsk (which had a long history of developing mine trawls and similar equipment) from 1975, based on the concept provided by Aleksandr A. Morov, the head designer of OKBTM in Omsk. The new IMR vehicle, which was developed under the prototype designation Obiekt-637, was accepted for service in 1980 as the IMR-2, with production commencing in 1982. The IMR-2 was originally planned to be assembled in Omsk, but the plant was already overloaded

The IMR-2, shown in these three photographs, was based on the T-72A chassis.

An IMR-2 in service with the post-Soviet Ukrainian Army.

with T-80 MBT production, so series production was transferred to UVZ in Nizhny Tagil where a new workshop for specialist vehicles was under construction. Because of delays with completion of the new workshop, the first ten IMR-2 vehicles were assembled on the main T-72 tank production line. Finally, UVZ concentrated on building the IMR-2 chassis while the engineer equipment was built and final assembly undertaken by the Novokramatorsk plant, located in the Ukrainian Soviet Socialist Republic.

The IMR-2 vehicle used the complete hull of the T-72A tank but with a rotating armoured turret mounting replacing the standard gun-turret, with a two-man crew of a driver-mechanic and commander-operator, as with the IMR-1. Since one of the primary reasons for its creation was clearing of obstacles and debris resulting from potential nuclear strikes, allowing armoured forces to continue to operate in a radioactive environment, the vehicle was from the outset provided with an anti-radiation liner (podboy) and SKZ overpressure system.

The IMR was fitted with several particularly useful hydraulically operated devices for its intended purpose. At the front was a large flexible twin-section bulldozer blade, which could be angled to use as a 3.4m-wide road grader or straightened out to serve as a 4.15m-wide bulldozer, as employed on earlier but far less specialized engineering vehicles such as the BAT-2. When split 'snowplough' style, the blade could sweep a width of 3.56m. The IMR was also capable of clearing heavy snow at 200–300m/hour or landslides at 160–200m³/hour.

RIGHT An IMR-2M on display in Nizhny Tagil.

BELOW LEFT An IMR-2M in travel order at Nizhny Tagil in 2000.

BELOW RIGHT The same IMR-2M with its boom and grab bucket extended.

The IMR's 'star performer' was a multipurpose extendable boom with a maximum reach of up to 8.8m, which was provided with a choice of two fittings: either a special claw assembly that could be used to lift trees or debris, or a backhoe bucket of $0.4m^3$ capacity which was capable of moving up to $40m^3$ of soil per hour. In claw mode the boom could lift large pieces of debris or fallen trees up to 2 metric tonnes in weight.

The original series production version of the IMR-2 was fitted with the UR-83 mine clearing system, mounted in boxes either side of the rear of the track guards. The UR-83 system fired a rocket that dragged an explosive filled 'hose' (a 'Bangalore torpedo' in British and US military parlance) out to a pre-determined distance ahead of the vehicle whereupon the 'hose' detonated it to clear mines 250–550m ahead of the vehicle, with each charge clearing a path 6m wide (in an anti-tank minefield) or 12m wide (in an anti-personnel minefield).

An IMR-2M in UVZ exhibition camouflage at the RAE-2013 exhibition. (Alexander Koshchavstev)

The demolition charges, cables, rocket motors and launching rails were placed in the large wooden boxes at the rear of the vehicle. There were two sets of charges in each box, i.e. four launches per vehicle. A dismountable portable version, the UR-83P, appeared in 1983.

Early production IMR-2 vehicles were sent to Afghanistan in 1985 for operational service trials with the 45th Engineer Regiment where the IMR-2 operated alongside the T-55 based IMR-1. In Afghanistan, it was quickly discovered that the mine clearing system was particularly vulnerable to small arms fire, and also prone to catching fire. The UR-83 system was thereby deleted from subsequent series production IMR-2 vehicles, as was the PKT machine gun mount fitted on the turret, which also proved ineffective. The UR-83 boxes mounted on the first IMR-2 vehicles were steel, but their location interfered both with the efficient operation of the manipulator and access to the engine deck grilles for routine servicing. The boxes were also vulnerable to damage when being loaded and unloaded, whereas the wooden crates were more damage resistant, though as noted they were vulnerable to catching fire and hence the system was deleted altogether in subsequent production.

The IMR-2 retained the PAZ anti-nuclear protection system, PPO fire suppression system, and TDA smoke generator system of the original IMR-1. Self-defence was originally via a 7.62mm PKT machine gun, later deleted.

An IMR-2M at the Army 2015 exhibition near Moscow. (Andrey Aksenov)

In 1986 when the Chernobyl nuclear power plant suffered a catastrophic meltdown, IMR-1 and IMR-2 vehicles were sent in to work there, but it was quickly discovered that the radiation shielding and PAZ system were not up to the task when subjected to 'real world' radiation conditions, particularly in the Chernobyl power station scenario. Most of the IMR-2 vehicles were thereby not used, and the T-55-based IMR-1 was fitted with heavy lead shielding and video cameras (the viewports were sealed up to prevent radiation leakage). Soviet planners thereafter reconsidered the concept of protection on a nuclear battlefield as having significant flaws.

A Soviet-era driver-mechanic serving his national service as a combat engineer and other tank-based vehicle operator noted the arrival of brand new IMR-2 vehicles to the 50th Separate Engineer Regiment in Sambor (today Sambir) near Lvov (today Lviv) in Ukraine, which was a reserve unit with equipment mobilized as required. The newly delivered IMR-2 vehicles were immediately put into newly erected garages for long term strategic storage. Meantime, the T-55-based IMR-1 continued to be used as required while the new vehicles were maintained in factory fresh condition for future use. The manuals were removed and kept secret even from the vehicle crews. The whole regiment, including its IMR-1s and pristine IMR-2s, was sent to Chernobyl nuclear power station in the last days of April 1986. Thereafter, the older IMRs were placed in an on-site storage 'graveyard' where they remain to this day.*

Series production of the modernized **IMR-2M** started in 1987, based on the series production T-72B chassis and its components, with better mine clearance capability. The IMR-2M can clear roads or mines at 6–12km/h, and clear 230–300m³ of earth or 300–350m³ of rubble in destroyed urban areas per hour. The IMR-2M has an adjustable dozer blade width of 3.55–4.35m. The 44.5 metric tonne IMR-2M is powered by a V-84-1 engine developing 840hp and can travel at 60km/h with a road range of 500km. The telescopic boom has a load capacity of 2,000kg. All controls are electro-hydraulic.

In 1990 an **IRM-2M1** was introduced; this was basically the same IMR-2M vehicle but without the aforementioned line charge clearing launchers.

Another improved version, the **IMR-2M2**, apparently taking into consideration the results of the use of IMR-1 vehicles at Chernobyl, was also introduced from 1990. This had improved radiation protection as well as a new bucket design fitted to the end of the manipulator boom for faster clearance of contaminated rubble. A remote-control variant, 'Klin-1' (wedge), was also developed immediately after the Chernobyl incident, with an Obiekt-033 'mashina upravleniye' (control vehicle) and an Obiekt-032 'mashina robot' (a remotely controlled IMR-2 vehicle).

The latest IMR version is the **IMR-2MA** or **IMR-3**, which was developed at UKBTM from 1996 and has a redesigned armoured housing with increased radiation protection lining for the operator, a modified 'universal work element' (URO) manipulator and also now mounts a 12.7mm NSVT or 'Kord' machine gun. The track width mine ploughs on the IMR-2MA/IMR-3 are additionally fitted with the KMT-RZ electromagnetic mine clearance system. The current IMR-3 is based on the T-90 chassis but is otherwise identical to the IMR-2MA.

A new vehicle proposal, Obiekt-153 UBIM (Robot-3), also developed at UKBTM in Nizhny Tagil, redesigns the concept into a vehicle similar to the German Leopard Bergepanzer 'Büffel' armoured recovery vehicle and a prototype was built in 2017, but this is now mounted on the T-90M chassis.

---

* The recollections are those of Andrey Aksenov, who clarified many technical aspects of this book and provided the artwork illustrations.

MTU-72 (MTY-72) BRIDGE-LAYER

Based on the overall success of the MTU-12, MTU-20 and MTU-55 series of bridge-layers, it was only natural that a T-72-based version would follow. Once again, the UVZ (Nizhny Tagil) and KBTM (Omsk) worked together to create a new model using the T-72A chassis. The new armoured bridge-layer tank was developed in the early 1970s by the A. A. Morov design team at KBTM in Omsk under the project designation Obiekt-632 'Triton'.

The same formula was followed: the turret was removed, crew was reduced to two men (driver-mechanic and commander), and the bridge-layer equipment mounted. An entirely new design of bridge was fitted, however, with an overall length of 20m when unfolded (11.64m in transport configuration), but with required footholds the span was 18m. Bridge width was 3.46m and capacity was

ALL ABOVE A selection of photographs of the Obiekt-632 (future MTU-72) bridge-layer prototype consisting of a three-section folding bridge on the T-72A chassis, which was developed under the project name 'Triton'.

(A) An MTU-72 with the bridge being deployed, RAE-2013, Nizhny Tagil. (Alexander Koshchavtsev)

(B) An MTU-72 bridge-layer in travel configuration, Nizhny Tagil, 2000.

(C) An MTU-72 in travel mode, RAE-2013, Nizhny Tagil. (Alexander Koshchavtsev)

(D) An MTU-72 in folded travel configuration. (Andrey Aksenov)

50 metric tonnes. With dry or shallow obstacles two bridges could be used to cover a gap of 30m by placing one on the other; they could not be connected end to end. The MTU-72 has a crew of two. Launch time was 3–6 minutes in daylight and 6–10 minutes at night, with daytime recovery being 8–10 minutes. The MTU-72 bridge-layer has a weight of 41 metric tons transporting the 6.4 metric tonne bridge, with a maximum road speed of 60km/h.

After testing, the prototype armoured bridge-layer was accepted for service with the Soviet Army on 26 July 1974 as the MTU-72, with production undertaken from 1974 to 1989.

The MTU-72 was the last series of 'scissors'-type bridges to be accepted for service. The newer MTU-90 based on the T-90A chassis uses a three-section sliding bridge instead of the older folding end type.

BMR-3 (БМР-3) MINE CLEARING VEHICLES AND SYSTEMS

The Soviets had taken 'defrocked' tanks and modified them with a modified or new casemate and other fittings such as a jib boom to serve as dedicated mine clearing vehicles. The BMR-1 (Bronevaya Mashina Razminirovaniya) was based on the short-lived SU-122-54 chassis, whereas the follow-on BMR-2 was based on a T-54B or later T-55 chassis. These vehicles could mount any of the mine clearing systems in use by the Soviet Army, with the latest one being the KMT-7 'Panas' mine trawl.

The new BMR-3 developed by BTRZ No. 103 in collaboration with UVZ under the project designation 'Kort-B' was based on the T-72A chassis. It had a new armoured casemate in place of the turret and provision to carry a mine trawl on its rear cargo deck, with a 5-tonne load capacity as well as lane markers to show cleared pathways. First shown in 1999, the new machine was designed to use the KMT-7 from the outset. This was a track-width mine roller system and a jib boom was mounted on the right side of the casemate to mount and demount the system. The five-man vehicle crew consisted of driver, commander and three combat engineer sappers to remove mines and help remove and mount the rollers. Many of the vehicles were operationally provided with a dog and handler for mine and IED detection based on experience from Afghanistan. A 12.7mm NSVT heavy machine gun was mounted for local defence.

A BMR-3 (3M) at the RAE-2013 exhibition. Note the ERA layout, KMT-7 mine clearance system, EhMT mine detonation, and command and control systems.

Soon after its introduction, the KMT-7 was upgraded by the fitting of the EhMT-1 electronic mine clearing device. Appearing as a large cylinder attached to the front of the roller assembly on each side of the tank, the EhMT-1 was designed to detonate electronically fused mines that were impervious to pressure detonation as with most other mines.

Three views of a BMR-3 at the Army 2015 exhibition. (Andrey Aksenov)

RIGHT A BMR-3 (3M) at the RAE-2013 exhibition. Note the ERA layout, KMT-7 mine clearance system, EhMT mine detonation, command and control systems.

The KMT-7 can also be fitted to standard T-72 tanks but requires external assistance from crane trucks or a BREhM-1 armour repair and recovery vehicle to install it. It may also use the similar KMT-6 or the KMT-8 track-width mine plough with the EhMT-1 fitted to it.

Production of the BMR-3 was later transferred onto the T-90 chassis, as the BMR-3M.

BREhM-1 (БРЭМ-1) RECOVERY VEHICLE

Even before World War II the Red Army tested tracked tractors and tank type recovery vehicles to recover damaged tanks from the battlefield. During the war, mechanically worn out 'Defrocked' T-34 and KV tanks (i.e. with turrets removed and plated over) served this purpose, but after the war was over research was carried out on creating dedicated vehicles for this purpose.

A series of BTS (BTS – Bronevirovaniy Tyagach Srednyy or medium armoured tractor) vehicles were produced, designed to tow damaged tanks to the rear for repair and fitted out to only undertake light repairs in the field. They only had a

RIGHT An early Soviet-era BREhM variant. (Sergei Popsuevich)

Three views of a BREhM-1 passing the burned-out Russian parliament building on 4 October 1993. (Aleksei Mikheev)

(A) A BREhM-1 parked up prior to the 9 May 1995 Victory Parade, Kutuzovsky Prospekt, Moscow.

(B) A BREhM-1 returning from the 9 May 1995 Victory Parade.

(C) A BREhM-1 at the edge of Red Square during the 9 May 2016 Victory Parade.

(D) A BREhM-1 at the Alabino training grounds near Moscow, April 2016. (Alexander Koshchavtsev)

LEFT A BREhM-1 at the Alabino training grounds near Moscow, April 2016. (Alexander Koshchavtsev)

ALL ABOVE A BREhM-1 demonstrating field repair capability on a T-64 MBT.

TOP LEFT A BREhM-1 in three-colour camouflage, Moscow, 9 May 2009.

TOP RIGHT A BREhM-1 passes the international Aerostar Hotel, Leningradsky Prospekt, Moscow, 7 May 2009.

RIGHT Rear view of a BREhM-1 returning from the Victory Parade in 2009. (Andrey Aksenov)

BOTTOM LEFT A BREhM-1 on Ulitsa Barrikadnaya, Moscow during the 7 May daytime full dress rehearsal for the 2016 Victory Parade.

BOTTOM RIGHT A BREhM-1 parked up on Ulitsa Tverskaya during a parade rehearsal on 5 May 2008.

light jib for minor repairs such as replacing road wheels. While they could carry a spare engine or transmission they could not lift or install it and required a separate crane vehicle to carry out that task.

LEFT Front view of a BREhM-1 returning from the 6 May daytime general rehearsal for the 2010 Victory Parade.

CENTRE A BREhM-1 returning to base after the 9 May 2011 Victory Parade in Moscow.

BELOW A BREhM-1 moving through Moscow on 7 May 2016.

ABOVE AND BELOW RIGHT A more typical weathered service BREhM-1 located at Kubinka, 1994.

(A) Rear view of a BREhM-1 at the Alabino garrison in 2019. (Esa Muikku) **(B)** A BREhM-1 in Ukrainian Army (VSU) service. (Sergei Popsuevich) **(C)** A BREhM-1 moving along Tverskaya Ulitsa, 3 May 2011. **(D)** A modified BREhM-1M, with myriad changes including to the stowage arrangements. Note the angled mounting of the external fuel tank.

(E) The BREhM-1 is also designed for deep wading. This BREhM-1 with training OPVT is shown in VSU (Ukrainian Army) service. **(F)** This overhead view of a BREhM-1 with training snorkel entering a river clearly shows the deck stowage arrangements. (Sergei Popsuevich)

The Soviets noted that the Americans and the Allies had recovery vehicles back in World War II, such as the M31 and M32 (M4 chassis), and post-war had developed the M74 (M4 HVSS), M51 (M103) and M88 (M48/M60) armoured recovery vehicles. All of them were fitted with a frame capable of lifting more than 4,500kg, with heavy recovery winches of 11,500kg or more that could extract many stuck vehicles. As a result, the Soviets finally developed their own version at KBTM in Omsk in the 1970s under the development designation Obiekt-608, the BREhM-1 (Bronevirovannaya Remontirnaya i Ehvakuatsionnaya Mashina) (БРЭМ-1) armoured repair and recovery vehicle. Accepted for service on 13 June 1975, the BREhM-1 was a state-of-the-art vehicle when introduced and had many things that the Soviets had desperately been missing over the years, replacing the earlier BTS-2 and BTS-4 types in service.

The BREhM-1 had a heavy-duty winch capable of 25 metric tonnes pull with a 200m cable for extraction. It now had a crane with up to 12 metric tonnes lift capability as well as a cargo platform with a 1.5 metric tonne capacity to carry spare parts such as complete engines, transmissions or sets of road wheels or tracks. Among its equipment was an EhSA-1 electric welding set and ST-10-1S generator set.

The vehicle had a crew of three – commander, driver and rigger. For defence it was armed with a 12.7mm NVST machine gun with 350 rounds.

In the 1990s the BREhM-1 was upgraded to the BREhM-1M with a new V-92S2 engine of 1,000hp and modifications that permitted the crane to lift 20 metric tonnes (25 with bracing) and fittings to permit the crew to connect the main cable to a stricken vehicle without exiting the vehicle.

In 2017 a further BREhM-1M modification appeared on the streets of Moscow during the 9 May Victory Parade, based on the T-90 tank chassis, and resembling the BREM but distinguished by minor changes to the hull stowage arrangements.

The Czechs developed a VT-72 version of the T-72M with a crane and the Poles had the similar WZT-3.

Soviet and now Russian armoured vehicles, as with all equipment, are provided with an identification tag with full description, here for a late model BREhM-1 (Obiekt-608.20.002sb).

BMPT (БМПТ) HEAVY ARMOURED COMBAT VEHICLES (OBIEKT-199 AND PREDECESSORS)

Soviet Army experience in Afghanistan showed the need for heavy combat vehicles better capable of dealing with light enemy units and targets at high elevation, such as on mountain sides or in buildings. The BMP-2 was created in

An Obiekt-781 BMPT prototype languishing in the storage field at Kubinka. This variant is also sometimes known as the Obiekt-781 Model A.

part to deal with this threat, but was too light to stand up to attacks by RPGs or ATGMs. As a result, the Chelyabinsk Tractor Plant (ChTZ) in collaboration with KBTM in Omsk began working on a series of prototype vehicles specifically to deal with these threats. The concept was referred to as a BMPT, which, depending on variant, translated as 'boyevaya mashina pekhoty – tyazhelaya' (BMP-heavy) or latterly 'boyevaya mashina podderzhki tankov' (heavy tank support vehicle), the latter vehicle type developed under the generic project name 'Ramka' (frame). A significant number of prototypes were built by Chelyabinsk and UVZ under such Obiekt-numbers as 745, 781, 782, 787, 193 and finally the Obiekt-199 'Ramka'. The common thread they shared was the use of a T-72 chassis for all of these prototype developments. Firepower consisted of one or two 30mm autocannon, a 7.62mm PKTM machine gun, two to four ATGM launchers, and at least one 30mm AG-17A or AG-17D grenade launcher.

One variant (Obiekt-781 variant B), developed at ChTZ KB under the direction of V. L. Vershinsky, mounted a low-profile turret on a T-72A chassis and fitted the turret with the twin gun armament (100mm 2A70 weapon and 30mm 2A72 autocannon) from the BMP-3, together with two 40mm 'Balkan' greanade launchers and four 7.62mm PKT machine guns, with a crew of seven. This Obiekt-781 prototype survives to the present day at the Kubinka Tank Museum (Patriot Park) near Moscow. Another variant, developed at the ChTZ KB in 1986 on the T-72B chassis and described by UVZ as Izdeliye-781 (article), mounted an unmanned turret with the main armament consisting of two 30mm 2A72 automatic cannon, with this prototype being today located at the UVZ museum in Nizhny Tagil.

The final variant of these T-72 based designs was developed at UKBTM as the result of an instruction from GABTU MO to develop a further BMPT design, which was developed under the project designation Obiekt-199. The first prototype (actually a moving mock-up) was demonstrated at the ViVT exhibition in Nizhny Tagil in 2000, armed with a single barrel 30mm 2A42 automatic cannon as used on the BMP-2, with a 7.62mm co-axial machine gun, four 'Kornet' ATGM launch tubes and two 30mm AG-17A grenade launchers. This original model was reworked and in 2002 a modified version, now an actual prototype, was demonstrated at the REA-2002 exhibition in Nizhny Tagil, now designated BMPT, with further changes being undertaken on the chameleon-like vehicle in the years 2004–05.

Four photographs of an Obiekt-781 prototype on display at the UVZ museum in Nizhny Tagil. The machine (referred to as Izdeliye-781 by the museum) was developed at GSKB-2 at ChTZ in 1986. This T-72B based variant is armed with two 30mm 2A72 automatic cannon with 1,100 rounds, two 7.62mm PKT machine guns with 4,000 rounds, a 30mm AG-17 grenade launcher with 300 rounds and two Konkurs/Fagot ATGM launch tubes with four missiles. Total crew is seven. (Esa Muikku)

TOP LEFT Another of several T-72-based BMPT prototype designs was the Obiekt-787 'gadyuka', developed to prototype stage by ChTZ in 1995–96 and seen here in the Kubinka storage field after evaluation trials.

TOP RIGHT The Obiekt-787 'gadyuka' (viper) has been restored and is now located at the Patriot Park museum at Kubinka. Armament was two 30mm 2A72 automatic cannon, two 12.7mm NSVT machine guns, two 7.62mm PKT machine guns and 12 ATGM rockets launched from tubes either side of the turret.

After such a protracted and wide-ranging development, the BMPT was, however, unexpectedly not accepted for service with the Russian Army in 2009, and, as with the earlier BMP-3, when the first limited production was undertaken in 2011 the BMPT was first sold abroad before being accepted into Russian service. After appearing at a number of shows over many years, the BMPT was finally first sold abroad to Kazakhstan in 2010. Although the official designation was (and remains) 'Ramka' (frame), it began to be nicknamed 'Terminator' after the famous Arnold Schwarzenegger movie character, with UVZ using the 'unofficial' title even in sales brochures. In August 2012, this led to the Russian State Duma demanding the sole use of a Russian name, with UVZ management advising that as and when the Russian Ministry of Defence (MO) adopted the vehicle, it would be designated 'Ramka-99'.

The somewhat belated series production model of the BMPT uses a T-72A (and later the T-90) chassis with stations for five personnel (driver, commander, gunner and two grenadiers) with an unmanned turret with elevated weapons station. It mounts twin 30mm 2A42 automatic cannon with 900 rounds, one 7.62mm PKTM machine gun with 2,000 rounds, and four 9K120 'Ataka-T' missile launchers. Twin 30mm AG-17D grenade launchers are mounted, one each in two small sub-turrets on either side of the driver's position, with a single 300-round belt feed and a range of 1,700m and 300 rounds. The grenade launchers can fire 420–480rpm. A set of Type 902A 'Tucha' smoke grenade launchers are mounted on the main turret, and the commander's sight is elevated at the rear of the turret assembly.

As noted, the chassis is that of a standard T-72A but now powered by a V-92S2 engine developing 1,000hp in place of the earlier V-46. The vehicle is also fitted with 'Kontakt-1' ERA.

The 30mm 2A42 cannon are provided with HE-FRAG or HE-T (tracer) on one cannon and AP-T on the other so it can engage either light armoured targets or troops with a selector switch. The 9M120-1 'Ataka-T' is a ground-based version of the missile used on the Mi-24 and Mi-28 series helicopters. Three missiles are available, with a tandem shaped-charge warhead with a range of 5,500m and a penetration capability of up to 800–950mm, a missile with an HE-FRAG warhead and a thermobaric warhead for use against fortifications or buildings.

The fire controls include the commander's B07-K1 sight and the gunner's B07-K2 sight, both of which have thermal viewers and built-in laser rangefinders. Either crewman can access the other's sight in case of damage. The vehicle is also fitted with a GPS/GLONASS system and an R-168 series radio set.

The BMPT can also use either the KMT-7, KMT-6M2 or KMT-8 mine clearing sets fitted with the EhMT-1 electronic mine clearer. It also possesses the same mobility as the T-72A, including fording to a depth of 1.2m without preparation and 5m using a snorkel.

Based on extensive testing, a new model, the **BMPT-72** or 'Terminator-2', was offered by UVZ in 2013, which was operationally tested in Syria in the summer of 2017, with the first batch of the new and now series production machine first being demonstrated in public on Red Square on 9 May 2018. This uses a rebuilt obsolete T-72B model chassis, with the only major difference being no provision for the grenadiers and their twin AG-17D grenade launchers. As it is a rebuild it can use either the older V-84 series engines or the newer V-92 series. The crew on the 'Terminator-2' is reduced from five to three. Maximum road speed for the 47 metric tonne BMPT is 65km/h and range is 550km.

These two photographs show a T-72-based BMPT prototype, the Obiekt-782, also sometimes known as the Obiekt-781 Model B. This version mounted the turret module from the BMP-3, armed with a co-axial 100mm 2A70 low pressure gun-launcher and 30mm 2A72 automatic cannon as main armament. The prototype is today located at the Patriot Park museum at Kubinka.

TOP LEFT AND RIGHT Another prototype in the protracted Obiekt-199 'Ramka' (frame) BMPT development story appeared at the turn of the 21st century, now beginning to use the unofficial name 'Terminator'. This early prototype, demonstrated in Nizhny Tagil in 2000, was armed with a single 30mm 2A72 automatic cannon. (Andrey Aksenov)

RIGHT The same Obiekt-199 'Ramka' on the polygon at Nizhny Tagil in 2000. (Andrey Aksenov)

BMP(T) HEAVY MICV PROTOTYPES

Combat results during the First Chechen War (1994–96) showed that the BMP vehicles used by the Russian Army were extremely vulnerable in city fighting to RPGs and anti-tank grenades used by the Chechens. Looking around for a solution, the Russian military studied the use of heavy armoured personnel carriers by the Israelis such as the 'Achzarit' which ironically was based on captured T-55 tank chassis.

KBTM in Omsk soon developed a version based on an obsolete T-55 chassis (the Russians were in the process of selling or scrapping most of these tanks at the time), and the result was a BMP vehicle capable of carrying a crew of two and up to nine desant troops in a heavily armoured vehicle with 'Kontakt-5' ERA built into the design. Armour and storage bins protected the troops inside a central casement, but the vehicle had a new blunt glacis to provide extra room. Two large protected hatches at the rear of the casemate opened onto the engine deck (with the top section providing protection for the troops as they exited the vehicle) and dismount steps were fitted to the rear of the hull in place of the auxiliary fuel tanks.

TOP LEFT AND RIGHT The Obiekt-199 'Ramka' continued to evolve, by 2012 now armed with twin 30mm 2A72 cannon and modified secondary armament. (Sergei Popsuevich)

CENTRE LEFT AND RIGHT The Obiekt-199 'Ramka' as demonstrated at RAE-2013 in Nizhny Tagil was again reconfigured into what would become its production specification. (Alexander Koshchavtsev)

LEFT The Obiekt-199 'Ramka', also now referred to as the BMPT-72, located at the Army 2016 exhibition near Moscow. (Andrey Aksenov)

These images show a BMPT during manoeuvres at the Alabino proving grounds in 2017. (Esa Muikku)

TOP LEFT The small series production BMPT made its public debut during the 9 May 2018 Victory Parade in Moscow. This BMPT is awaiting starting orders for the 6 May full dress rehearsal.

TOP RIGHT BMPT vehicles traverse Red Square during the 9 May 2019 Victory Parade.

CENTRE AND LEFT The T-72 origins of the BMPT are evident from these side views of the machine. (Andrey Aksenov)

TOP LEFT A BMPT-72 at speed on the Moscow 'Sadovaya Koltso' (Garden Ring) inner ring-road.

TOP RIGHT A BMPT during the Russian-termed Special Military Operation in eastern Ukraine, mounting the additional soft KDZ armour protection mounted on the side skirts, as introduced on the T-72B3.

The BMP(T) prototype showed lots of promise but there was no interest after the First Chechen War in having to retain multiple chassis types. General-Lieutenant Sergey Mayev complained that at that time the Russians had around 30 different types of tanks and tank chassis on the books with many parts that were not interchangeable. So KBTM went back to the drawing board and developed a BMP(T) based on the T-72 chassis which is effectively the same vehicle as the BMO-T described below, with a vehicle crew of two plus seven desant infantry, a combat weight of 43.9 metric tonnes, with its 840hp engine providing a maximum road speed of 60km/h. The principal difference from the BMO-T is the installation of a BM combat module armed with a remote controlled 12.7mm heavy machine gun. The BMP(T) and BMO-T designs are so closely related that they are best described as differently configured variants of the same vehicle.

BOTTOM Three photographs of an early BMO-T prototype at the VTTV-2007 exhibition in Omsk. (Andrey Aksenov)

A decade later, the BMO-T at the Army 2016 exhibition at Patriot Park, now provided with upgraded side skirt armour and other detail modifications. (Andrey Aksenov)

BMO-T HEAVY FLAMETHROWER VEHICLE

Around the same time as the Russians began to come up with new vehicles for urban combat, one other vehicle was suggested by chemical troops as a heavy flamethrower vehicle. KBTM again undertook the development work and came up with the **BMO-T** (boyevaya mashina ognemetov – tyazhelaya or heavy armoured flamethrower vehicle). This is not as severe a reworking of a standard T-72 chassis as the BTR-T vehicle but has some of the same features.

The glacis of the vehicle has been extended up to meet the front of the new casemate replacing the turret, and it also has the armoured storage bins on the sides of the hull replacing the older chassis' fenders. It has the same hatch arrangement at the rear of the casemate for troop egress under fire and also has a commander's cupola with a 12.7mm machine gun. The crew is normally seven – commander, driver-mechanic, and five desant troop flame weapon operators.

Its primary weapons are 42 RPO-A 'Shmel' (bumblebee) hand held 'flamethrowers' for delivery of thermobaric and other munitions to pinpoint targets.* These are 93mm rocket propelled systems which come in one of three pre-loaded types: RPO-A thermobaric, RPO-Z incendiary, or RPO-D smoke. The rockets have a range of 20 to 1,000m and use a clip-on firing control with sights and a discardable tube with the rocket to form a complete weapon.

---

* The generic system name is RPO-A, with different rockets designated A, Z and D as noted. Though labelled as a 'flamethrower' and operated by chemical troops, the RPO-A is primarily a thermobaric weapon with a similar desant-infantry purpose to the tracked TOS-1A.

TOP LEFT AND RIGHT A BMO-T at the Army 2017 exhibition near Moscow. (Andrey Aksenov)

ABOVE The BMO-T, shown in these four photographs, is a highly specialized vehicle, designed to transport desant infantry armed with RPO-A thermobaric flamethrower weapons. The origins can be traced back to the T-55-based heavy MICV concept developed in Omsk at the turn of the 21st century.

The vehicle has built-in 'Kontakt-5' ERA armour protection. Unlike the prototype BMP(T) vehicle, the BMO-T has been fielded by the Russian Army with a platoon of three vehicles assigned to every chemical company.

TOP LEFT AND RIGHT A BMO-T at the Alabino polygon in 2018. (Esa Muikku)

ARTILLERY SYSTEMS

2S19/M/M1/M2 'MSTA-S' SELF-PROPELLED GUN-HOWITZER

The T-72 chassis was directly used for only one artillery variant, the TOS-1/TOS-1A, but the base chassis also contributed to the design of the 2S19 'Msta-S' 152mm self-propelled gun. The original prototype, Obiekt-327, developed from 1976, was an open mounting based on a modified T-72 chassis, later evolving in the 1980s into the 2S19 self-propelled gun-howitzer with a large new enclosed turret for mounting the 152mm 2A64 ordnance, which was modified from the towed 2A65 'Msta-B' gun-howitzer.

The 2S19 was designed under the development index Obiekt-316 by the Ural Transport Machinery Factory (Uraltransmash) in Ekaterinburg in the late 1980s under the direction of chief designer Yu. V. Tomashov in collaboration

LEFT The Obiekt-327 was an open mounted competitor to the Obiekt-316, which would enter service as the 2S19 Msta-S.

TOP LEFT The Obiekt-327 'Shaiba', based on a modified T-72 chassis, during trials in 1987. The armament installation was the 152mm 2A33/2A36 gun-howitzer.

TOP RIGHT The late Soviet-era 2S19 had a protracted development and delayed service introduction due to the break-up of the Soviet Union.

CENTRE AND RIGHT The late Soviet-era 2S19 had a protracted development and delayed service introduction due to the break-up of the Soviet Union.

(A) The 2S19 'Msta-S' made its public debut in Moscow during the 9 May 1995 Victory Parade, held uniquely on Kutuzovsky Prospekt to the west of the city centre rather than Red Square.
(B) The 2S19 on parade on 9 May 1995. The 2S19 was in 1995 joined by the last public appearance of the 2S3 'Akatsitya'. **(C, D)** A 2S19 at the Kantemirovskaya Tank Division, September 1997. The 2S19 was designed to replace the 2S3 'Akatsiya' and the 2S5 'Giasint'.

(A) There were no military parades in Moscow involving 'tekhnika' between 1995 and 2008. A 2S19 is parked up on Ulitsa Tverskaya awaiting a parade rehearsal on 5 May 2008.
(B) 2S19M1 Msta-S vehicles on parade on Red Square during the daytime Victory Day rehearsals on 5 May 2008. (Andrey Aksenov)
(C) A 2S19M1 passing the Aerostar Hotel on Leningradsky Prospekt en route to a parade rehearsal on 7 May 2009. **(D)** This view of a 2S19M1 gives a perspective on the not inconsiderable size of the turret. The 2S19M1 has integrated automatic battery-level day-and-night-all-weather fire control. **(E)** A 2S19M1 column in three-colour camouflage returning from a parade rehearsal in Moscow, 7 May 2009. (Andrey Aksenov)

ABOVE A 2S19M1 moving towards Red Square for a parade rehearsal on 3 May 2011.

LEFT A 2S19M2 (Msta-SM) parked on Tverskaya Ulitsa awaiting a parade rehearsal on 7 May 2014. The 2S19M2 was adopted for service in June 2013 and had its public debut in May 2014. Note the distinctive side skirts on the last production model in the 2S19 series.

ABOVE 2S19M2 self-propelled howitzers during parade rehearsals at the Alabino polygon, 20 April 2016. (Alexander Koshchavtsev)

RIGHT 2S19M2 self-propelled howitzers traversing Red Square during the Victory Day parade on 9 May 2016.

with OKB-2 at the 'Titan' TsKB (central design bureau) at the Barrikady plant in Volgograd, Plant No. 9 (the Motovilikha Plant) in Perm and the KBP design bureau in Tula. The 2S19 in its various guises has had a constant crew of five.

The 2S19 was intended to replace the 2S3 and 2S5 152mm self-propelled gun-howitzers in Soviet tank and motorized rifle divisions. It used a modified T-72 hull with lightened armour and T-72 and T-80 transmission assemblies, chassis components and running gear, and was powered by the V-84A engine developing 780–840hp. The ordnance provided a maximum range of 24.7km (28.5km with rocket-assisted projectiles) with an initial continuous rate of fire of 7–8 rounds/minute. The 2S19 can also fire 'Krasnopol' guided munitions. The 42 metric tonne 2S19 was a mobile vehicle considering its size, with a 60km/h maximum road speed and a range of 500km. The 2S19 was accepted for service in 1989 and entered production in 1990, but this stalled due to the break-up of the Soviet Union. The 2S19 was first seen in public at the 50th Anniversary Victory Parade held on Kutuzovsky Prospekt in Moscow on 9 May 1995.

The 2S19 has undergone several modifications since first originally introduced into service, including the 2S19M and 2S19M1, with improvements in fire control accuracy (including the introduction of the ASUNO-M (АСУНО-М) integrated fire control system) and battery fire control integration. The 2S19M1, first seen in public in 2008, was modernized at TsKB 'Titan' from 2001 as the 'Uspekh-S', with an automatic targeting and fire control system and day-and-night all-weather operational capability, with earlier 2S19 variants also upgraded. The 2S19M2 'Msta-SM' was accepted for service in June 2013, with 108 ordered for use in six divisions, with the system having its public debut on 9 May 2014. The 2A64Ms ordnance provides an increased rate of fire of ten rounds/minute and has automated battery fire control integration at divisional command level, and the 2S19M2 can operate at 3,000m above sea level, with vehicle road range increased to 600km.

TOP LEFT An overhead view of a 2S19M2 during a Victory Parade rehearsal, 5 May 2016. (Alexander Koshchavtsev)

TOP RIGHT A 2S19M2 on Barrikadnaya Ulitsa, Moscow, 6 May 2018. Some 2S19s are prone to emitting significant exhaust smoke. (Andrey Aksenov)

TOP 2S35 SPGs entering Red Square for the 9 May 2016 Victory Parade.

CENTRE The much-enlarged turret is evident in this view of 2S35 self-propelled guns at the same 2016 parade.

BOTTOM 2S35 SPGs during training at the Alabino proving grounds on 20 April 2016. (Alexander Koshchavtsev)

2S35 'KOALITSIYA-SV' SELF-PROPELLED GUN HOWITZER

The same base chassis as used for the 2S19 'Msta-S' and later variants was used for the 2S35 'Koalitsiya-SV' artillery system, which was developed in collaboration by Uraltransmash, Uralvagonzavod (UVZ) and OAO Burevestnik from 2011. The first two prototypes were built and tested in 2013, with the system making its public debut at the 70th Anniversary Victory Parade in Moscow on 9 May 2015. The series production 2S35 uses the same mixed chassis and running gear configuration as the 2S19, but now based on the T-90A chassis.

TOP LEFT This overhead view of a 2S35 moving into Moscow on 5 May 2016 shows the sensors for the automated battery/divisional level fire coordination system. (Alexander Koshchavtsev)

TOP RIGHT This overhead view of a 2S35 SPG awaiting the 9 May 2016 Victory Parade clearly shows the significantly enlarged turret compared to the 2S19. (John Ham)

LEFT A 2S35 returning from the 9 May 2017 Victory Parade in Moscow.

TOP LEFT The original TOS-1 at the VTTV Omsk exhibition in June 1999. (Andrey Aksenov)

TOP CENTRE A TOS-1 with its launcher cover fitted, Nizhny Tagil, 2000. (Andrey Aksenov)

TOP RIGHT A TOS-1A on display at VTTV-2003, Omsk. (Andrey Aksenov)

RIGHT Two TOS-1 prototypes were operationally tested in Afghanistan in the 1980s.

TOS-1 (TOC-1) 'BURATINO' AND TOS-1A (TOC-1A) 'SOLNTSEPYOK' HEAVY FLAMETHROWER SYSTEMS

The Soviet Union began to undertake research into the concept of thermobaric weapons in the 1970s as an effective means of destroying hardened targets such as bunkers, reinforced concrete buildings and closed armoured vehicles. Work was concurrently conducted on effective delivery systems for such weapons.

The basic concept behind a thermobaric weapon is simple: fuel-air explosive projectiles release a mist of highly explosive and flammable fuel into the air a split second before they are detonated. The resulting cloud delivers a massive amount of pressure on its target that can literally go around corners, through doors or hatch opening cracks, and crush or burn whatever they reach. Further, all the air in the vicinity of the detonation is consumed, creating a vacuum which can cause further damage when all of the surrounding air roars back in to fill the void.

Firing is oriented by using a laser rangefinder to determine range to target and then two rockets are simultaneously fired at the target. As the rockets impact, a 30cm-long probe at the front of the rocket triggers an inert burster charge to disseminate the fuel and after a short delay the mixture is detonated with enhanced lethality. Due to the probe's appearance, the system was later nicknamed 'Buratino' – the Russian name for the famous children's story of Pinocchio.

TOP LEFT A TOS-1A in standard three-colour camouflage, VTTV-2005, Omsk. (Andrey Aksenov)

TOP RIGHT The modified 24-round TOS-1A at the VTTV-2007 exhibition, Omsk. (Andrey Aksenov)

CENTRE AND LEFT TOS-1A BM vehicles parked on Tverskaya Ulitsa awaiting the 6 May 2010 daytime Victory Parade rehearsal.

(A) TOS-1A BM vehicles returning from the 9 May 2010 Victory Parade. (Andrey Aksenov) **(B)** A TOS-1A BM vehicle returning from a live-fire launch exercise, RAE-2013, Nizhny Tagil. (Alexander Koshchavtsev) **(C)** A TOS-1A PU vehicle awaiting the 9 May 2020 Victory Parade after a decade long absence from such parades. (Andrey Aksenov) **(D)** A rear view of the 24-round launcher unit. Note the convoy light. (Andrey Aksenov)

TOP LEFT AND RIGHT A TOS-1A parked on Pushkin Square, Moscow, awaiting the 9 May 2020 Victory Parade. (Andrey Aksenov)

CENTRE A TOS-1A in Moscow, 9 May 2020. Note the extreme rear mounted elevation mechanism and stabilizer jacks. (Andrey Aksenov)

LEFT A column of TOS-1A PU vehicles moving towards the 9 May 2020 Victory Parade. (Andrey Aksenov)

These views show a TOS-1A at the Army-2017 exhibition in 2017. (Esa Muikku, Andrey Aksenov)

At the time of development, the Soviets had the longer range 122mm 'Grad', 220mm 'Uragan' and 300mm 'Smerch' multiple rocket launchers, but experience in Afghanistan showed that they were too long-ranged and not accurate enough to deal with smaller targets closer in to troops.

From as early as 1971 until 1979, KBTM in Omsk under the direction of A. A. Morov in collaboration with Plant No. 9, the 'Motovilika' plant in Perm (responsible for the launcher system), developed what became the **TOS-1** 'Buratino' system* with its tracked Obiekt-634 launch vehicle. The prototype passed trials in 1980 and was recommended for service.

As the Soviet Union considered thermobarics a 'flame' weapon, the system was named the Tyazhelaya Ognemotnaya Sistema or Heavy Flamethrower System. The result was a three-component system: a launcher vehicle, a projectile, and a reloader vehicle. The TOS-1 BM (Boevaya Mashina – combat machine/launcher) was based on a T-72A chassis, with the TZM – (Transportno–Zaryazhayushaya Mashina / Transport–Reload Vehicle) originally envisaged with a KrAZ-255B 6x6 truck as the reload vehicle.

The first TOS-1 prototypes based on the T-72 chassis were completed between 1978 and 1979 under the direction of A. A. Lyakhov. Two TOS-1 BM launcher vehicles were sent to Afghanistan for evaluation in the early winter of 1988–89, with the weapons being used to great effect during Operation *Taifun* in the southern Salang region in January 1989 in the final weeks of the Soviet occupation of Afghanistan.

The original launcher design was a 'honeycomb' casing with 30 tubes in an 8-8-8-6 configuration, fitted to a rotating and elevating platform and operated

---

* Due to the TOS-1 thermobaric systems being classified as heavy flamethrowers, they are normally operated by RKhBZ chemical troops.

by a crew of three (driver, commander, gunner). Each rocket was a 220mm projectile designated MO.1.01.04 for the initial round and MO.1.01.04M for a longer-range round. Experience in Afghanistan led to the unarmoured KrAZ-255 6x6 TZM vehicle being replaced by a tracked TZM vehicle also based on the T-72A chassis, so that development continued with the Obiekt-634 (BM-1) launcher and the Obiekt-563 dedicated TZM. The original TOS-1 'Buratino' system was officially taken into service with the Russian Army in 1995. It was later operationally deployed in the Second Chechen War, with one recorded operation being with the 1st MBr RKhBZ (a chemical warfare unit) during the taking of the village of Komsomolskoe in the Urus-Martanovsky District on 7 March 2000.

The original rockets used by the TOS-1 were 220mm in calibre, 3.3m long and weighed 173kg. Range on the early rockets was from 400 to 2,700m. To provide greater range as requested by the Russian Army required an elongated rocket, the combined weight of which significantly increased the overall combat weight of the BM vehicle, and hence the launch unit was redesigned in a 24-round, 8-8-8 configuration as the Obiekt-634B. The later rockets were

TOP LEFT A TZM-T in UVZ exhibition camouflage at the RAE-2013 exhibition, Nizhny Tagil. (Alexander Koshchavtsev)

TOP RIGHT The TZM-T reload vehicle for the TOS-1A, VTTV-2003, Omsk. (Andrey Aksenov)

LEFT A TZM-T at the Army-2017 exhibition at Patriot Park. (Andrey Aksenov)

3.7m long and weighed 217kg, with an increased range of 1,200 to 6,000m. The new TOS-1A, capable of firing either rocket, was accepted for service on 4 April 2001, with the BM-1 launcher and TZM-T reload vehicle both mounted on the T-72B chassis. The modified system is designated **TOS-1A 'Solntsepyok'** (sunbeam) and was first seen in public on Red Square at the Victory Parade held on 9 May 2010. The system is at the time of writing deployed in Ukraine and was also used during the Ukrainian incursion into the Kursk region of Russia. Later exports to Azerbaijan and Kazakhstan were mounted on the later T-90 chassis.

The tracked TZM-T dedicated reload vehicle carries two pods of 12 rockets each for reloading, but reloading is done one at a time with the use of an onboard crane. Reloading a TOS-1A vehicle via the on-board 1,000kg capacity jib crane takes 24 minutes.

1K17 'SZHATIYE' SELF-PROPELLED LASER WEAPONS SYSTEM

Although not technically an artillery system, mention must be made of the 1K17 'Szhatiye' (compression) tactical laser weapons system, developed at NPO 'Astrofizika' under the direction of N. D. Ustinov (the son of D. F. Ustinov). The system was a continuation of earlier electronic warfare jamming research work based on the T-72 chassis, and on the earlier 1K11 'Stilet' laser system based on a GM-100 series (i.e. SU-100P SPG related) chassis. The 1K17 was based on the T-72 chassis modified at Uraltransmash, with the heavily modified turret being that of the 2S19 'Msta-S', the turret being fitted with a large mount holding 12 high-energy ruby lasers that were originally intended to disrupt enemy electro-optical systems on the battlefield. A separate generator set was fitted to provide the power for the lasers. It was backed up by a 12.7mm NVST machine gun for defence against helicopters and infantry. The 1K17 was powered by a standard V-46-6 engine developing 840hp, giving the vehicle a maximum road speed of 60km/h and a range of 500km.

BOTTOM LEFT The 1K17 'Szhatiye' prototype self-propelled laser system (SLK) was developed from the late 1980s and actually accepted for service in 1992 but not series produced due to the break-up of the Soviet Union.

BOTTOM RIGHT The 1K17 was based on the same chassis as the 2S19 SPG, with a modified turret from the same vehicle.

LEFT The UBIM (Obiekt-153) was first seen as a model in 2017 and is seen here as a prototype in 2018. The Ural KBTM (UVZ)-developed UBIM, originally described as on the T-72/90 universal chassis, is proposed as the next generation of BREhM, BMR and IMR. Series production is expected to be based on the T-90M chassis. (Esa Muikku)

Two 1K17 prototypes were completed in December 1990 and tested from 1990 until 1992. The vehicle was recommended (and accepted) for service in 1992, but as with many prototypes at the time was hit by the financial difficulties resulting from the break-up of the Soviet Union, and as such did not enter service with the Russian Army.

One of the prototype 1K17 vehicles, serial number Zh12ShT2205, is now retained as a museum exhibit at the Muzei Tekhniki at Chernogolovka near Moscow.

RKHM (PXM) NBC RECONNAISSANCE VEHICLE

A single prototype of an NBC reconnaissance vehicle designated RKhM was built on the T-72 chassis and evaluated for service, but did not enter series production.

BOTTOM LEFT AND RIGHT The UMZ-G 'Kleshch-G' (mite) universal tracked minelayer is a self-propelled mine laying vehicle based on the T-72 chassis powered by a V-84MS engine developing 840hp and developed by OMTM in Omsk. Seen here during its debut at the Army 2019 exhibition near Moscow, the vehicle mounts three rows of three rotating drum launchers for launching up to 270 anti-personnel or anti-tank mines. (Esa Muikku).

CHAPTER 5
COMBAT USE

A T-72B/B1 with KDZ (T-72 'BV' as described abroad) during the First Chechen War, 1994.

OVERVIEW

Unlike past Soviet tanks, there were some major differences in the combat use and results achieved by the T-72 main battle tank.

Firstly, the T-72 tank had increased mobility due to the installation of a more powerful engine, 7-speed transmission inherited from the T-64 and new tracks. While the tank had the same good range (up to 700km on roads) and better speed than previous tanks, test usage in in the mountainous southern Soviet republics showed that in mountainous conditions the tank was very fatiguing to drive due to the narrower power band of the more powerful V-46 engine and the constant need to shift the transmission to maintain speed. In years ahead, the T-72 was operated by both the Russian and Georgian armies in and around South Ossetia and Abkhazia where the rugged terrain such as near the Kodori Gorge in Abkhazia proved hard going for T-72 driver-mechanics.*

Secondly, the use of the autoloader both helped and hindered its use in combat. Kartsev and Venediktov were proven right when the T-64 went into combat in Transnistria and the T-80 was deployed in Chechnya. If their fighting compartment was penetrated and the tank had a nearly full load of ammunition, the exposed propellant charges were detonated, causing a catastrophic explosion and often the complete destruction of the tank.

With its protected charges in the 'Zhelud' autoloader the T-72 was far less likely to suffer this form of damage or destruction, but in its case if it had a full load of ammunition – stowed around the inside of the fighting compartment – it too could 'cook off' and suffer the same fate. As a result, starting

---

* Soviet and Russian sources indicate that the T-64 was sent to Afghanistan with a single motorized rifle regiment of the 40th Army, but the tanks proved complex to operate and maintain and were thereby removed within three to four months and replaced with T-62 tanks. The T-72 by contrast is not known to have been deployed in Afghanistan, although the T-72 chassis based TOS-1 thermobaric rocket launcher and IMR-2 engineering vehicle were deployed on operational trials during the conflict.

A T-72 fitted with 'Reshotka' grille armour at Kubinka in 1996, the additional armour having been tested in Chechnya in 1995 as a retrofit for T-72B tanks.

in Chechnya the Russians developed a new series of tactics for using the T-72 which they called the 'fire carousel'. This tactic consisted of using a platoon of T-72 tanks fitted with ERA when attacking positions in Chechnya. One T-72 would load only its autoloader with ammunition – 22 rounds, usually only HE-FRAG – and then move forward just behind the infantry. They would identify targets and call them out to the tank commander for suppression. When the T-72 had fired all 22 rounds, it would back out of the engagement as a second tank moved up to take its place. While the first one reloaded its autoloader, about a 20-minute operation, the third T-72 would be on standby. When the second one went 'dry' the third one would replace it, and the first one would be moved up to standby. This tactic proved highly successful and the tanks proved nearly invulnerable to damage as they only presented their frontal 60-degree arc to the fighters. One tank noted taking at least eight direct hits from RPGs (the ERA defeated them) while carrying out its mission.

Thirdly, most of the Western analysis of T-72 combat performance was based on combat between armies provided with Western tanks using the latest ammunition versus export versions of the T-72 in the hands of as-then-defined Third World armies with highly variable training and skill sets. The conclusion that the tank was 'easy meat' was rather hasty considering none of the forces in contact were dealing with domestic Soviet-built tanks like the T-72A or T-72B with much better armour protection and ammunition, nor with better trained Soviet tank crews. This initial foreign analysis has changed in recent years, with feedback from countries such as Syria for instance where later versions of the T-72 and the newer T-90 were fielded, which showed that tanks lost were attacked from either broadside or behind, aspects that are usually far more favourable to the attacker than the defender. Head-on attacks on T-72 and T-90 tanks appeared to be relatively ineffective from information that filtered back from the Syrian battlefields.

Recent events on either side of the Ukrainian border have however shown that in the hands of competent operators any T-72 model, in fact any tank, may be vulnerable to the current generation of modern anti-tank weapons. No tank has ever been designed to defeat the new top attack type weapons being used during the conflict in Ukraine, and the T-72 is no exception. Meanwhile, the appearance of drones on the battlefields of Ukraine and later the Kursk Oblast in the Russian Federation has proven a major threat to all tank types operating in the conflict, whether of Russian, Ukrainian or foreign origin.

THE SOVIET WAR IN AFGHANISTAN 1979–89

As noted above, the T-72 is not documented as having been deployed in Afghanistan, as the tank and motorized rifle units there were equipped with the T-62, with the few T-64 tanks deployed being withdrawn within four months of arrival. The TOS-1 and IMR, both mounted on the T-72 chassis, were however deployed, with the former used in combat operations during the near decade-long Soviet campaign in the country.

THE IRAN–IRAQ WAR 1980–88

Iraq was one of the first non-Warsaw Pact recipients of the T-72 tank, receiving 100 export versions of the original T-72 'Ural' in 1979–80, with the TPD-2-49 optical rangefinder, reduced turret frontal armour, a limited ammunition complement, and without a PAZ protection system.

In the first year of the Iran–Iraq War, there were major armour clashes between Iraqi and Iranian forces, including in January 1981 when approximately 300 Iraqi T-62 tanks engaged a similar number of Iranian M60 and Chieftain tanks. The first documented use of the T-72 during the war was in fighting near Basra in 1982 when the Iraqi 10th Brigade launched a flank attack on Iran, during which Iranian forces reportedly lost 200 tanks, though they in turn destroyed many Iraqi tanks, the T-72 included, and recovered several operational examples. The last major armoured engagement of the war was several years later, when on 17 April 1988 Iraq mounted a major counter-offensive with a reported 200,000 troops supported by Iraqi Republican Guard units equipped with T-72 tanks. The assault petered out for logistical reasons, resulting in a negotiated peace agreement.

The Soviet Union had initially censored all reporting on the deployment of the T-72 in Iraq, even within Iraqi military reports, the restrictions being lifted in 1985. As a consequence of the Iraqi attack on Iran using Soviet-built tanks, the Soviet Union in 1980 temporarily banned tank exports to Iraq, but lifted the ban two years later, as in early 1982 Poland had filled the vacuum with the sale of 250 T-72M tanks, with the majority of the 1,100 T-72 tanks received by Iraq during the entire Iran–Iraq War having been Polish-built examples. Soviet- and allied-supplied tanks were mainly used by Iraqi Republican Guards units, the 1st and 2nd Armoured Divisions, the 3rd and 6th Mechanized Divisions and the non-Republican Guard 3rd Saladin Tank Division.

Iraq possessed a single battalion of T-72s at the start of the war, but as they showed such good results in combat, the country purchased ongoing additional lots of T-72, T-72M and T-72M1 tanks from the USSR, Poland and

ABOVE AND RIGHT T-72B1 tanks in Dagestan, 1998–99.

Czechoslovakia (purchased in batches and receiving different tanks in each batch). They found them superior to most of the Iranian tanks they were fighting against, but for the most part the Iraqis used them in a defensive mode of operations and not in open combat. As is often the case, numbers are conflated, though Iraq is noted as having lost approximately 500 of their staple T-62, and by contrast only 60 T-72 tanks during the eight-year war.

The Iranians rated the T-72 highly, more so than their own Chieftains. Complaints about the latter were focused on lack of mobility and the ill-suited power plant that constantly overheated in the terrain and climate where it was operated, rather than on the armament or armour. An Iranian Chieftain tank commander, Adar Foruzyan, later told of two separate Chieftains he commanded being destroyed by T-72 tanks that were more agile and not prone to constant overheating and breakdown, leaving them a 'sitting duck'. He also noted that while Iraqi T-55 and T-62 tanks could be engaged frontally by the Chieftain at range, the T-72 had to be outflanked to destroy it from the side or rear. He also noted that on a personal level the capture of an operational T-72 was considered a special event.

Iran was so impressed with the performance of the Soviet- (in fact primarily Polish-) supplied T-72 tanks against their own American- and British-supplied tanks during the war that some years later, when they needed to replace their own ageing inventory, Iran contracted with the Russian Federation for the purchase of 300 T-72S tanks, which were assembled under licence in Iran between 1993 and 2001. Iran also purchased further T-72 tanks from Poland and Belarus, while also developing their own variant with Western sub-systems, designated the 'Zulfiqar'. The sanctioned status of Iran following the events of 1979 will without doubt have also played a major role in assisting Soviet T-72 export sales.

OPERATION *PEACE FOR GALILEE* 1982

The IDF went into Lebanon in 1982 to silence Hezbollah fighters backed by Syrian forces in the Beqaa Valley. While the Syrians considered their troops part of an 'Inter-Arab Peacekeeping Force', the Israelis disagreed as Palestinians and Hezbollah used them as protection to fire rockets into Israel, and so on 4 June 1982 the IDF rolled into Lebanon.

There were combat engagements between Syrian T-72s and Israeli M48 and M60 'Magach' tanks and also the new Merkava main battle tank. The battles included some of the first confirmed T-72 losses in combat (the specific events of the Iran–Iraq War being generally more opaque), with Israeli M60A1 tanks destroyed in the same engagements.

Results varied according to engagement, with the most consequential loss to the IDF (and ultimately the US and NATO) being an M48 fitted with 'Blazer' ERA that was sent back to the USSR for evaluation, that same tank being located today at the Kubinka Tank Museum near Moscow. The Merkava turned out to be robust and performed well but took losses from the T-72. A Syrian tank officer, Mazina Fauri, apparently personally witnessed a T-72 firing a HE-FRAG round (having run out of armour-piercing sub-calibre ammunition) blow the turret off a Merkava tank.

While ten to 12 T-72s were claimed as destroyed in combat, the IDF reportedly only had a short period of time to investigate one before they were forced to withdraw and did not recover any of the tanks for more detailed examination. Syrian T-62s were not so lucky, and several were either captured or destroyed during the battles. It would be another five years before a T-72 was delivered intact into Western hands for evaluation by NATO countries.

Syrian tank officers (who were trained in the Soviet Union) gave the T-72s high marks, while President Hafez al-Assad himself declared during an interview that the T-72 was 'the best tank in the world'. The tank had established itself as more than capable of engaging peer tanks delivered to the Middle East by NATO countries.

As a direct consequence of engagements with the T-72, the IDF subsequently re-armed the Merkava with the Rheinmetall 120mm smoothbore gun and also developed far more lethal APFSDS rounds for both the British L7/US M68 105mm gun and the Rheinmetall 120mm gun.

ETHIOPIAN-SOMALI BORDER WAR 1982

Reportedly the Ethiopians used some T-72s on the border against Somali forces.

SRI LANKAN CIVIL WAR 1987

India reportedly used some of their significant T-72 tank inventory in combat against the Tamil Tigers in support of the Sri Lankan government.

OPERATION *DESERT STORM* 1991

One Soviet client who particularly liked the T-72 was Saddam Hussein. The Iraqi Army, and especially the Republican Guards, much appreciated them as they had proven very effective against the Iranians, and when Saddam invaded Kuwait they led that assault. At that time most of the Republican Guards Forces Command (RGFC) armoured and mechanized divisions, especially the Hammurabi, Medina and Tawakalna divisions, were fully equipped with T-72s of one or another version. The 3rd Armoured 'Saladin' Division had a full

A rear view of two T-72B tanks, Dagestan, 1998–99. Note the stowage on operational tanks.

brigade of T-72s and the 5th Mechanized 'Muhammed-ibn-al-Kasem' Division had one regiment in one of its mechanized brigades. Overall, the Iraqis probably had close to 1,000 T-72s of all types, including some semi-knocked down Polish T-72M1 tanks they dubbed 'Asad Babil' (Lion of Babylon).*

But what had worked well against Iran was another story when placed up against Western forces and latest generation tanks. The Allied Coalition had nearly 1,500 modern tanks like the M1A1 Abrams and Challenger Mk 1 in country prior to the breakout of the ground war, and all of their crews were very well trained. When the ground war broke out on 24 February 1991 there was little doubt how things would go.

This was the first time that these modern Western tanks came into direct combat with members of the Soviet-era T-72 family. While the results were pretty one-sided, it was more due to the fact that the Iraqis were not particularly adept at tank combat. They were also not inclined to engage for reasons outside the scope of this book, with many tanks being abandoned rather than destroyed, and the T-72M1 export models engaged were not armoured or equipped to the same standard as those used by the Soviet Army.

While the USAF claimed at one point as many as 60,000 vehicles destroyed from the air, and US tank forces claimed numbers as high as 4,000 Iraqi tanks destroyed, the score among tanks as determined by after-action analysis was

---

* This refers to tanks that were exported in component form and were re-assembled by the customer upon arrival.

RIGHT A T-72B1 on the move, Dagestan, 1998–99.

BELOW LEFT An emplaced and partially camouflaged T-72B1 in Dagestan, 1998–99.

BELOW RIGHT Another emplaced T-72B1 during the same operation in Dagestan.

1,860 armoured vehicles knocked out in combat, with most assessed damage due to artillery fire and BGM-71 Tow-2 ATGM systems, with the majority of T-72 tanks destroyed by their own crews before being abandoned, having run out of fuel and/or ammunition.

Of those knocked out, Iraq probably lost in the aggregate half of its T-72s, while units like the Tawakalna RGFC Division lost almost all of their tanks (estimated at around 200 tanks), as did the 3rd Armoured Division and the 5th Mechanized Division.

The other two premier Iraqi armoured divisions, the Hammurabi and Medina, apparently were able to save many of their tanks by retreating across the Tigris River as US President George H. W. Bush called it a no-fire line and any forces across that river were not to be attacked. Some units lined up in easy sight of Coalition forces to taunt them about being 'safe' and at least enjoyed the fact that nobody violated the order.

TOP LEFT Georgian tanks were rebuilt using equipment from several foreign contractors. Note the main rangefinder-sight on this tank.

TOP RIGHT A row of T-72AV and T-72B series tanks captured from Georgia during the short war in 2008.

LEFT A T-72B destroyed in the short war in Southern Ossetia and Georgia, 2008.

The First Gulf War also witnessed one of the first cases of the T-72 series being used by both sides in a conflict. Kuwait had earlier purchased Yugoslavian M84 tanks and deployed them against the Iraqis during the war.

The Soviet Union was meanwhile focused internally on its own immediate future in 1991 rather than on events in the Middle East. Soviet tank designers nevertheless assessed the results of the war as it related to Soviet tank technology. The use of thermal imaging, allowing engagement at up to 3,000m at night and in poor weather conditions, was noted as a major advantage for Coalition forces ranged against Soviet armour, as was the use of depleted uranium rounds. The Iraqi T-72M1 tanks were provided with 3BM9 armour-piercing APFSDS rounds dating from when the T-72 entered service in 1973, at a time when the aforementioned British and American tanks were still in the development stage. The Soviets, soon to be the Russians, took note of failings observed during the First Gulf War, whether technical or operator related, and made appropriate changes.

GEORGIAN CIVIL WAR 1991–93

The Georgians suffered a civil war that broke out after a coup removed Zviad Gamsakhurdia from power in September 1991 and a new government headed by Eduard Shevardnadze took power. Gamsakhurdia loyalists fought to retake the government but failed. With all of the disruption in the country, Abkhazia later tried to break away and the Georgian Army was sent in in August 1992 to put down the rebellion, during which time Gamsakhurdia tried to take back power, but was finally defeated and died in December 1993 under suspicious circumstances. T-72 tanks were used by all parties in the above simmering conflicts.

NAGORNO-KARABAKH CONFLICT 1988–2020

With the break-up of the Soviet Union, ethnic tensions boiled over in several former Soviet republics, with one of the longest conflicts being that between Armenia and Azerbaijan over the region of Nagorno-Karabakh. Tensions pre-dated the break-up of the Soviet Union but became an open conflict in the early 1990s, with a ceasefire signed in 1994 but a second short conflict erupting in 2020. The T-72 tank was widely used during the first conflict, where the early production model T-72s deployed suffered some problems with turret rotation in mountainous conditions. The tanks used in the conflict were already obsolete, and the known problem was addressed in the T-72A/T-72B with a more powerful electric turret traverse drive, but, as in all conflicts, lessons were learned from combat experience versus peacetime training.

BREAK-UP OF YUGOSLAVIA 1991–2001

Yugoslavia was a country formed of six subordinate republics after the end of World War I. The dominant leader emerged as Josef Broz Tito, who turned it into a Communist country at the end of World War II when his partisan forces took over the country after Nazi occupation. Tito did not trust the Soviets, and (rather successfully) played 'both sides of the street' with NATO and the Warsaw Pact.

This worked well until Tito died and power inside the country eventually devolved upon Slobodan Milosevic in 1989. While he did loosen some of the iron controls on the country, the six subordinate republics – Croatia, Bosnia and Herzegovina, Serbia, Macedonia, Slovenia and Montenegro – and the breakaway section of Kosovo all had very different ideas about independence and soon began to declare their freedom from Belgrade.

The result was a long and bloody war inside the country, with the bulk of the fighting falling on Kosovo, Croatia and Bosnia and Herzegovina. Sporadic outbreaks of fighting took place with UN and later NATO troops deployed to the area from 1996 to prevent further bloodshed; the fighting did not completely stop until 2002.

All sides in the conflict had access to either M84 or T-72 tanks as well as many other armoured vehicles, including World War II remnants such as US M18 and M36 tank destroyers. There is no accurate record of who used which tanks against which threat force and where.

THE AUGUST 1991 PUTSCH IN MOSCOW

When Mikhail Gorbachev oversaw the disintegration and collapse of the USSR, many in the Soviet government concluded he must be forcibly replaced and a new government take control to prevent any further disintegration. Personalities such as Defence Minister Dmitriy Yazov called on the army to back up their 'putsch' (the August coup), but Army Commander General Pavel Grachev refused to inject the military into politics and only used the Moscow garrison units like the 2nd Tamanskaya Guards MRD with its T-72B tanks to secure the capital. Boris Yeltsin, the future President of the Russian Federation, himself stood on a T-72B tank outside the Russian parliament building to address the nation. The putsch soon collapsed.

THE CHECHEN WARS 1991–96 AND 1999–2003

For over 150 years, the Caucasus region has been politically volatile, and within the USSR that especially included the various small autonomous regions within the Caucasus. With the break-up of the USSR in 1991, the Chechens pushed for independence, and former Soviet VVS General-Major Dzhokar Dudayev was named as the head of the new government of the Chechen Republic of Ichkeria, with Grozny being established as its capital. The Russians were initially too engaged with post-Soviet economic impacts to do much about it at the time, with resistance forces in the country unable to make headway. In December 1994 President Boris Yeltsin decided to put down the rebellion by force.

The T-72 tank was deployed by the Russian Army during both subsequent wars in the Russian autonomous region of Chechnya, where fighting in rugged mountainous terrain and street fighting with inexperienced Russian crews at first took a heavy toll on Russian forces operating there. The T-72A was also used by Chechen forces. According to a report of the Northern Caucasus Military Region (VO) in June 1992 there were 108 armoured vehicles located around Grozny, including 42 T-62 and T-72 tanks.

The 1994 Russian invasion of Chechnya by a peacetime conscript Russian Army without combat experience for the most part was fraught with difficulty.

Many of the tanks used were drawn from strategic storage with little time to ensure proper return to service, and tanks consequently suffered from the ravages of long-term storage on long route marches. On the move from bases north of the republic into Chechnya some 2,200 vehicles of various types suffered failures, mostly due to a combination of the aforementioned long-term storage and poor preparation; rubber parts and cooling systems were the primary systems and items that failed. Some 20 per cent of the T-72 and T-80 tanks deployed in the first assault – mainly the early 'scrap candidate' T-72s that had undergone two to three capital repairs and were mechanically worn – had at least one breakdown en route. There were also early problems with fuel logistics, as is often the case with a transit from peace to wartime operation.

On 31 December 1994 T-72 and T-80 tanks were sent into the capital Grozny, but the fuel consumption of the T-80 tank, which burns nearly as much fuel at idle as at running speed, created logistics issues, as in a matter of hours almost all of the tanks ran out of fuel. Since they had no backup auxiliary power units for the control systems they were rendered helpless, and once in such a predicament the Chechens came out of concealment and destroyed nearly all of them.

The storming of Grozny was by a combination of units including the 131st Maikop Separate MRB and the 81st Guards MRR. During the engagement, 22 T-72 tanks belonging to the 131st 'Maikop' were recorded by the Russian Army as lost in action.

The initial weeks of the conflict in Chechnya were a hard lesson for the inexperienced tank crews deployed there. One motorized rifle unit deployed from Ekaterinburg received its ERA packages only en route for the storming of Grozny, with not enough time to install them on all tanks before they were operationally deployed, an oversight that lost tank crews their lives and for which responsibility was never taken by senior officers. Tanks were initially lost due to a combination of psychologically unprepared conscript crews,* logistics blunders and terrain, including urban combat, the bane of all tank units.

After this initial combat debacle many T-80 tanks, which were over-complex for such operations, were switched out for T-62- and T-72-equipped formations, but even so they also had problems. Some of the tanks that initially went into Chechnya were not fitted with the 4S20 flyer plates installed in their 'Kontakt-1' containers, so if hit by RPG or ATGM projectiles they were penetrated and frequently knocked out. Once this oversight was fixed and the tanks were properly prepared, losses dropped accordingly. The Russian Army's priority was the elimination of T-62 – and a few T-72 – tanks in the hands of the Chechens, which was quickly executed.

---

*   In many cases, early tank losses were due to crews not appreciating that they were regarded as the enemy in enemy surroundings, being ambushed by grenades dropped through open hatches, etc.

The war in Chechnya was brutal for combatants and civilians alike. As regards the T-72, there are recorded incidents of T-72 tanks and the realities of their combat environment. One T-72B, turret No. 436, not fitted with its prescribed ERA armour due to the logistics problems noted above, was caught in street fighting and hit on the side by a PG-9V 73mm round from an SPG-9 recoilless anti-tank weapon, which detonated the ammunition complement, with the crew killed as a direct consequence of the noted logistics issues in the higher command. In the capital, Grozny, tanks were engaged from several directions simultaneously, with Chechen rebels, also well versed in tank technology due to prior Soviet military service, specifically targeting the most vulnerable top deck and engine compartments to disable tanks.

In January 1995, T-72B turret No. 259 of the 'Maikop' MRB was simultaneously hit by rockets from several RPG-7 and SPG-9 launchers. The tank managed to disengage from the firefight, and on later inspection the crew counted seven hits on the hull and turret, luckily with none penetrating the armour.

Later in the war in March 1996, in an engagement to take the village of Goiskoye south of Grozny, a T-72B-equipped MRR tank company from the Urals Military District (UVO) was engaged by Chechen forces armed with the 9M111 ATGM system. Fourteen rounds were fired at the tank unit, of which 12 hit their targets, with one tank hit by four rockets. The latter tank disengaged and survived, but with the turret optics and air defence machine gun destroyed. The following month, T-72 tanks travelling in convoy on a mountain road with hatches open and tank crews seated on the tank exterior were engaged by a 9M111 ATG system from nearly 2km range. An ammunition container stowed on the hull was hit and detonated, with the tank commander seated outside the hull instantly killed. The tank again survived, but with hard lessons learned. Such was the reality of the close-combat fighting during the First Chechen War.

As of February 1995, of the 2,221 armoured vehicles used in the conflict 225 were written off, including 62 tanks, of which approximately half were T-72s belonging to the 131st Motorized Rifle Brigade.

Dudayev was killed by Russian forces in April 1996, but the Russian government agreed a ceasefire with the separatists and pulled forces out, leaving them in charge of the republic. The unresolved situation simmered for some years, flaring back up as President Yeltsin was forced from power, handing the presidency over to Vice President Vladimir Putin in December 1999. Fighting had in the meantime broken out between the self-declared republic in Chechnya and Dagestan in August 1999, with the latter prevailing. There followed a second invasion of Chechnya by a completely reorganized and better-trained Russian military.

In the Second Chechen War, which lasted from October 1999 until August 2000, the Russians quickly and ruthlessly overwhelmed all rebel forces and took back control of the region, quickly turning over many duties to pro-Russian Chechen forces. T-72 tanks were again used in combat as part of what the Russians called 'Reconnaissance Fire Operations' in which all types of firepower – missiles, artillery, rockets, fighter-bombers and helicopters – were used to suppress an area where the fighters were trapped and then the tanks and infantry would go in to mop up. T-72s made use of the 'fire carousel' tactics in these operations, but in general wheeled BTRs were used far more extensively than tanks during the second campaign in Chechnya, with no tank or tank crew losses. Military operations technically ended in April 2002 and Ministry of Internal Affairs (MVD) troops took over much of the now much reduced fighting against the rebels. Operations were only formally ended in 2009.

MOLDOVA-TRANSNISTRIA CONFLICT 1992

In 1992 the province of Transnistria broke away from Moldova and caused a short and sharp war between the two entities. Russian forces came in on the side of the separatists. While the only tanks identified in the conflict were T-64s, with the total destruction of some tanks demonstrating why UVZ was correct in not having an open mechanical loader in their tanks, it is likely the Russians did use some T-72s and also provided weapons to the breakaway province.

TADJIKISTAN CIVIL WAR CONFLICT 1992

The break-up of the Soviet Union led to significant conflict in and between several former Soviet Socialist Republics. In May 1992 regional groups from the Garm and Gorno-Badakhshan regions of Tadjikistan rose up against the newly formed Tadjik government in the capital Dushanbe in a civil war that would rage for a year and simmer until June 1997. The T-72 tank was used by both sides during the conflict.

RUSSIAN CONSTITUTIONAL CRISIS 1993

The political turmoil in the Russian Federation in the early 1990s led to intense factional intergovernmental rivalry, and in October 1993 this broke out into open conflict between the Duma and the president of the country.

The conflict in Moscow was between President Yeltsin and his supporters led by Viktor Chernomyrdin against Vice President Rutskoy and Speaker Khasbulatov and their supporters. With the government split, Yeltsin called for the support of the Russian Army to settle the problem. After some considerable debate with the army, the Moscow garrison forces were called in to put down the rebellion and cornered the plotters in the Russian 'Beliy Dom' (White House) – the Russian parliament building. T-72B tanks from the 4th 'Kantemirovskaya' Guards Tank Division were used to block access to the city while the T-80UDs from the 2nd 'Tamanskaya' Guards MRD were used to fire on the Russian 'Beliy Dom' building.

OPERATION *IRAQI FREEDOM* 2003–11

After the 1991 Gulf War the situation inside Iraq remained stable until a crisis in 2003, when in ultimate response to the well-documented and subsequently disproved weapons of mass destruction case for invasion. a Coalition ground force built up in Saudi Arabia and Kuwait and invaded in April of that year. It took 21 days to take over the country, mostly due to the fact that the Iraqi Army did not present any meaningful defence but simply melted away.

Some tanks and other military hardware were destroyed, either from the air or on the ground when troops did put up a fight, but for the most part Iraqi Army equipment was captured intact. Most of the surviving T-72 tanks were turned over to the new Iraqi Army formed by the US after the country fell.

Saddam Hussein was captured in 2003 and executed in 2006, by which time continued resistance within Iraq had gradually faded, although sporadic fighting would continue for many years. The T-72 was widely used in the Second Gulf War, but in much less dramatic and loss-heavy engagements than during the First Gulf War due to the aforementioned lack of major direct tank clashes.

SOUTH OSSETIA AND ABKHAZIA (GEORGIAN) WAR 2008

In the years following the Georgian Civil War of 1991–93, the situation in the region continued to simmer. In the summer of 2008, the pro-Russia population of South Ossetia declared independence from Georgia, with Abkhazia simultaneously declaring independence. Russian armoured forces crossed the border on 7 August 2008, beginning active conduct on 8 August in what was described as a peacekeeping expedition into the two provinces. Russian troops quickly occupied and secured both of the provinces as well as parts of Georgia proper, with T-72 tanks operating in difficult mountainous terrain such as the Kodori Gorge area, where Chechen rebels were also located.

BOTTOM LEFT The turret of a captured Georgian T-72AV. Compare the Kontakt-1 ERA layout with the T-72B ('BV').

BOTTOM RIGHT This view of a destroyed Georgian T-72B tank turret clearly shows the typical layout of Kontakt-1 ERA blocks.

RIGHT Maskirovka and the fog of war. Described at the time as a TOS-1A in service with DNR forces in Donbass, it is in fact a badly damaged T-72B with the turret traversed and a fabricated 'TOS-1A' structure.

OPPOSITE PAGE A Russian T-72AV during the Russian-termed Special Military Operation in Ukraine in 2022–23.

BOTTOM LEFT AND RIGHT A 2S19 in service with VSU (Ukrainian Army) forces in eastern Ukraine 2014–15. (Sergei Popsuevich)

The T-72 tank was employed by both sides during this conflict that lasted for less than a week. Georgia started the war with a combination of 191 T-72AV and B tanks, many upgraded to the T-72 Sim-1 level, together with a number of US-supplied systems and leftover Soviet weapons systems. Recorded Russian losses included two T-72s and one T-62. Georgian losses were significant, with many tanks captured intact by Russian forces.

LIBYAN CIVIL WAR 2011

Libya descended into internecine fighting following the 'Arab Spring' and the death of Muammar Gaddafi in 2011. Before Gaddafi's death, approximately 150 T-72 tanks were used by the Libyan Army, with the Russian Federation selling

new tanks and undertaking some capital modernization of older Soviet-era tanks. As the country descended into anarchy, tanks had been divided up between tribal based factions, with T-72s to be found fighting for any number of factions at the same time. The current number of T-72 tanks operating in Libya is unknown.

SYRIAN CIVIL WAR 2011–PRESENT

With the death of Hafiz al-Assad in 2000, and subsequently his son Bassel, his other son, Bashar al-Assad, a former ophthalmologist in London, was recalled to Syria to assume the reign. Bashar was not the iron-fisted dictator his father had been, but was also unable to solve many of the problems the country faced. The complexities of the 'Arab Spring' and the labyrinthian politics of the Middle East are beyond the scope of this work, but insurrections beginning in 2011 led to a large section of the country being declared a caliphate. This brought in first the United States and then Russia to eliminate the threat, with tens of thousands of Syrians killed and hundreds of thousands displaced by a war that ultimately resulted in the collapse of the Syrian government, al-Assad fleeing into exile and the country descending into chaos.

During this prolonged agony for Syria, T-72 tanks were at the forefront of Syrian army efforts to eliminate fighters of all stripes. While Assad was able to purchase newer Russian tanks like the T-72B3 and T-90 to arm his forces, older T-72 tanks underwent both formal and informal upgrades. The formal ones include installation of 'Kontakt-1' ERA suites and other upgrades. The informal ones – a programme that American troops usually refer to as 'hillbilly armour' – consists of fitting baskets of rebar to the turrets and hull fronts and filling them with rocks or broken concrete chunks for added protection. Some have been fitted with locally designed 'Reshotka' grille armour or even standard Russian suites. Tanks in Syria are condemned to street

Small calibre round and shrapnel damage to the aluminium thermal sleeve on a Georgian T-72AV or B tank.

fighting, which is brutal and exacts a toll. Various militias also used captured T-72s against the Syrian army, but they were always fewer in number.

The designers at UKBTM in Nizhny Tagil took note of the urban warfare as conducted in Syria and local Syrian modifications to better protect their T-72 tanks in such an environment, leading to a 'Gorodskoy' (urban warfare) version of the T-72B unveiled at the RAE-2013 exhibition in Nizhny Tagil. It also led to the development of additional 'Reshotka' grille packages, including overhead protection at both factory and field rebuild level, as extensively used in the Russian-defined Special Military Operation in Ukraine which was launched in February 2022.

SUDAN-SOUTH SUDAN CONFLICT 2013–PRESENT

After the Republic of South Sudan broke off from Sudan in 2011, tribal warfare and internal conflict broke out between the tribes and the government with a major rebel group, the Sudanese People's Liberation Movement, being the main one. A bloody civil war followed in which government forces have T-72s and have used them against the rebels.

DONETSK, LUGANSK AND CRIMEA 2014–22

Following the break-up of the Soviet Union 1991, Crimea attempted full autonomy before settling for autonomous status within newly independent Ukraine, while Russia and Ukraine eventually agreed to split the Soviet Black Sea Fleet based at Sevastopol, with Russia concluding a long-term lease with Ukraine for use of the naval base and its facilities.

Following political turmoil in Ukraine in 2014, conflict broke out in the eastern regions of Donetsk and Lugansk and several years of internal fighting followed between Kiev (Kyiv) and the breakaway Donetsk and Lugansk regions (DNR and LNR respectively), with the regions later declaring full autonomy as republics. The first full year of fighting culminated in the defeat of Ukrainian and foreign forces at the Battle of Debaltsevo in January–February 2015, with the contentious Minsk II Agreements providing a degree of peace and stability for the next years, but sporadic shelling and fighting continued until 2022.

During this initial period of heavy fighting in 2014–15, the breakaway republics used a variety of Soviet-era tanks and equipment, including T-64 and T-72 tanks, with tank losses on both sides of the conflict. The Ukrainian Army (VSU) did not have enough of the later domestic 'Oplot' or 'Bulat' models to gain overall momentum, and Ukraine eventually had to bring out a number of mothballed T-72s from long-term strategic storage to make up for the losses.

ABOVE A Russian T-72B coming to a stop to receive orders during the Russian-termed Special Military Operation in Ukraine.

RIGHT Another Russian T-72B during the war in eastern Ukraine. Note the mix of markings.

IRAQI CIVIL WAR 2014–17

While Iraq remained unstable after the defeat of Saddam Hussein in 2003, by 2007 the US had managed to eliminate most of the opposition in the country to the new government. But in 2014 a large swathe of the north and west of the country was taken by ISIS forces that joined with ISIS fighters in Syria to form 'The Caliphate' under their new leader al-Baghdadi.

With US backing, the Iraqi Army moved to attack these combined forces and after three years was able to force them out of the country. The Iraqi Army used both T-72s and US M1A2 Abrams tanks in suppressing the fighters, but with a combination of assistance and interference by Iranian forces inside Iraq in a region with complex historical and religious loyalties.

RUSSO-UKRAINIAN CONFLICT 2022 TO THE PRESENT

After the Battle of Debaltsevo in early 2015, sporadic fighting in what was still ostensibly a civil war continued in the industrial regions of eastern Ukraine, primarily as an artillery war. On 21 February 2022 Russia recognized the DNR and LNR as 'independent republics' and three days later, on 24 February 2022, launched its Russian-termed Special Military Operation and invaded Ukraine, setting the scene for what is a full-scale war fought with combined arms forces on the edge of Europe.

A Russian T-72B3 tank photographed during the war in July 2023.

LEFT AND BELOW A destroyed T-72B1 displayed on Khreshchatyk, Kyiv. (Sergei Popsuevich)

The war has rewritten tactical warfare, with the mass use of anti-tank weapons and also drones. It has seen modern NATO armour pitted against Soviet-era and current tanks, with the T-72 in large-scale use in numerous modifications on both sides of the conflict. The T-72 has been central to the fighting, being operated by both Russian and Ukrainian (VSU) forces. T-72 and other tanks operating in the war in Ukraine and in late 2024 in the Kursk Oblast of Russia have rarely been used in tank-on-tank engagements, rather providing fire support for infantry, mechanized or otherwise, in the manner of the 'sniper' role assigned (at least on paper) to the T-62 tank when introduced into service. The war has become one of precision missile, artillery, anti-tank guided weapon and drone warfare, with the individual merits of particular tank technology being negated

TOP LEFT AND RIGHT The reality of war. A destroyed T-72B M-1989 (also seen designated as T-72BA) on display in Kyiv. Note the 1K13-49 sight for the 9K120 'Svir' ATGM system from the earlier T-72B and the retained L-4A IR projector.

by the application of new weapons ranged against them, this applying to foreign tanks as much as to the T-72 or any other Soviet origin design, Russian or Ukrainian. The necessary use of field-rigged additional screening to ward off top-attack ATGMs and drones is reminiscent of the sandbags applied to Allied tanks in World War II or the grille 'bedspring' armour applied to tanks entering Berlin in the spring of 1945, simply a case of adaptation to new threats that evolve at lightning pace during wartime. In all of this, the T-72 has remained a staple and stable tank, performing its designated role without fuss or unduly arduous maintenance requirements.

Most Russian losses in the war have been ascribed to Western ATGM and RPG weapons (and now drones), specifically the US Javelin ATGM and the British NLAW RPG systems. Both of these weapons have a top-attack mode where the missile pulls up and dives on the target from above, attacking the thinner top armour on the turret or roof of the target. From the number of catastrophic losses observed in the early months of the war, it would seem that the inexperienced T-72 crews did not observe the lessons learned in Chechnya with the use of the 'fire carousel' tactic and were using fully loaded T-72s with all 44–45 rounds of ammunition on board. Once penetrated, these tanks tended to blow up and become a total loss.

The Ukraine war has also added the use of German Leopard 2, Abrams and Challenger 2 tanks donated to the Ukrainians. While tank vs tank combat is somewhat sketchy and prone to anecdotal evidence, all tanks in the conflict, of whatever origin, have proven vulnerable to ATGM and drone attack.

Ukrainian drones initially used a tactic where they hovered over a tank looking for an open hatch. If they saw one on video the operator would order the drone to drop an 82mm or 120mm mortar bomb into the open hatch, with the resulting internal explosion destroying the tank.

Early attempts to fit tanks with a grille armour screen over the turret as well as grille armour on the turret sides to prevent this sort of attack were not particularly successful, being easily penetrated by at least the Javelin missiles with their tandem warheads. But in wartime experience is rapidly accumulated and developments are quick, and current models of this roof defence show a mix of ERA bricks attached as well as mesh nets to keep drones from attacking from the sides.

The most bizarre modifications seen in the full-scale Russia–Ukraine war which started in 2022 are the so-called 'cherepakhi' (turtle) tanks, where a large lightweight welded metal barn-like structure has been built to hide the entire tank within, with open rear and front openings protected by the aforementioned anti-drone mesh. The cumbersome looking but highly effective fabricated frames essentially provide good protection from overhead attack but are vulnerable to snaring and damage in typical operating environments.

SUMMARY

As of the time of writing in 2025, the T-72 main battle tank is currently involved in its greatest operational deployment in history, being used on both sides in a war between two former Soviet states some 50 years after its service introduction with the Soviet Army. Meanwhile, the T-72 also soldiers on with several other nations, many of which have been involved in smaller conflicts, with results hard to isolate. Combat in Ukraine has shown that the T-72, like all tanks, is vulnerable to new anti-tank means, but many of those losses – like those in the hands of foreign forces – are due more to crew inexperience or tactical misuse than failures of the tank to carry out its designed functions. 'Penny packet' use of the tank has seen many of them isolated and destroyed by small units of infantry, often with ATGMs carried on fast all-terrain vehicles. The T-90, basically the developed T-72BM tank from 1992, has suffered many of the same problems and results as any other tank involved in the conflict, on the basis that a tank is an instrument of war, and in war things get destroyed.

Those T-72 tanks that remain in operational condition after the current conflict, with a consequent build-up of operational wear, maintenance and rebuild, will doubtless remain in service with the Russian Federation for years to come, with further modifications and upgrades such as those carried out on the T-72B3M. The current T-72B3 modernization programme in its various forms

was originally introduced as a cost-effective upgrade for an older tank model. But it became a unique and paradoxical case of an older tank being modernized to such an extent that it was almost as combat effective, and at the same time more financially viable to produce, as the T-90A tank originally designed to replace it in production. The T-72 today serves alongside its production replacement not as an older tank kept current until mechanically worn out as in the past, but rather as a late 1960s tank design having been given a second life as a tank model that both militaries and accountants approve of. A similar modernization programme has also been undertaken with the T-80BVM.

The sheer number of T-72 tanks still in service both domestically and abroad in many countries ensures that the full story of the T-72 tank family remains a work in progress, to be retold many years into the future.

T-72 tanks of all modifications have been fitted with 'Reshotka' grille type anti-drone frames on the turret roof during the war in Ukraine, with factory designed structures later fitted to new-build tanks.

CHAPTER 6
MANUAL EXTRACTS

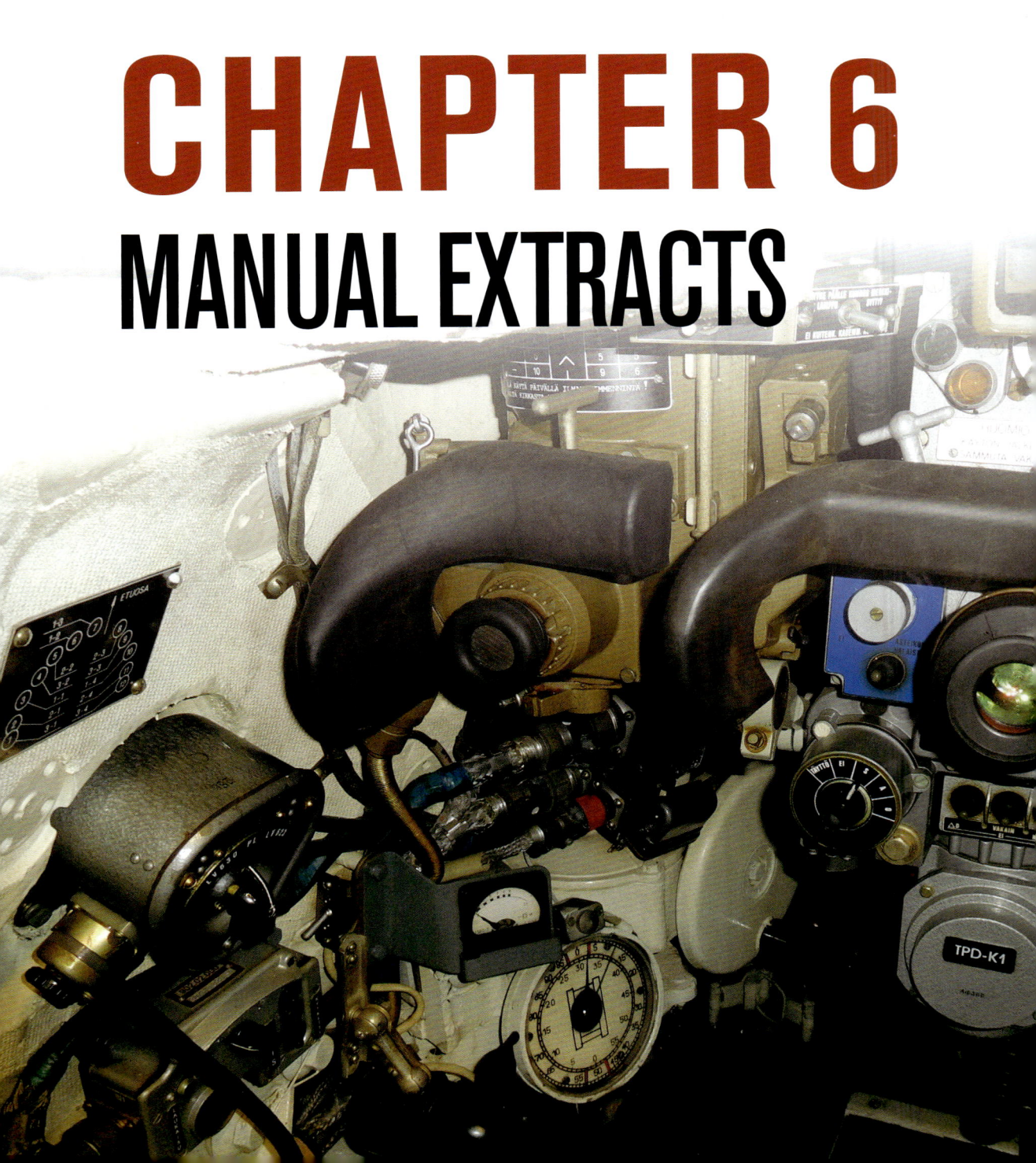

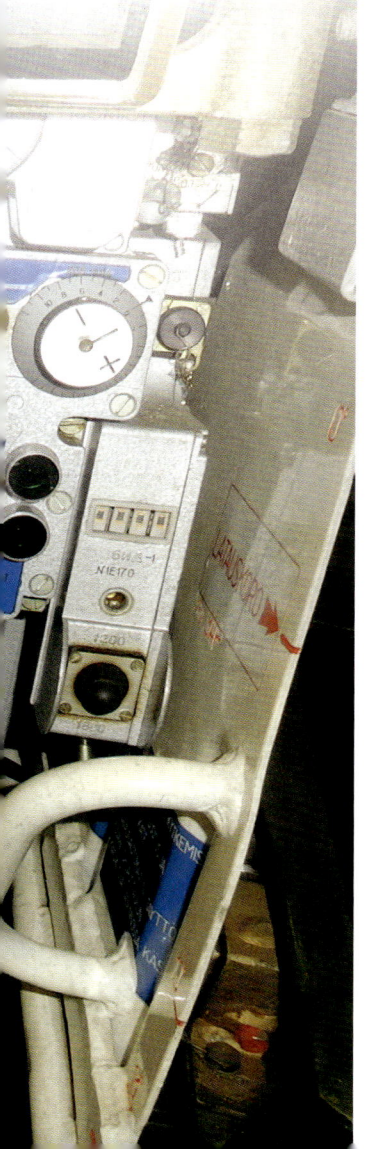

TPD-K1 gunner's sight/rangefinder as mounted on a T-72M1 export tank built in 1988 and exported to Finland (Ps 264-122).

The T-72 was built in several domestic and additional export variants, with all tanks subject to medium and capital rebuild and modernization. In consequence, there are myriad fitments and modernizations to consider when reviewing any given tank model. The operator's manual extracts provided here are from original Soviet (rather than Warsaw Pact or export) manuals for an early Soviet Obiekt-172M, a Soviet T-72A and Soviet T-72B. Some photographs provide clarification on specific components where clearer than in the manuals. Many details change from model to model, some obvious, some more subtle; for example the driver-mechanic's control panel on the Obiekt-172M and the T-72A are quite different. Photographs of components labelled Ps264-122 are from an at the time Finnish operational T-72M1 built at UVZ at Nizhny Tagil in the Soviet Union in August 1988, courtesy of Esa Muikku. The photographs also illustrate where the original equipment is missing from the T-72A tank detailed in the Walkaround chapter. The authors would like to express their thanks to the Museum of Russian Military History at Padikovo for internal access to their ex operational T-72 built in 1978 with one capital rebuild in 1988 during its service life.

BELOW TKN-3 commander's sight in an export T-72M1 built in Nizhny Tagil in 1988.

(A) Obiekt-172M Operator's Manual Cover. Note the manual is entitled Obiekt-172M rather than T-72.

(B) T-72A Operator's Manual Cover.

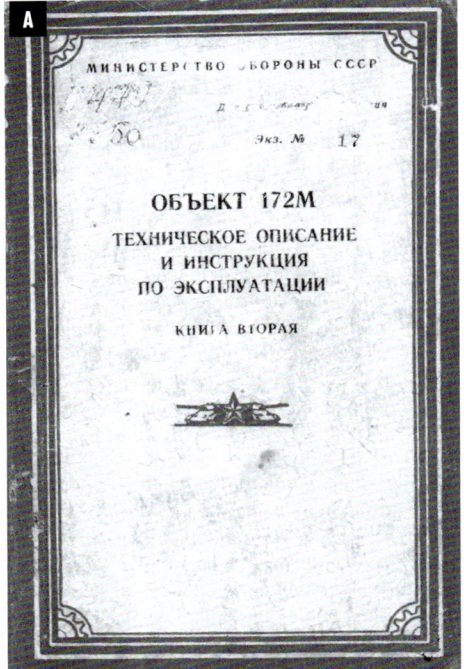

(C) T-72B Operator's Manual Cover.

(D) TPD2-49 gunner's sight and fire control system.

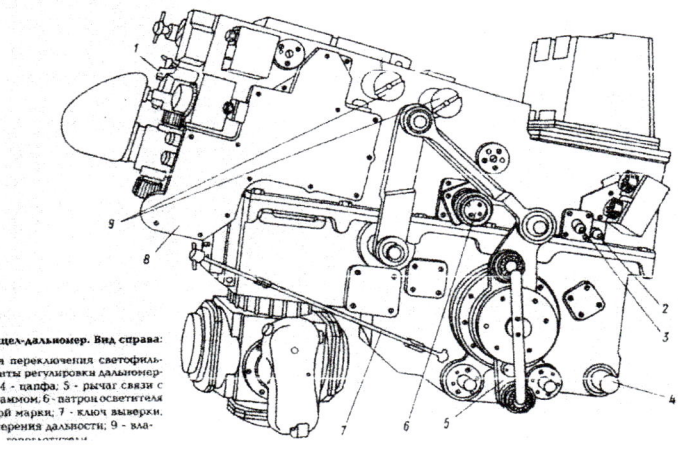

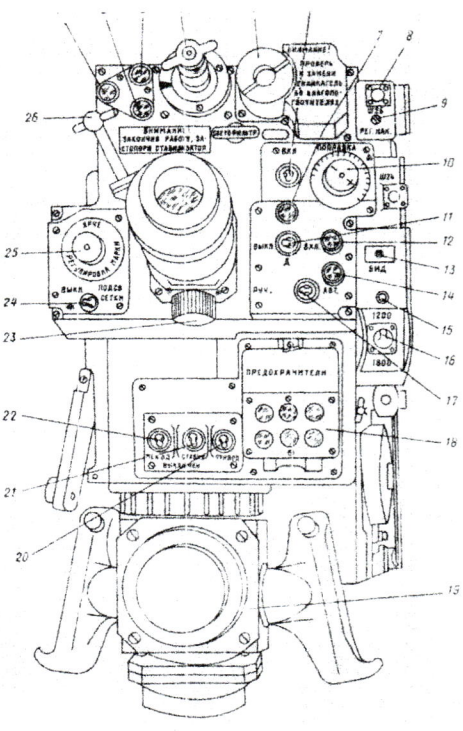

(E) TPD2-49 gunner's sight on T-72 serial number 4152 built February 1978, with capital rebuild in 1988.

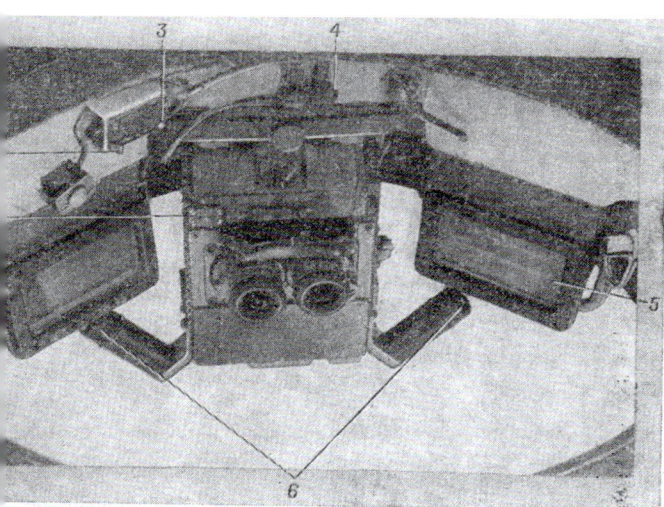

Рис. 20. Смотровой прибор ТКН-3:
1 — выключатель прибора; 2 — налобник; 3 — рукоятка шторы; 4 — упор; 5 — головка; 6 — замок; 7 — рукоятка диафрагмы; 8 — корпус; 9 — рукоятка переключения зеркал; 10 — окуляры; 11 — патрон осушки; 12 — зажим; 13 — рукоятка

(F) TKN-3 commander's sight.

Рис. 22. Установка прибора ТКН-3:
а электрообогрева окуляров; *2 — переключатель осветителя ОУ-3ГК; 3 —* ль электрообогрева; *4 — разветвительная колодка; 5 — призменный прибор ТНП-160; 6 — кнопки*

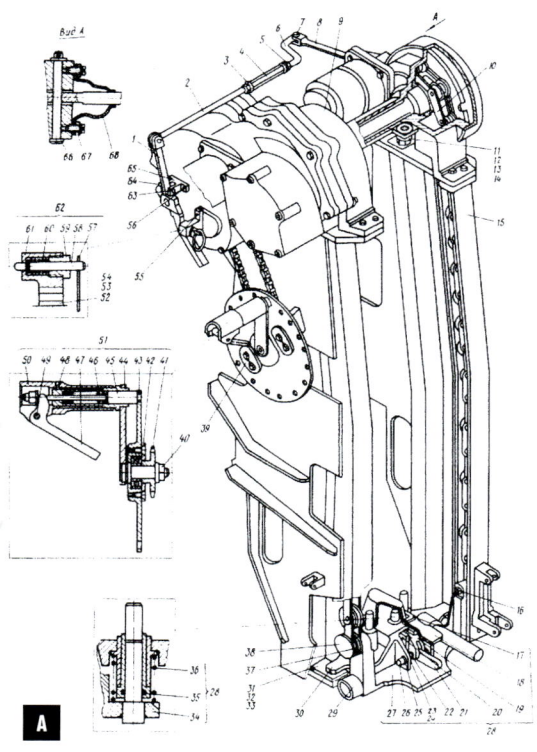

(**A**) Autoloader and case ejection system.

(**B**) Autoloader and case ejection system in a Soviet T-72A built in 1978.

(**C**) 125mm 2A46 gun breech (Finnish export T-72M1, Ps 264-122) at the Motovilikha Museum, Perm (Esa Muikku)

(**D**) 125mm 2A46 gun breech. (Finnish export T-72M1, Ps 264-122).

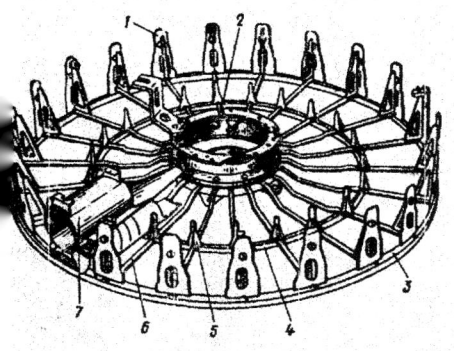

Рис. 53. Каркас ВТ с погонным устройством

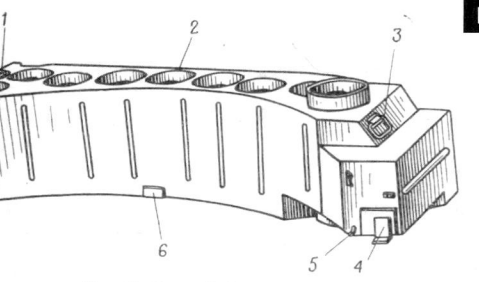

Рис. 48. Средний бак-стеллаж:

фланец для установки крана отключения наружных топливных баков; 2 — трубы для укладки боекомплекта; 3 — ручка для транспортировки бака; 4 — лапа крепления бака; 5 — направляющая трубка троса к заслонке ОПВТ; 6 — уголок; 7 — заборная трубка

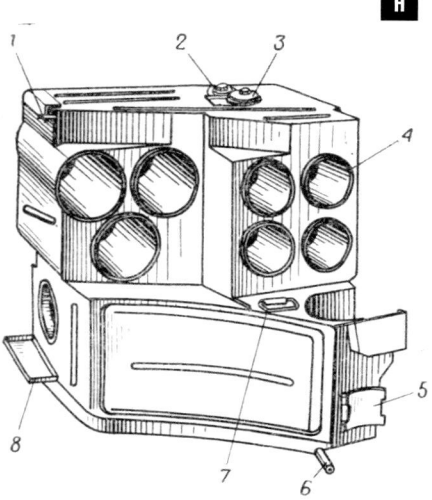

Рис. 47. Передний бак-стеллаж:

1 — трубка выпуска воздуха из левого носового бака при его заправке; 2 — фланец для установки топливомера; 3 — фланец заправочной горловины; 4 — труба для укладки боекомплекта; 5 — кронштейн для крепления баллона ППО; 6 — патрубок для соединения со средним баком-стеллажом; 7 — ручка для транспортировки бака; 8 — лоток для запасного смотрового прибора

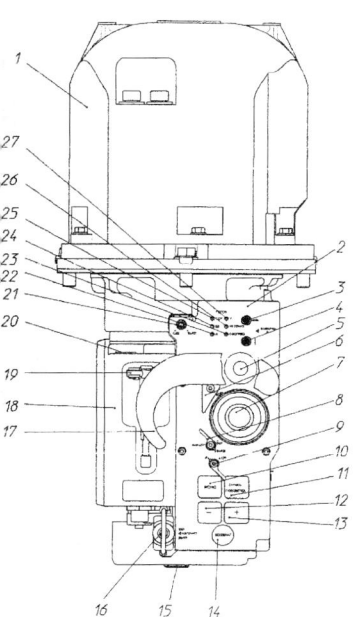

(E) Autoloader base carousel mechanism.

(F) Rear 'bak-stellazh', Obiekt-172M.

(G) The 'Sosna-U' sight as introduced on the later T-72B3.

(H) Front 'bak-stellazh' (literally fuel/ammunition stowage) container, Obiekt-172M.

(A) Driver-mechanic's seat, Obiekt-172M.

(B) Driver-mechanic's seat (Finnish export T-72M1, Ps 264-122).

(C) Power distribution and fuse panel, Obiekt-172M.

(D) Driver-mechanic's control panel, Obiekt-172M.

(E) Driver-mechanic's control panel, T-72A.

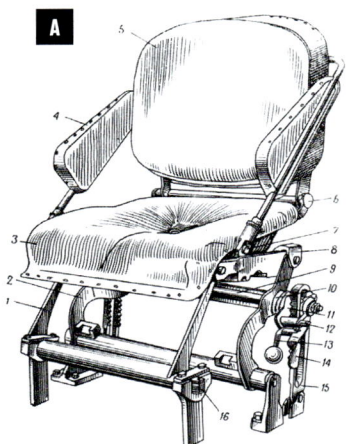

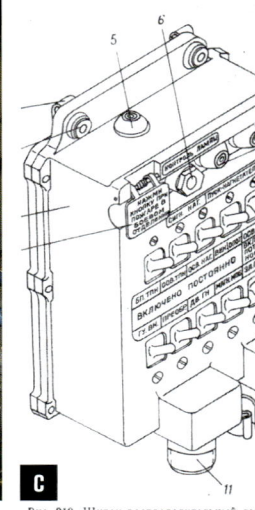
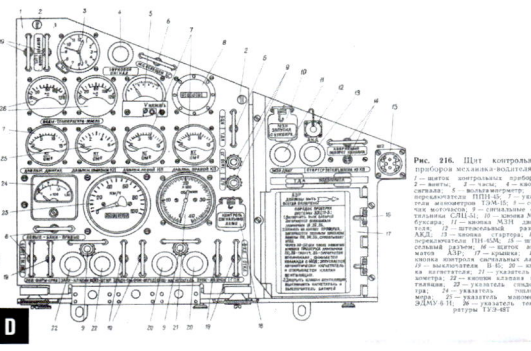
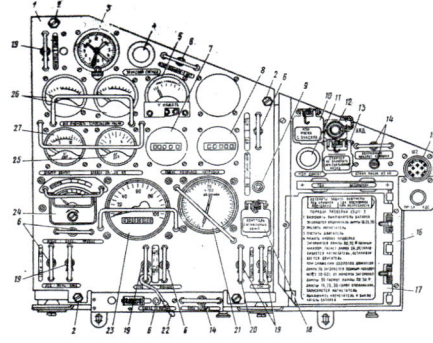
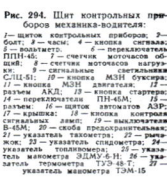

(F) Driver-mechanic's control panel, T-72A built in 1978.

(G) Driver-mechanic's position (Finnish export T-72M1, Ps 264-122).

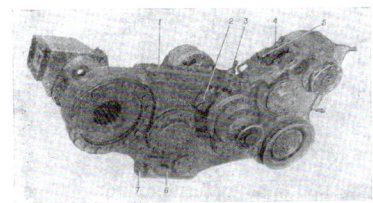

(H) The V-46 engine. (Sergei Popsuevich)

(I) The V-46 engine as mounted in all early production T-72 tanks.

(J) The later V-84MS engine at the UVZ museum, Nizhny Tagil. (Esa Muikku)

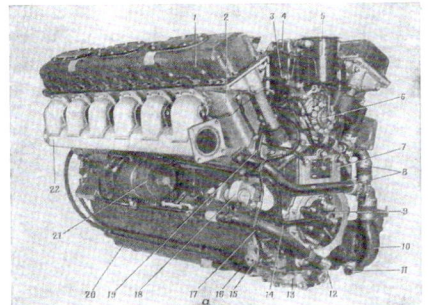

Рис. 120. Гитара (общий вид):
1 — верхняя крышка с каналом подвода масла; 2 — датчик Д-20; 3 — штуцер подвода масла; 4 — рычаг; 5 — стопор рычага; 6 — лапа гитары; 7 — нижняя крышка

Рис. 121. Гитара (общий вид):
1 — штуцер для подсоединения к сапуну; 2 — задняя крышка гитары; 3 — трубопровод смазки; 4 — подвод масла в привод СТ; 5 — фильтр компрессора; 6 — кожух компрессора; 7 — компрессор; 8 — трубопровод слива масла из компрессора; 9 — нагнетающий насос гитары; 10 — трубопровод подвода масла к разбрызгивателю

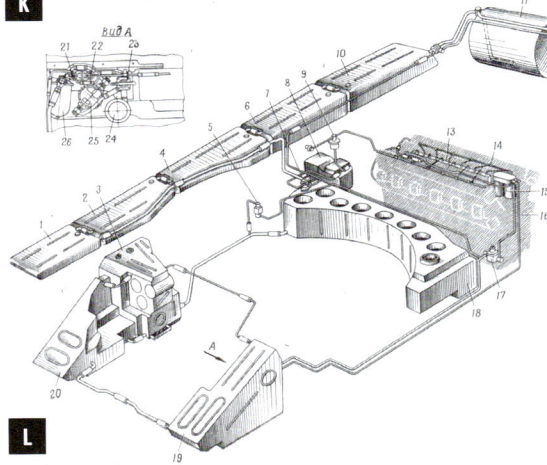

Рис. 44. Система питания топливом:
1 — первый наружный бак; 2 — второй наружный бак; 3 — передний бак-стеллаж; 4 — третий наружный бак; 5 — топливный насос подогревателя; 6 — четвёртый наружный бак; 7 — кран отключения наружных топливных баков; 8 — расширительный бачок; 9 — поплавковый клапан; 10 — пятый наружный бак; 11 — правая бочка; 12 — левая бочка; 13 — топливный насос высокого давления; 14 — форсунка; 15 — топливный фильтр тонкой очистки; 16 — двигатель; 17 — топливораспределительный кран; 18 — средний бак-стеллаж; 19 — левый носовой; 20 — правый носовой; 21 — клапан выпуска воздуха; 22 — сливной штуцер; 23 — топливораспределительный кран; 24 — бензиновый центробежный насос; 25 — ручной топливоподкачивающий насос; 26 — топливный фильтр грубой очистки

1.1.6. Крыша над силовым отделением

Крыша над силовым отделением (рис. 6) состоит из:
— крыши 7 над двигателем;

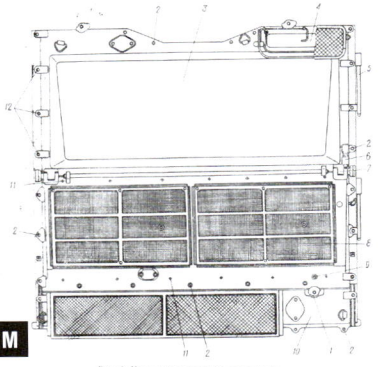

Рис. 6. Крыша над силовым отделением

(K) The 'guitar' power transfer system.

(L) Fuel system and ammunition 'bak-stellazh' racks, Obiekt-172M.

(M) Engine deck, Obiekt-172M.

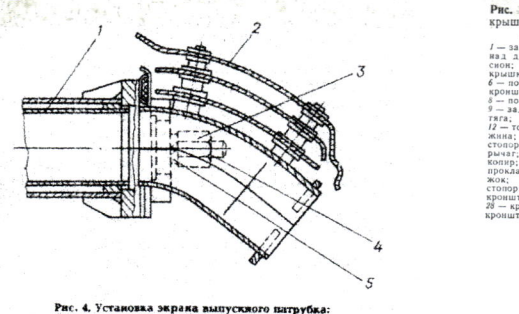

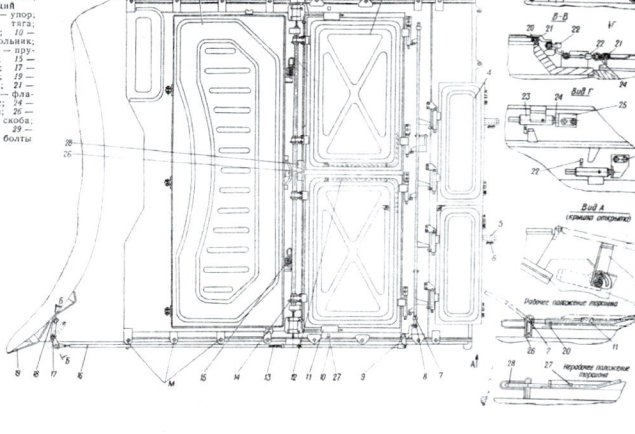

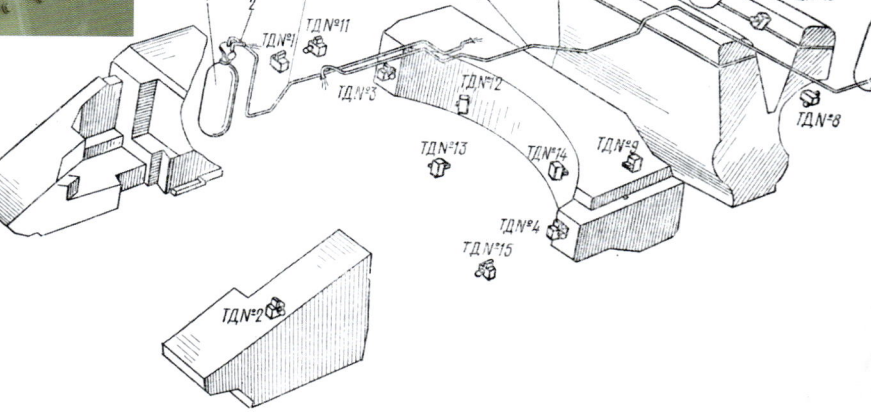

(A) Late model T-72A onward 'Silfon' exhaust port with heat dissipation, as fitted on tanks with the V-84MS engine installation.

(B) The 'Silfon' exhaust port on a T-72A built in 1979.

(C) Engine deck with covers closed, Obiekt-172M.

(D) T-72A PPO fire suppression system.

(E) Front wheel suspension mounting, Obiekt-172M.

(F) Self-emplacing dozer blade and KMT mounting points on a T-72A (M-1983).

(G) Self-emplacing dozer blade, Obiekt-172M.

(H) Early T-72 track.

(I) Early T-72 track as used on Obiekt-172M, T-72, T-72A and early production T-72B tanks.

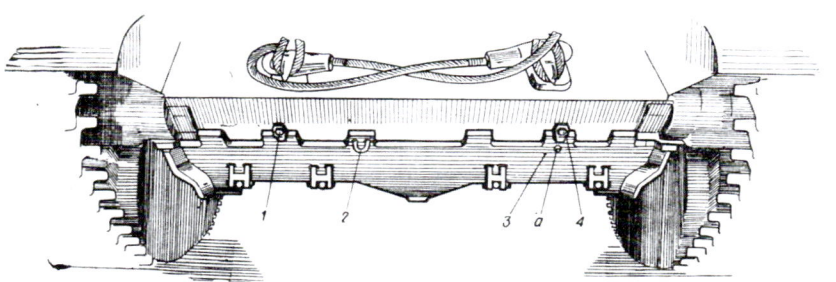

Рис. 253. Отвал в походном положении:
1 — болт; 2 — скоба; 3 — отвал; 4 — зажим; а — отверстие

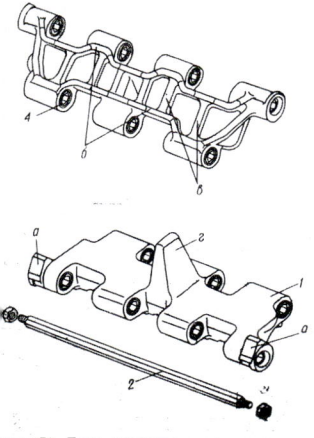

Рис. 171. Трак гусеницы с резинометаллическим шарниром:
1 — трак; 2 — палец; 3 — гайка; 4 — втулка; а — проушина цевки; б — грунтозацепы; в — ребра; г — гребень

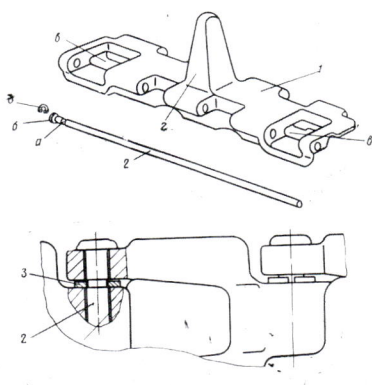

Рис. 172. Трак гусеницы с открытым шарниром:
1 — трак; 2 — палец; 3 — кольцо пружинное; а — проточка; б — головка пальца; в — цевочные окна; г — гребень

(A) The R-124 component of the R-123/124 radio and intercom system, Obiekt-172M.

(B,C) An R-123M-based communications system installed in a Soviet-built Finnish T-72 (Ps 264-122).

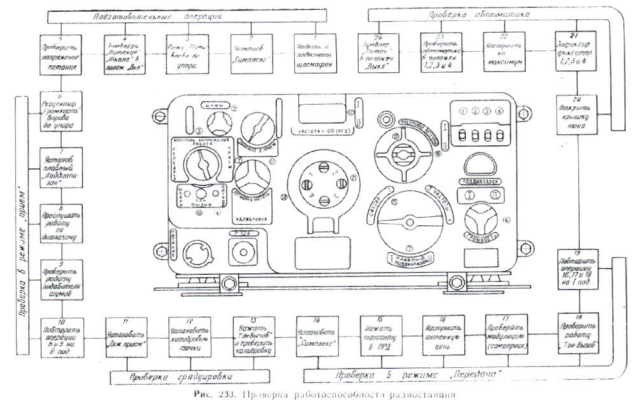

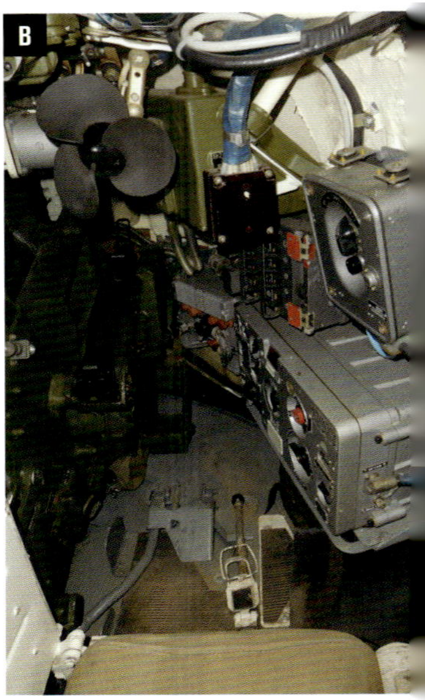

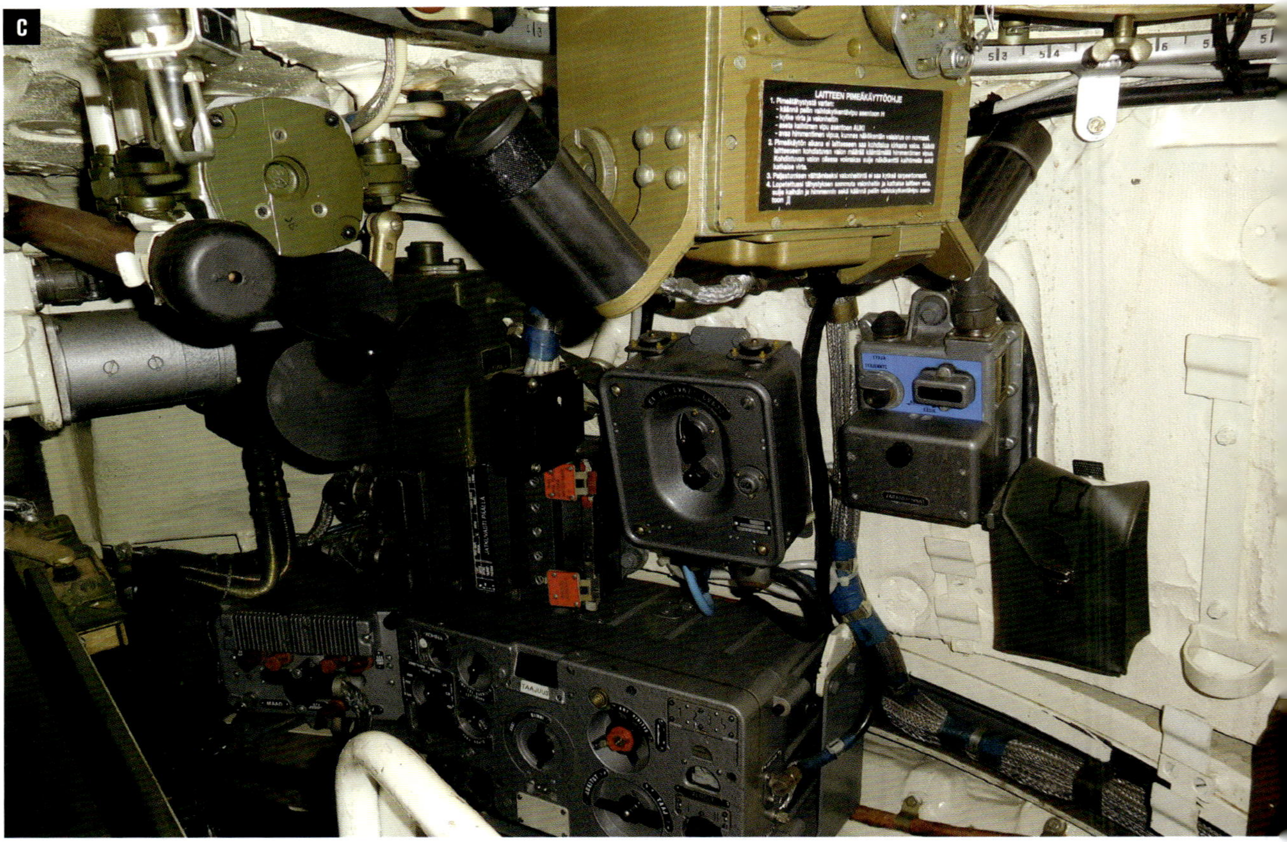

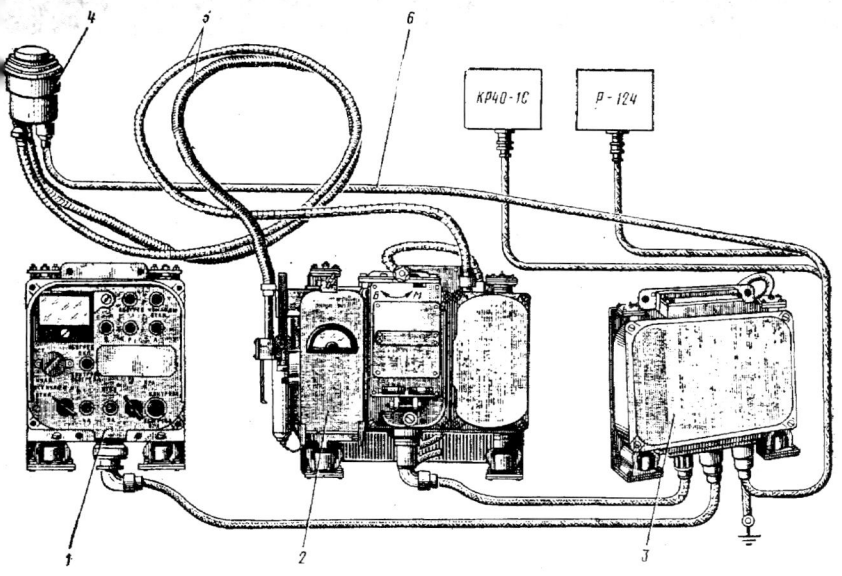
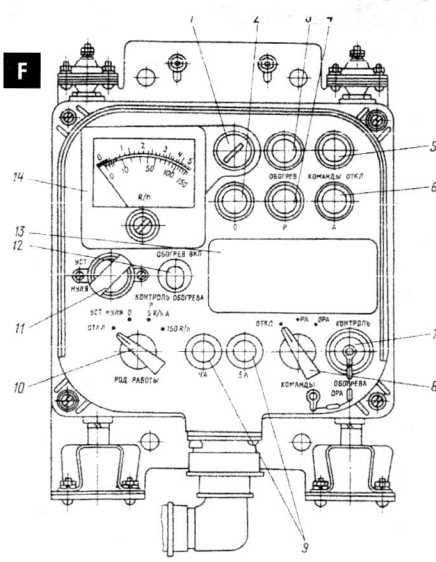

Рис. 315. Комплект прибора радиационной и химической разведки (ПРХР):
1 — измерительный пульт Б-1; 2 — датчик Б-2; 3 — блок питания Б-3; 4 — воздухозаборное устройство с циклоном; 5 — трубки обогрева; 6 — резиновая трубка

Рис. 61. Измерительный пульт Б-1:
1 - патрон; 2, 4, 6 — сигнальные лампы О, Р, А; 3 - сигнальная лампа ОБОГРЕВ; 5 - сигнальная лампа КОМАНДЫ - ОТКЛ; 7 - заглушка кнопки КОНТРОЛЬ ОБОГРЕВА ОРА; 8 — переключатель КОМАНДЫ; 9 - держатели предохранителей; 10 - переключатель РОД РАБОТЫ; 11 - ручка УСТ. НУЛЯ; 12 - переключатель ОБОГРЕВ ВКЛ. - КОНТРОЛЬ ОБОГРЕВА; 13 - табличка; 14 — микроамперметр

(D) The PRKhR NBC control system as fitted on the T-72A.

(E) Stowage and 'service items' layout on the Obiekt-172M.

(F) B1 control box for the PRKhR NBC control system.

Рис. 286. Укладка табельного имущества:
1 и 8 — чехлы для комплектов ПХЗ; 2 — противогаз; 3 и 5 — плавательные жилеты; 3 — изолирующий противогаз; 4 — чехол для сухого пайка; 6 — вещевое имущество; 7 — прибор ТДП-2; 9 — плащ ОП-1

CHAPTER 7
WALK AROUNDS

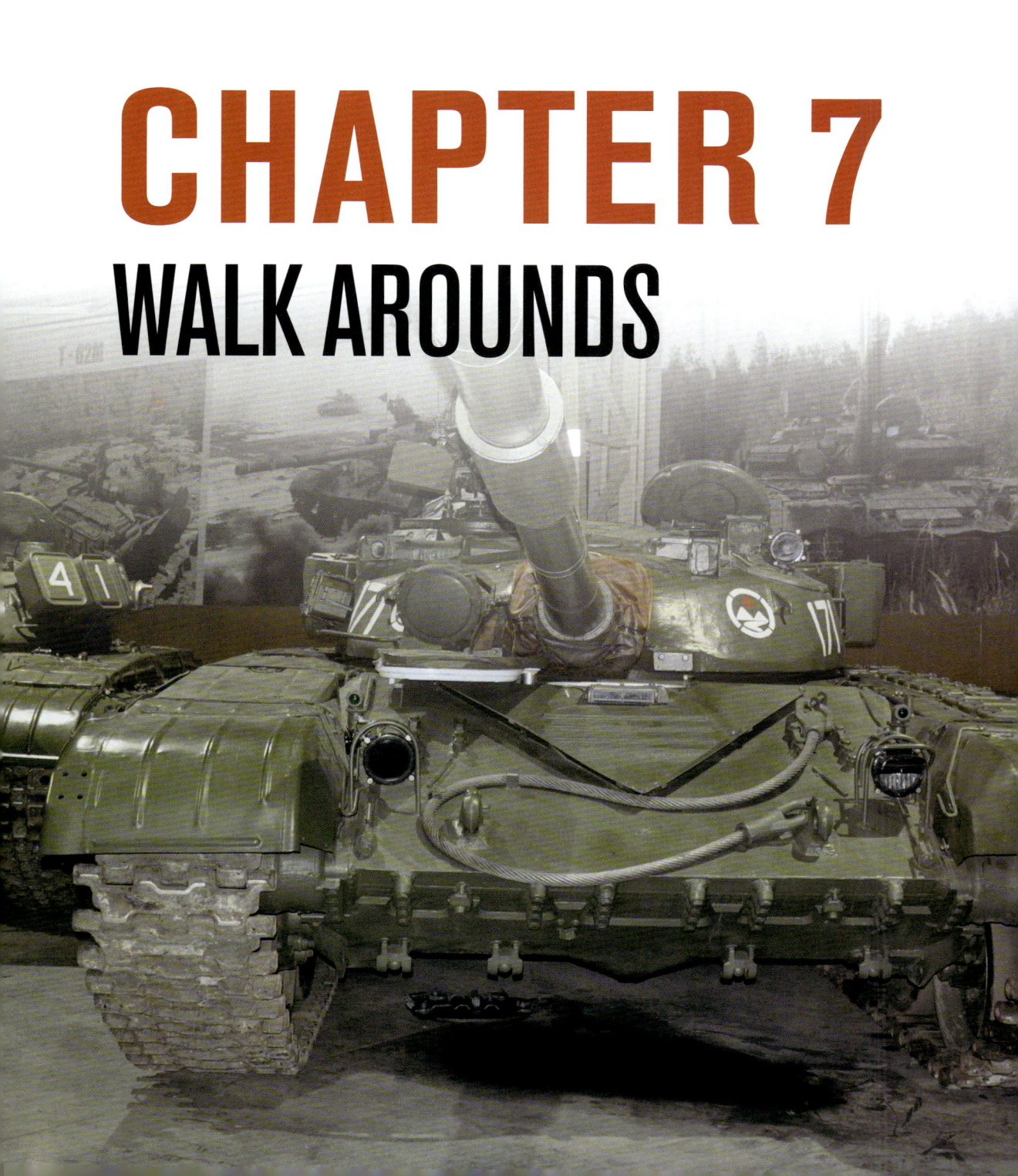

T-72 № 4152 produced at UVZ in February 1978, rebuilt at BTRZ №143 in 1988.

The T-72 featured in the following pages is located at the Museum of Russian Military History at Padikovo in the suburbs of Moscow. The tank is T-72 № 4152, assembled at UVZ in February 1978. It had one capital overhaul during its service life by BTRZ № 143 at Kaunas in the Lithuanian Soviet Socialist Republic in 1988. Newly built T-72 tanks were factory fitted with the 'nadboy' anti-neutron radiation layer from 1983; older tanks were retrofitted in army depots or during overhaul at repair plants.

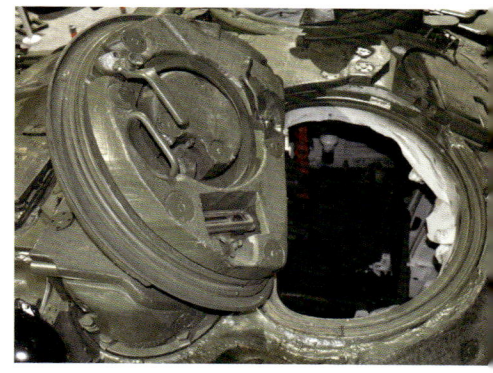
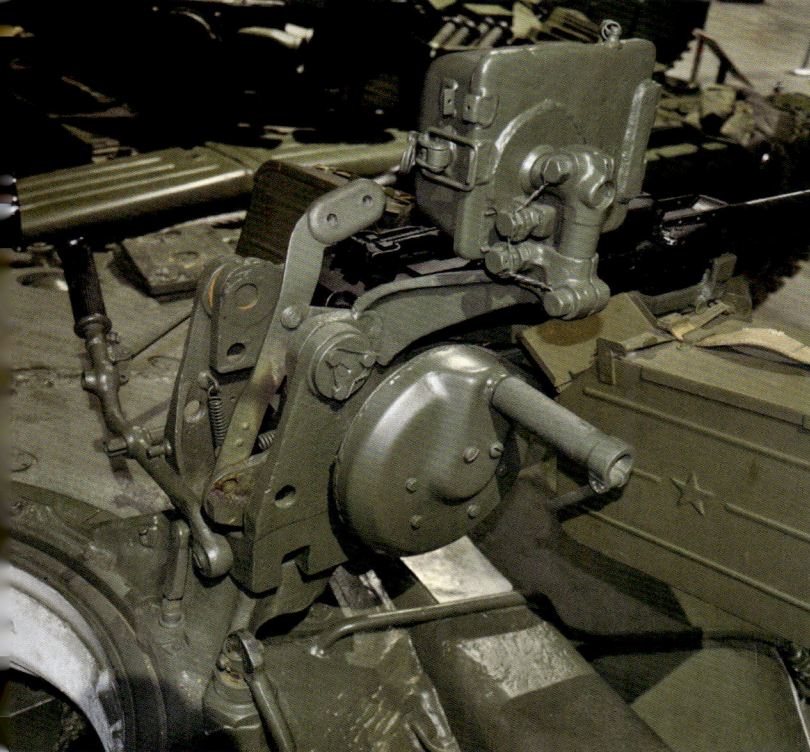

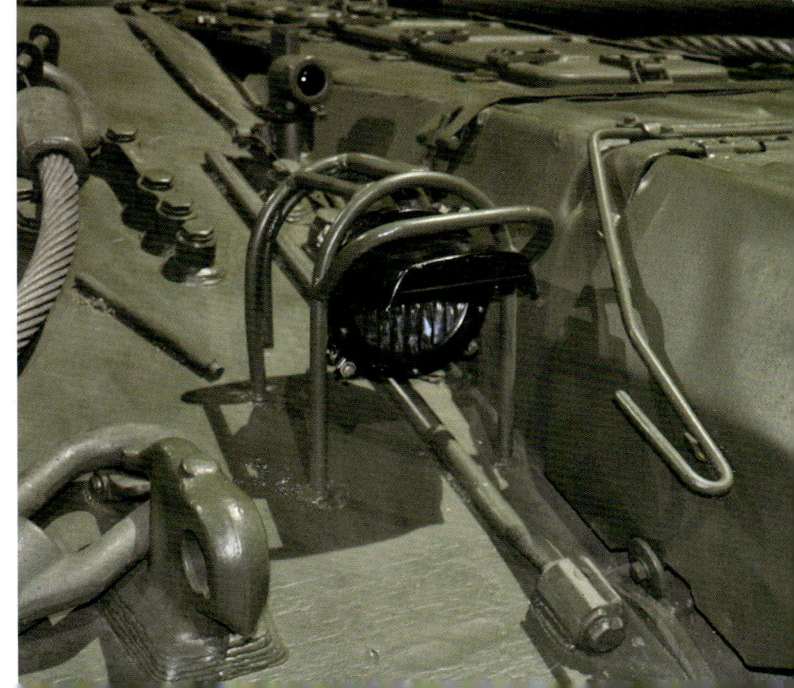

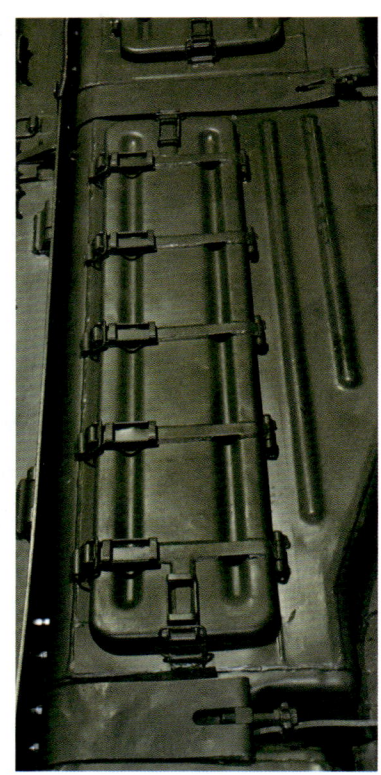

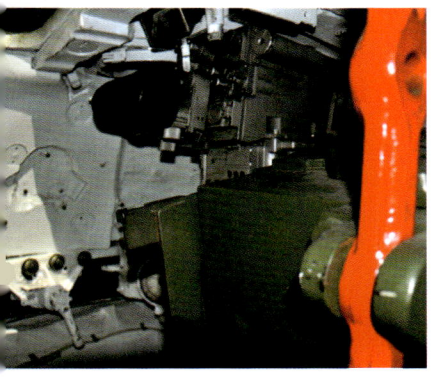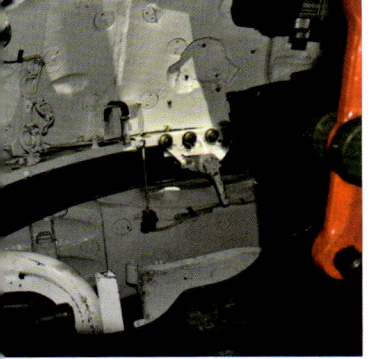

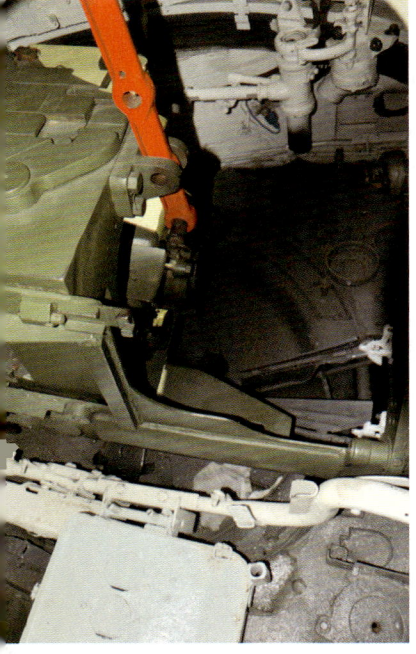

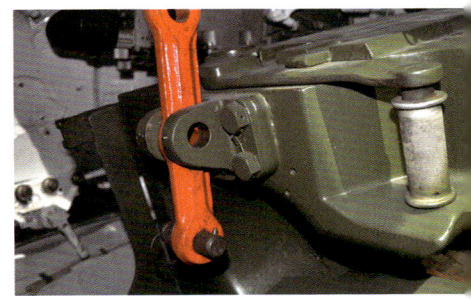
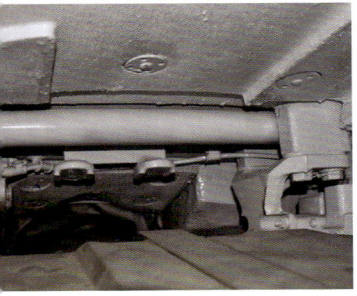

T-72A built at UVZ in November 1987, located at the Muzei Tekhniki, Arkhangelskoye, Moscow.

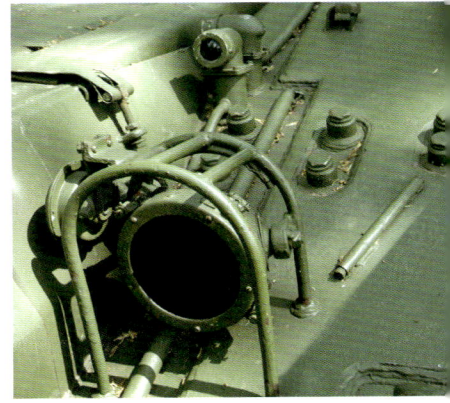

T-72A M-1983 UVZ production tank located at Partizanskaya Polyanna, Bryansk.

CHAPTER 8
FOREIGN PRODUCTION AND SERVICE

Belarus inherited a T-72 tank inventory with independence and has continued to both use the tank and modify it for potential export. This T-72AV is at the MILEX-2001 exhibition in May 2003. (Sergei Popsuevich)

Soon after the Yom Kippur War in the Middle East in 1973, many Soviet customers began to complain that their current inventory of tanks was not effective against American and British tanks supplied to their enemies and wanted a better tank to field against them. After a field trip by senior Soviet tank designers and personnel including Leonid Kartsev in his GBTU persona, a Soviet state decision had to be made about what tanks to sell and to whom.

The main problem was at the time there were three tanks undergoing testing in the USSR to determine which one would be the new Soviet Army main battle tank – T-64A, Obiekt-172M (T-72) and Obiekt-219sp2 (T-80). When the T-72 was accepted for service, it was then felt that perhaps this 'inferior' tank (in the mind of Dmitriy Ustinov) could be offered to foreign governments with only a few changes from Soviet Army standards. Ustinov was on this occasion also being pragmatic, in that of the three tank types the T-72 was the simplest to operate and maintain outside the confines of Soviet Army support infrastructure.

One thing to keep in mind is that for years Western analysts always derisively referred to many simplified export versions of Soviet weapons as 'monkey models'. This is something of an oversimplification as in reality they tended to produce multiple levels of weapons systems for different customers, albeit with the full Soviet standard equipment package never being offered for export until after years of Soviet service. For example, the first versions of the MiG-29 fighter used a frequency-agile radar with 32 different possible frequencies; those sold to the East Germans had 24 frequencies, but those sold to Iraq only had four. The same sort of convention was used with T-72 tanks that were either built for the USSR, built exclusively for the Warsaw Pact, or those sold to so-called 'Third World' customers.

The first versions of the **T-72** offered for sale in 1975 were the **Obiekt-172M-Eh** and **Obiekt-172M-Eh1**. The Eh (Э) was for the Warsaw Pact and the Eh1 (Э-1) was for the rest of the Soviet customer base. The Eh was virtually identical to the Soviet T-72, but the Eh1 had a different design of turret and glacis armour protection as reduced NBC collective protection and a limited selection of ammunition that was sold along with

RIGHT A Polish T-72M located at Fort IX Czerniaków, Warsaw.

BELOW A column of T-72M tanks of the German NVA.

the tanks. (Warsaw Pact countries did get a wider selection of ammunition but the Soviets kept the best rounds for their own use.)

The next version to enter production concurrent with the Soviet T-72A in 1979 was the **T-72M** which came in **Obiekt-172M-Eh3** and **Obiekt-172M-Eh4** variants, again the former for the Warsaw Pact and the latter for the rest of the world respectively. Poland, Czechoslovakia and Yugoslavia also purchased rights to build the T-72M variant domestically. Once again, they had a different design of turret and glacis armour (essentially monolithic and not composite) and the Eh4 lacked full Soviet NBC protection. (It remained with the Warsaw Pact vehicles, as they would be considered to be fighting side by side with Soviet tanks on the same battlefield and required similar levels of protection.) These tanks were provided with laser rangefinder and modified fire controls systems, but were not fully identical to those of the T-72A.

In 1982 the next version appeared, the **T-72M1** (**Obiekt-172M-Eh5** and **Obiekt-172M-Eh6**), which had a revised armour layout for the turret and glacis. The glacis received a 16mm appliqué plate to increase its protection and the turret received extended cheeks (now some 10cm thicker) to provide better protection from APFSDS projectiles. Once again, Warsaw Pact vehicles had a better NBC protection suite than the foreign models. The Obiekt-172M-Eh5 models may have had the upgraded turret protection with quartz rods, but the Eh6 ones clearly did not.

In response to demands for more standardized models of the tank, in 1987 the Soviet Union finally relented and offered an export version of the T-72B and T-72B1 as the **T-72S** and **T-72S1** and the T-72S 'Shilden' (**Obiekt-172M-Eh8**). The T-72S was much closer in performance and protection to the later T-72B models and offered either the complete 1K13 and 9K120 system with the 'Svir' missile, or without it as the T-72S1. The Obiekt-172M-Eh8 tank was marketed for export in the 1990s as the T-72S 'Shilden' (the 'Shilden' variant having originally been developed specifically for export to Iran, with a V-92S2 diesel engine developing 1,000hp), with the emphasis being on the ability to fire the aforementioned barrel-launched missile and the provision of first-generation 'Kontakt-1' ERA on export models. Once again, the T-72S in its various guises did have some differences in its armour protection and NBC provisions, but it also listed one item on its 'options' lists not found in the Soviet model: air conditioning. In this case the compressor was part of the engine fittings and the condenser unit was mounted in a ZIP-bin shaped container that was mounted on the left rear of the turret. It had vents for air circulation through the condenser. Some T-72 tanks built as T-72S 'Shilden' tanks for export were later re-absorbed into the Russian Army as domestically labelled T-72B/B1 tanks.

ABOVE A T-72M1 captured from Iraq at the Aberdeen Proving Ground in the US.

LEFT A T-72M captured by Iran from Iraq during the Valfajr-8 operation in February 1986. (Alexander Morzhitsky)

TOP LEFT Many T-72 tanks in museums abroad were obtained during the First Gulf War. This privately owned early production T-72 Ural is shown on display during a War and Peace show in Great Britain.

TOP RIGHT Ukraine with independence in 1991 inherited a significant number of T-72 tanks, and has its own subsequent history of the tank model. These T-72AVs are undergoing rebuild in Ukraine in the 1990s.

When the Russians announced the T-72B2 'Rogatka' upgrades, a similar package was offered for the T-72M1 tanks as the **T-72M1M or Obiekt-172M2A**. This mounted much of the equipment offered for the domestic B2 but used the M1 with an underlying lesser degree of protection as the basis.

The main customer for export T-72 tanks has been India, which after much more extensive plans in the mid 1970s also ordered a small quantity of T-72M1 tanks in the mid 1980s in order to begin local manufacture, having previously purchased a small number of T-72 'M-1975' tanks. Some specialized upgrades specifically for the Indian Army have also been undertaken.

All versions of the export T-72 family also had K model command tanks and some of the later M1 tanks also had a V model with 'Kontakt-1' ERA.

RIGHT A Belorussian T-72B, photographed at the MILEX-2009 exhibition in Minsk in 2009. (Sergei Popsuevich)

TOP LEFT AND RIGHT
Belorussian T-72B tanks during a parade in Minsk. (Sergei Popsuevich)

LEFT A Belorussian Army T-72B in green parade livery. (Sergei Popsuevich)

T-72B1MS 'BELIY OREL' EXPORT TANK (2012)

As time went on, the post-Soviet Russian Federation decided to upgrade the T-72B1 tanks for sale as export vehicles, and as a result conceived the T-72B1MS 'Beliy Orel' (white eagle) tank. The prototype, which was shown at the Technology and Machinery Construction Forum 2012, was painted white in accord with its new name. (A T-80 derivative was dubbed 'Cherniy Orel' or black eagle, so UVZ wanted a similar striking name.)

TOP LEFT A Georgian T-72B1, captured by the Russian Army in August 2008. The turret 'Kontakt-1' KDZ armour layout can be compared with the T-72AV on the right as viewed.

TOP RIGHT This Georgian T-72B1 tank, fitted with KMT-6 series mine ploughs, has a typical KDZ block arrangement on the hull glacis and turret.

CENTRE A Georgian T-72B captured by Russian forces in 2008. The KDZ blocks and mountings on the hull skirts are remarkably resilient to wear and tear damage.

BOTTOM LEFT The end of the Cold War. Ex Czech- and Polish-built NVA T-72M1 tanks stored in Germany awaiting sale or dismantling. (Esa Muikku)

BOTTOM RIGHT Two columns of ex Czech- and Polish-built NVA tanks in Weißkeißel, Germany. Finland acquired 99 of these DDR surplus tanks, which were shipped to Finland in 1992 (97) and 1994 (two). (Esa Muikku)

This T-72M1K which served in the Finnish Army as Ps265-20 was built by ZTS in Czechoslovakia in 1987 and purchased from Germany as ex-NVA inventory. It is shown marked with its German service number while still at Weißkeißel in Germany in December 1991 prior to shipment to Finland. (Esa Muikku)

Developed under the 'Proryv-2' (breakthrough) development plan, this tank added a number of new systems to the design. These included the PKP-72 all-weather panoramic commander's sight, the PN-72 'Sosna-U' gunner's sight, a new digital ballistic computer and automatic target tracking device and a remote-control 12.7mm machine gun mount. The driver-mechanic also received a 'glass cockpit' panel showing him the status of all vehicle systems at a glance.

Now redubbed the T-72MS, these tanks began being exported in 2016 to Nicaragua, Laos and Serbia. Laos meantime released some long-since exported T-34-85 tanks back to the Russian Federation to participate in the 75th Anniversary Victory Parade held on Red Square on 9 May 2020, an interesting case of re-import and a testament to the durability of Soviet tank designs, re-imported as most in the Soviet Union had long since been installed on plinths as war memorials or scrapped.

ABOVE This Finnish T-72M1 (Ps264-309) was built at Bumar-Łabędy in Poland in 1987 and also acquired from Germany as ex-NVA inventory. It was subsequently modified in Finland. (Esa Muikku)

WARSAW PACT PRODUCTION OF THE T-72

Poland and Czechoslovakia also produced the T-72M and T-72M1, with some minor changes made by each country. Poland built around 1,500 of the tanks and the ČSSR also produced 1,700 tanks. After the collapse of the USSR, around 1,700 were sold to customers in the Near East and Middle East, including Syria and Iraq. Former Yugoslavia also produced several hundred as their M-84 series of tanks, usually identifiable by a wind sensor mast behind the main gun on the front of the turret.

RIGHT A Finnish T-72M1K1 (Ps266-38) built at Bumar-Łabędy in Poland in 1987. The M1K1 has two R-123M radio sets and other command tank modifications. (Esa Muikku)

This T-72M1 at the Shrivenham Defence Academy in Great Britain is a typical M1 export model, also built in Poland. Note the uncluttered turret roof devoid of Soviet service model NBC warfare fitments. (John Ham)

FOREIGN VERSIONS OF THE T-72

Both China and North Korea produced derivative tanks based on technology from the T-72. After the break-up of the Soviet Union, the Chinese bought mid-1970s examples of the T-72 in Eastern Europe and the Middle East which were evaluated, with many design features reproduced on future Chinese tank designs, but China also did not make a direct copy of the Soviet T-72 design.

The Chinese used the 125mm gun and autoloader produced under licence in both their **ZTZ-96** and **ZTZ-99** series tanks as well as copies of the road wheels and other details, but the rest of the tank was an indigenous design. No firm numbers on production are available but it is estimated several hundred ZTZ-96 tanks are in service, the tank type being the current standard base model MBT.

The North Koreans also did not directly copy the Soviet T-72 design, but did use concepts from the T-72 tank design with their late variants of the **'Chon'ma VI'** tank: the 'Juche-93' or 'Chon'ma-216' version used a stretched hull riding on six road wheels per side with a T-72 styled engine deck and hull rear to differentiate it from earlier models. However, they also crammed all sorts of external weaponry onto the turret (a cast T-62 turret with appliqué armour fittings), such as a 14.5mm heavy machine gun, ATGMs, and MANPADs for air defence.

The later **'Pokpo'ong'** ('Juche-98' or 'Seon'gun-913') used a hull design based on the T-72 with a steeper glacis and centrally placed driver's position. It also uses the extra turret armament but surprisingly retains the 115mm gun from the T-62 and does not use the 125mm gun. There are no firm numbers on how many 'Chon'ma' and 'Pokpo'ong' tanks have been built but battalion sets have been paraded in Pyongyang.

CHAPTER 9
UKRAINIAN POST-SOVIET SERVICE AND VARIANTS

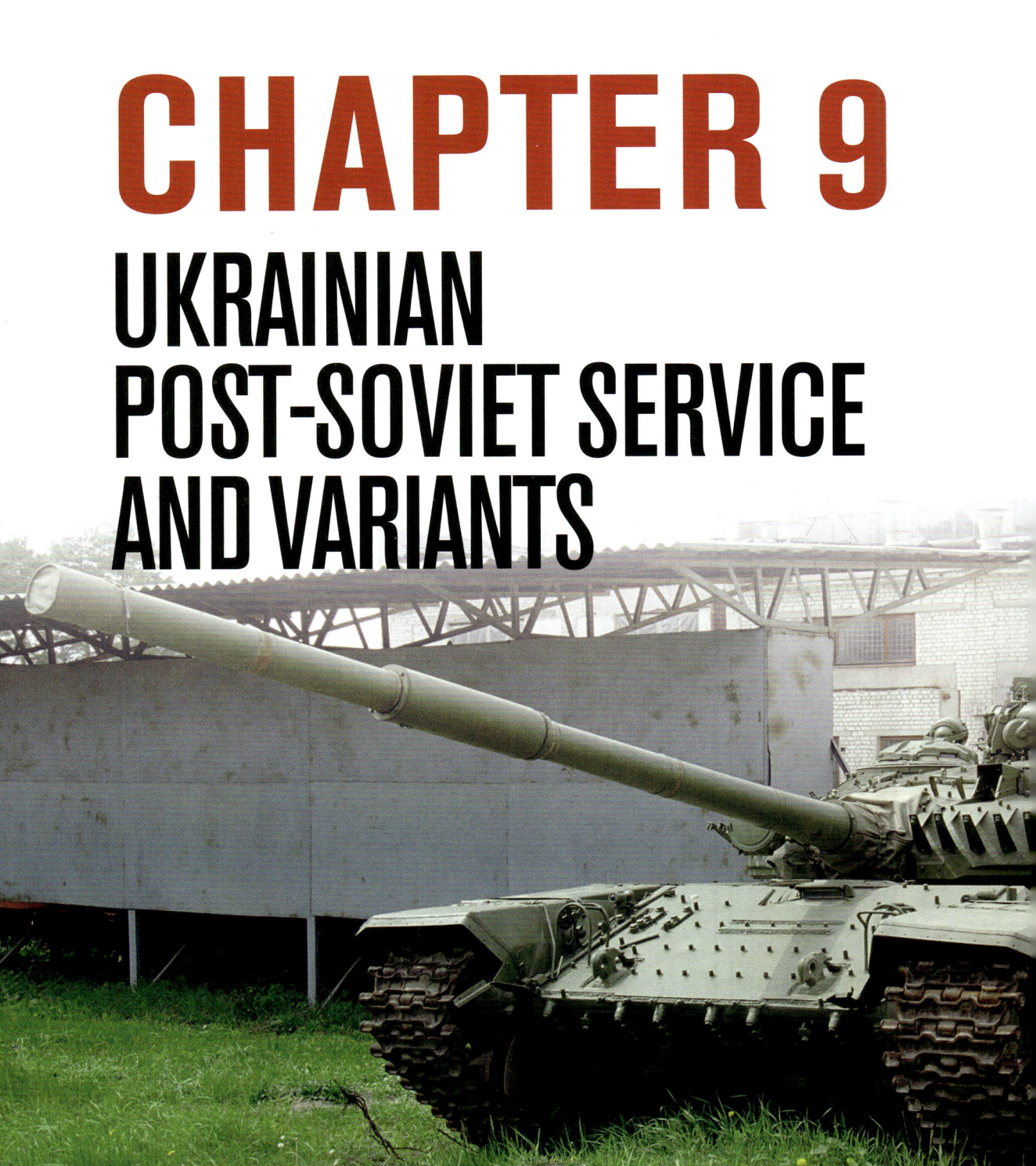

A T-72AV awaiting rebuild in Ukraine.

Prior to the break-up of the USSR, KhKBM in Kharkov did not concentrate on development of the UVZ-developed T-72 MBT as it was an 'NIH' product (not invented here – a standard engineering situation worldwide) and the plant concentrated on T-64 and later T-80UD production. After 1991, all of the former Soviet republics found themselves inheriting whatever tanks were within their borders, and in the case of Ukraine that included a large number of Nizhny Tagil-built T-72 tanks of all types.

Concurrently, the 'Malyshev' plant found itself bereft of orders and without a saleable product to offer to foreign buyers. The last new Soviet-era tanks they had built were 200 T-80UD tanks fitted with the 6TD version of the Kharkov-opposed piston diesel engine, and while they were still able to produce those tanks there was no interest from foreign potential clients. Eventually they modified the tank for new production as the T-84, but that still did not solve what to do with all the T-72s left in the country, which

RIGHT T-72 turrets being rebuilt at Kharkiv Tank Repair Plant in the 1990s. (Sergei Popsuevich)

BELOW A familiar sight in the countries of the former Soviet Union in the early 1990s, an Obiekt-172M stripped to its hull and turret prior to a total rebuild at a Ukrainian BTRZ. The turret in the foreground has the distinctive turret bulge added to borrowed T-64A turrets to accomodate the T-72 autoloader.

(A) After years of economic recovery, a T-72AV undergoing capital rebuild in Ukraine in the late 1990s. (Sergei Popsuevich) **(B)** The BTRZ in Kiev in the 1990s with T-72 and other tanks, including an ISU-T under rebuild. (Sergei Popsuevich)
(C) A T-72AV undergoing rebuild in Ukraine in the 1990s.
(D) T-72A tanks awaiting rebuild in Ukraine.
(E) A T-72AV rebuilt and modernized in Ukraine in the late 1990s.
(F) T-72B and T-72AV tanks after rebuild in Ukraine.
(G) The same T-72B with 'Kontakt-1' KDZ armour after capital rebuild in Ukraine. Note the directional markings on the armour blocks. **(H)** A T-72B1 in strategic storage in Ukraine in the 1990s.

though repaired and rebuilt in Ukraine during the Soviet era were of Russian factory origin. Post 1991, this meant that maintenance and spares became more problematical than even for the Kharkov-built T-80UD. The Russian Federation faced the exact same problem in reverse with domestic stocks of the Soviet-era T-64 as built in Ukraine.

The result was that since many other countries had purchased Soviet-era T-72s – and as the T-64 was never offered for foreign sales in Soviet times – Ukraine began to rebuild T-72s for sale abroad, with BTRZ No.7 (Kiev) (now Kyiv) and BTRZ No.17 (Lvov) (now Lviv) also being active in rebuilding T-72 tanks for export with V-46-6 or V-84 engines, and modified fire control and sighting systems. Since the Ukrainians now had a viable engine in the 6TD series they of course would retrofit the domestic engine to the T-72 and use that as a selling point – slightly ironic considering that the T-72 had been created to use a V-2 type engine descended from the original V-2 diesel built in Kharkov for the T-34 – instead of the Kharkov 5TDF, the new engine's predecessor. The Ukrainian view was that all

(I, J, K) A Ukrainian T-72B on a firing range. The original 'Kontakt-1' DZ blocks have been removed from the turret but remain fitted on the side skirts. Note the modified gunner's sight. (Sergei Popsuevich)

(L) A T-72A after rebuild in post-Soviet Ukraine. (Sergei Popsuevich)

(A) A T-72AV on display in Kharkov, September 1997. (Viktor Maskovsky) **(B)** The T-72 UMG was modernized by Kyiv BTRZ in Ukraine, 2002. (Sergey Popsuevich) **(C,D)** The T-72 UMG during winter trials. **(E)** The T-72 UMG prototype during mobility trials in 2002. (Sergey Popsuevich) **(F,G,H,I)** The same T-72 UMG during summer testing in 2002. (Sergei Popsuevich)

LEFT The Ukrainian T-72AG post-Soviet modernization of the Soviet-era T-72, with a 125mm 2A46M (KBA-2) gun, 'Duplet' KDZ, 6TD engine built in Kharkiv and other local modifications. (Sergey Popsuevich)

of the production line equipment was still set up for the T-80UD/T-84, so this conversion was not difficult.

The first offering developed from 1992 and first seen in in 1995 was the **T-72AM 'Banan'** (Banana), which essentially took a T-72A chassis and upgraded it to nearly the same standards as the T-80UD tank. It was fitted with a 6TD series engine (either 6TD-1 of 1,000hp or the 6TD-2 producing 1,200hp) and with a new rear hull section. This then had to use the T-64 type OPVT system with twin snorkels. It also received a complete suite of 'Kontakt-1' ERA.

A second and more extensive KhKBM redesign and upgrade to the tank was the **T-72AG,** which merged many more of the T-80UD design features with the T-72A chassis, and was also originally intended for export clients. It also used either the 6TD-1 or 6TD-2 engine developing up to 1,200hp along with a new air filter and cooling system (recall the Kharkov engines used 'ejection cooling' with the exhaust providing for air flow through the radiators) as well as the T-64 type snorkels.

The Ukrainians fitted their 1A43 version of the 1A45 'Irtysh' fire control system with the 1G46 day sight, PNK-4S commander's day/night combination sight, and TPN-4 or the TPN-4 merged with the 'Buran' and French 'Catharine'

ABOVE LEFT The Ukrainian T-72AMT, a modified T-72B tank, armed with a 125mm 2A46M (KBA-2) gun, with thermal imaging, 'Nozh' KDZ secondary armour and a combination of T-72 and T-80 components, grille armour and other modification, was developed and built at the Kyiv Tank Plant (the former Kiev BTRZ tank repair plant). (John Ham)

ABOVE RIGHT A rear view of the same T-72AMT, showing the extensive use of 'Reshotka' grille armour. Approximately 70–80 T-72AMT tanks were rebuilt from existing chassis between 1999 and 2016. (Sergei Popsuevich)

Three photographs of a captured T-72AG on display at Paklonnaya Gora in Moscow in May 2024. The tank uses the skirt armour and other components from the T-80UD previously built in Ukraine. Note the digital camouflage used on Ukrainian armoured vehicles.

(labelled as 'Sanoet' in brochures) thermal viewer, and T01-K01 'Buran' gunner's sight, the combination providing target detection of 5,000m in daytime and 3,000m at night, with overall coordination via the 1V528 ballistic computer. It was also compatible with firing the 9M119M 'Invar' through-the-bore ATGM. This used the 2A46 (2A46M1) gun mated to the 2Eh42M stabilizer for increased accuracy.

For protection the tank now received a suite of the upgraded 'Kontakt-5' ERA around the hull, with a reinforced glacis, and on the turret. The tank used additional side shielding as previously used on the T-80U. The 45.5 tonne T-72AG had a maximum road speed of 65km/h, with a claimed all-terrain speed of 45–50km/h.

In 1997 another attempt at modernizing the T-72 was made in the form of the **T-72MP**, which used the 6TD-1 engine developing 1,000hp combined with a French Sagem SAVAN 15MP fire control system. This used a multichannel SAVAN 15MP thermal sight for the gunner and an SFIM VS580 sight for the commander. While a vast improvement over the base sighting system it was still paired with the older 2Eh42-2 stabilizer system and the earlier 2A46M gun (with the option of the Ukrainian 125mm KBM-1M weapon), so it could not provide a totally modern fire control set.

(A) A general view of the BMT-72, which from this angle looks quite conventional. (Sergei Popsuevich)

(B,C,D,E,F) The BMT-72 was a drastically modified Ukrainian T-72 development. Both combat vehicle (BM) and tank (T), the BMT-72 featured a lengthened hull with additional wheel station and a compartment behind the turret for three desant infantry.

(A,B) An IMR-2M in Ukrainian Army service in the 1990s. (Sergei Popsuevich)

(C) A Ukrainian Army IMR-2M at an exhibition in 2008. (Sergei Popsuevich)

(D) Ukraine inherited a large number of BREhM-1 vehicles with the break-up of the Soviet Union. (Sergei Popsuevich)

It was also the first tank to offer either (Soviet-origin) 'Kontakt-5' ERA or the new Ukrainian 'Nozh' (knife) system that was advertised as providing protection from both HEAT and APFSDS ammunition. It was also noted it could be fitted with the Ukrainian 'Shtora-2' version of the 'Shtora-1' (curtain) active protection system then fitted to the Russian T-90 tanks.

The tank was a joint venture by KhZTM along with Sagem of France and PSP Bohemia from the Czech Republic.

In order to appeal to customers preferring Western/NATO-standard armament, another effort was the **T-72-120** option developed in 1997, which paired a chassis upgraded to either T-72AG or T-72MP standards with a new turret fitted with a French GIAT-designed 120mm KBM-2 smoothbore gun and using French designed ammunition. An improved 2Eh42M stabilizer system was fitted and it used the GIAT turret bustle design of autoloader in place of the carousel; this carried 22 rounds in the loader and 20 more rounds stowed in the fighting compartment.

In the second decade of the 21st century, further Ukrainian designs primarily intended for export markets included the T-72E and E1 (2011), and the T-72UA1 (developed for Ethiopia) and T-72UA4 (developed for Kazakhstan).

(E,F,H,I) Ukraine inherited a large number of BREhM-1 vehicles with the break-up of the Soviet Union. These photographs show BREhM-1 vehicles in Ukrainian Army (VSU) operational service in the mid 2000s. **(G,J,K)** The BREhM-1 is also capable of deep wading, seen here in Ukrainian VSU service with training OPVT snorkel fitted. (All photographs Sergei Popsuevich)

(A,E,F) This BTS-5 photographed in Ukraine in 2009 is of an entirely different configuration to the Soviet origin UVZ-built series production BREhM-1. **(B,C)** The BTS-5 Ukrainian-built version of the BREhM-1. **(D)** A BREhM-1 during a Ukrainian VSU exercise, 2014. (Sergei Popsuevich) **(G)** A BTS-5B during conversion from a standard T-72 gun-tank chassis in Ukraine. (Sergei Popsuevich) **(H,I)** Ukraine inherited a significant quantity of late Soviet era self-propelled artillery. This 2S19 is on a Ukrainian firing range. (Sergei Popsuevich)

A 2S19 during firing practice on a Ukrainian polygon. (Sergei Popsuevich)

In 2017, Ukraine unveiled a further T-72-based indigenous design, the T-72AMT, based on the T-72A, which was developed at the Kyiv Tank Plant (the former BTRZ tank repair plant in Kiev) with many major and detail changes from earlier developments, and the drive sprocket, tracks and other components borrowed from the T-80. The T-72AMT is armed with the 125mm 2A46M tank gun with 44 rounds, including 'Kombat' rounds, with a 12.7mm NSVT (6P17 'Utes') air defence machine gun and secondary 7.62mm PKT. The tank uses the 1A33-1 fire control system, with the commander having a TKN-3UM combination sight and the gunner a 1K13-49 sight. The driver has an SN-300M 'Bazalt' land navigation system and a TVNE-4BU type night vision device. The tank is provided with 'Nozh' ERA, a local development of the Soviet-era 'Kontakt-1' and additional screening for the turret rear and engine area. Power is provided by a V-84-1 engine developing 840hp, giving the tank a power-to-weight ratio of 19hp/tonne. The tank is fitted with K-2RB 'Libid' radio communications.

TOP LEFT AND RIGHT
Ukrainian VSU 2S19 self-propelled gun-howitzers in digital camouflage await the Independence Day Parade on Khreshchatyk, Kyiv, 24 August 2016. (Sergei Popsuevich)

One curious offshoot to the Ukrainian development of the T-72 tank was the **BMT-72.** This was a Ukrainian redesigned and lengthened T-72 fitted with the 6TD series engine, which featured a compartment behind the turret for three desant infantry. To support the vehicle's new compartment, the tank hull was extended and a seventh road wheel added with a small interval between it and the original sixth road wheel. The BMT-72 did not progress past the prototype stage.

The last major redesign effort the Ukrainians made with the T-72 design was the **T-72UA1,** which was not as expensive as other options. This was one reason sales of the other models were close to non-existent (the other factor was incompatibility with stocks of T-72 tanks already owned by foreign customers).

The T-72UA1 once again replaced the V-46 engine. Originally, they wanted to install the improved 6TD series engines, but due to space constraints they went with the 5TDFMA engine developing 1,050hp and fitted with a larger cooling system suitable for tropical environments. It was fitted with an EA-10-2 auxiliary power unit (APU) providing 10kW of power when the main engine was shut down, saving fuel and avoiding wear on the highly stressed engine.

The gun and fire controls remained unchanged from previous models (this tank was based on a T-72B chassis and not the previous T-72A models), but it now mounted 'Kontakt-1' ERA on the hull and the new Ukrainian-developed 'Nozh' system on the turret; 'Nozh' modules are interchangeable with 'Kontakt-1' and the hull can be upgraded per the customer's specifications.

An air conditioner was offered as an option with installation, similar to that offered in the Russian T-72S series.

This tank did sell, and Ethiopia reportedly purchased some 170 T-72UA1 tanks, with another 30 being purchased by the Ukrainian Army.

Three photographs of the KhVT-72, developed as a crew training tank. The T-62 was similarly converted in the same plant.

CHAPTER 10
T-72 TANKS PRESERVED IN MUSEUMS

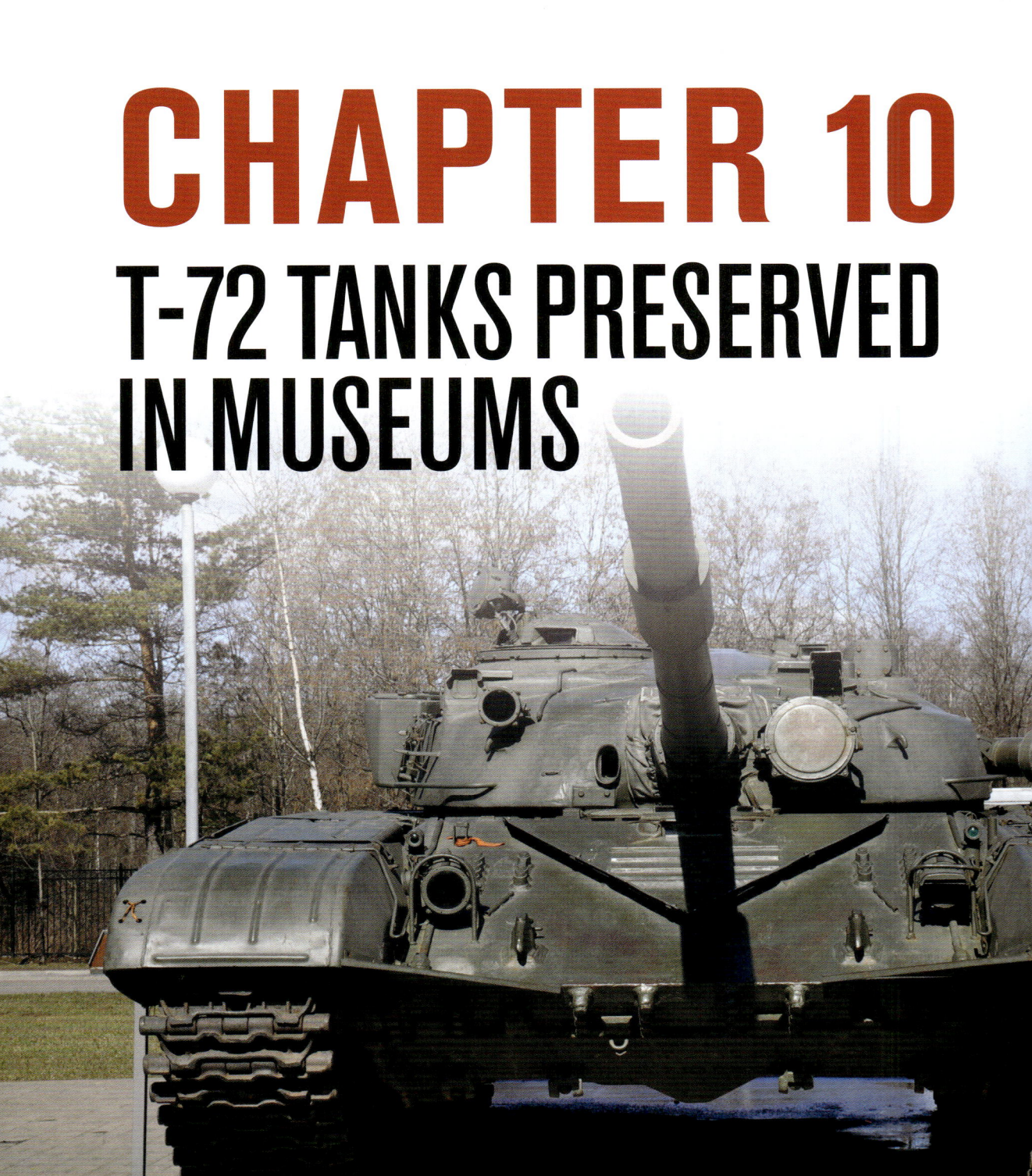

An Obiekt-172M (T-72 Ural) with later upgrades, located at the Leningrad Proriv (breakthrough) memorial complex at Nevsky Pyatachok east of St Petersburg where the siege of Leningrad was broken.

At the time of publishing, more than 50 years after the T-72 entered service with the Soviet Army, there remain several thousand operational T-72 tanks and variants in service in different countries around the world. Relative to the numbers produced and exported, however, there are few T-72 tanks in museum collections outside the Russian Federation. The majority of T-72 tanks abroad have been accumulated in museum collections either as a result of the end of the Cold War, with for instance former East German NVA tanks being commonly acquired by museums, or as a result of the two Gulf Wars during which large numbers of Iraqi tanks were captured intact.

The T-72 has seen extensive combat in recent years, particularly in the Middle East/West Asia and North Africa, and has been used during the wars in Chechnya, South Ossetia/Georgia and most recently in Ukraine and the Kursk Oblast of the Russian Federation. The T-72 is however a case of reviewing military history in the present tense. In contemporary times captured Russian T-72 tanks have been displayed in Ukraine, and captured Ukrainian T-72 derivatives displayed in Russia as the T-72 is used on both sides of a conflict between two former Soviet states on home soil. As yet none of these most recent

BELOW This T-72 tank located at the Museum of Russian Military History, Padikovo is covered in detail in the Walkaround section of this book.

(A) This Obiekt-172M located at the Technical Museum in Toliatti has been subject to later rebuild and modification that obscure its origins, including much of the entire turret roof having been rebuilt.

(B) An original Obiekt-172M located at the UVZ museum in Nizhny Tagil. Note the early road wheels with eight rather than six bolt mounting points. (Esa Muikku)

(C) A T-72A located at the T-34 Museum, Sholokovo, near Moscow. The tank is identified by the museum as a T-72 M-1978. Note the turret external radiation lining.

(D) This T-72A at the Muzei Tekhniki (The Vadim Zadorozhny Museum) at Arkhangelskoe near Moscow is a T-72 M-1979 specification, but was built in November 1987. Note that though a later tank, it has no radiation lining, which was not fitted on all tanks.

(E) This T-72 is one of few surviving early production T-72 tanks fitted with an early modified T-64 turret as fitted on early Obiekt-172M prototypes and trials tanks. The tank and turret are not original to each other. (Andrey Malyshev)

(F) This T-72A tank with much of its original fittings stripped for display purposes is located as a memorial to UVZ in Nizhny Tagil. (Esa Muikku)

(G) This T-72A (M-1983 model) is located at the Partizanskaya Polyanna Museum near Bryansk. As a museum example its original fittings are remarkably well preserved.

(H) This is an early Obiekt-172M later rebuilt to T-72A (M-1979) specification. The tank retains its original cast eight-bolt mounting road wheels. (Alexander Koshchavtsev)

(I,J) These two images are of the same T-72 Ural tank located in Ekaterinburg. Note the commander's cupola on this early production Obiekt-172M (T-72), the early road wheels and the use of 'parts bin' restoration for museum display. Although the same tank, the two views indicate how different T-72 models can appear depending on viewing angle. (Vyacheslav Belogrud)

(A) An early T-72 Ural later rebuilt to mid 1980s T-72A standard is located at a regional military headquarters also in Ekaterinburg. Notice the retained early L-2 infrared projector location on the left side of the barrel. (Esa Muikku) **(B)** An original T-72AV at the NII-38 Institute Museum at Kubinka in 2009. For those that visited the museum in early years when it retained the aura of 'secret museum' status, the backlighting remained a major challenge. **(C)** This T-72A M-1983 located at Patriot Park according to the serial Number F10VT5951 was built at UVZ in October 1983. (Esa Muikku) **(D)** A T-72A M-1983 located at the Muzei Bronevoi Tekhniki at Prokhorovka near Belgorod, the central location of the Battle of Kursk in 1943. **(E)** This T-72A is located at the UVZ museum in Nizhny Tagil. (Esa Muikku) **(F)** An early T-72 Ural tank with subsequent capital rebuild located at the Urals Military Glory Museum in Verkhnyaya Pyshma near Ekaterinburg. The tank has Serial Number A07VT5400, built at UVZ in July 1975. (Esa Muikku) **(G)** Many T-72 tanks located abroad are foreign production or Soviet export models. This T-72M1 at the Tank Museum in Bovington in Great Britain is an ex German DDR NVA example. Most T-72M1 tanks in NVA service were Czech- or Polish-built.

(H,I) The T-72M1 at the Shrivenham Defence Academy is also an ex German NVA example with the same heritage as that located at Bovington. (John Ham)

(J) A T-72M1 (ex NVA) in running order at Tankfest, Bovington, in the UK in June 2025.

(K) A T-72B1 at the Park Patriot Museum complex near Moscow.

(L) A Finnish T-72M1, Ps264-122, built at UVZ in August 1988, today located at the Parola Tank Museum in Finland. (Esa Muikku)

(M) Another Finnish T-72M1, Ps264-231, with KMT-6M2 mine plough was also located at the Parola Tank Museum, but has now been replaced with a tank in better condition, Ps264-202, built in Czechoslovakia in March 1987. (Esa Muikku).

(N) A T-72B1 without its 'Kontakt-1' KDZ armour fitted, located at the Omsk Tank Academy.

(A) A privately owned T-72 Ural on display at a War and Peace Show in Great Britain. The tank was captured in Iraq. **(B)** An ex-Iraqi T-72A (M) located at the Islamic Revolutionary and Holy Defence Museum in Tehran. The tank has the early production T-72 features including the original road wheel type. (Alexander Morzhitsky) **(C)** A T-72B as described by UVZ located at the UVZ Museum in Nizhny Tagil. The tank is a T-72B (M-1989) with the original 1K13-49 sight as mounted on the earlier T-72B for the 9K120 'Svir' ATGM rather than the later 'Sosna-U' based gunner's sight. (Esa Muikku) **(D)** The UVZ Museum also has a BREhM-1 vehicle on display. Note the early wheels. (Esa Muikku) **(E)** This BREhM-1 is located in Maikop, near Krasnodar, as a memorial to soldiers who lost their lives in Chechnya. **(F)** In recent years several previously unknown prototypes have been restored and placed in museum collections. This Obiekt-781 BMPT prototype is also located at the UVZ museum in Nizhny Tagil. (Esa Muikku)

A 2S19 at the Artillery Academy, Ekaterinburg. (V. Belogrud)

combat-served tanks have appeared in museum collections, but doubtless many will do so in the immediate future to commemorate their participation in what has become the greatest and deadliest military conflict of the 21st century.

The list below is far from exhaustive, and is but a snapshot of some of these tanks to be found on display in various museums in the Russian Federation and abroad. For tank locations more generally, readers are recommended to consult the preserved tanks and shadock websites on the internet.

T-72 Tanks Preserved in Museums and as Memorials

Country	City/Town	Location	Tank Type	Comments
Australia	Cairns (Queensland)	Australian Armour & Artillery Museum	T-72M1	Czech production
Belarus	Minsk	Shabanakh region	T-72A	Plinth mounted outside Wargaming company offices
Canada	Borden	Borden Military Base	T-72M1	
	LeBreton Flats	Canadian War Museum	T-72M1	
	Oshawa (Toronto)	Canadian Tank Museum	T-72M1	Ex NVA (DDR)
Finland	Parola	Parola Tank Museum	T-72M1	Built in USSR August 1988 for export to Finland. (Ps264-122)
			T-72M1	Built in Czechoslovakia March 1987. Purchased by Finland from ex NVA (DDR) stock. (Ps264-202)
France	Saumur	Musée des Blindés	T-72	
Germany	Münster	Deutsches Panzermuseum	T-72M1	Ex NVA (DDR)
	Hammelburg	Lager Hammelburg	T-72	
	Koblenz	War Technology Museum	T-72M	Cutaway Training Tank
	Sinsheim	Auto & Tekhnik Museum	T-72M1	Ex NVA (DDR)
Great Britain	Bosworth	Armourgeddon Museum	T-72M	
	Bovington	Tank Museum	T-72M1	Ex NVA (DDR)
	Duxford	Imperial War Museum	T-72M1	
	Shrivenham	Shrivenham Defence Academy	T-72M1	Ex NVA (DDR)
	Private ownership	N/K	T-72M1	Ex Iraq
Country	City/Town	Location	Tank Type	Comments

Country	City	Museum	Model	Notes
Iran	Tehran	Islamic Revolutionary & Holy Defence Museum	T-72M1	Ex Iraq
Israel	Latrun	Yad La-Shiryon Museum	T-72M1	
Jordan	Amman	Royal Tank Museum	T-72M1	Polish production. Ex NVA (DDR)
Poland	Warsaw	Fort IX Czerniaków	T-72M	
	Bydgoszcz	Land Forces Museum, Lądowych	PT-91M	Polish modification of the T-72M, modified glacis & turret ERA
	Poznan	Citadel Museum	T-72M	
	Żagań	Polish Armour Centre	T-72M	
Russian Federation	Bryansk	Partizanskaya Polyanna	T-72A	T-72A M-1983 model
	Chelyabinsk	Victory Garden	T-72	Tank with T-64A turret as fitted on some early T-72 tanks
	Ekaterinburg	Military HQ Building	T-72 Ural (early)	Capital repair rebuild
		Military Museum	T-72 Ural	
	Ekaterinburg (Verkhnyaya Pyshma)	Museum of Urals Military Glory	T-72 Ural	Built in USSR July 1975, with later rebuilds
		Artillery Academy	2S19	
	Kamensk Shakhtinsky (Rostov Oblast)	Park Pobeda – Engineering Forces affiliate	IMR-2	
	Kemerovo	Plinth mounted memorial	T-72A	
	Khasayurt (Dagestan)	Plinth mounted memorial	T-72A	
	Krasnogorsk (Arkhangelskoe – Moscow)	Muzei Tekhniki Vadim Zadorozhny	T-72A	Built in November 1987
	Kubinka (Moscow)	Kubinka Tank Museum	Obiekt-172	
			Obiekt-172M	
			T-72AV	
			T-72B1	
			Obiekt-781	Early BMPT Prototype
			Obiekt-782	Early BMPT Prototype (also known as Ob.781 Model B)
			Obiekt-787	Early BMPT Prototype
			BREM-1	Installed as a memorial to the wars in Chechnya
			M-84	Yugoslav-built version of T-72
		Patriot Park	T-72A	Built in USSR October 1983
			T-72B1	
	Moscow	Paklonnaya Gora (Victory Park)	T-72B	
		Marfino region - Plinth mounted memorial	T-72A	
		Solntsevo region - Plinth mounted memorial	T-72A	
	Maikop	Within the town	BREM-1	
	Nizhny Tagil	UVZ Museum	Obiekt-172M	
			T-72A	
			T-72B (M-1989)	
			BREM-1	
			Obiekt-781	Early BMPT prototype
		UVZ monument in city	T-72A	
	Omsk	Tank Academy	T-72B1	Plinth mounted outside the Tank Academy
			T-72B1	Located in a display of armoured vehicles outside the Tank Academy
			BREM-1	
	Padikovo (Moscow)	Museum of Russian Military History	T-72 Ural	
	Prokhorovka	Muzei Bronevoi Tekhniki	T-72A	T-72 M-1983 model
			2S19	
	Sholokovo	T-34 Museum	T-72A	Built in 1978

	St Petersburg	Artillery, Engineer, Communications Troops Museum	2S19	
	St Petersburg (Nevsky Pyatachok)	Leningrad Blockade Breakthrough Museum	Obiekt-172M	
	Toliatti	Technical Museum (VAZ)	Obiekt-172M	
	Volgograd	Battle of Stalingrad Panorama Museum	T-72B	
	Yelets	Plinth mounted memorial	T-72A	
Sweden	Strängnäs	Arsenal Museum	T-72M1	1 of 5 former DDR T-72M1 tanks purchased from Germany in 1992 for evaluation
Switzerland	Full	Swiss Military Museum	T-72	
United States	Aberdeen, Maryland	US Army Aberdeen Proving Grounds	T-72M	For many years the most accessible T-72 tank in the US. Now relocated
	Fort Benning, Georgia	National Armor & Cavalry Museum	T-72M	
	Fort Hood, Texas	1st Cavalry Division Museum	T-72M	
	Fort Knox, Kentucky	General George Patton Museum	T-72M	
	Fort Lewis, Washington State	Fort Lewis Army Base (Lewis McChord)	T-72M	Ex Iraq
	Rochester, New York State	US Naval & Marine Corps Reserve Center	T-72M	
	Stow, Massachusetts	American Heritage Museum	T-72M	Ex NVA (DDR) Ex Military Vehicle Technology Foundation (Jacques Littlefield)
	Triangle, Virginia	National Museum of the Marine Corps	T-72M	
	Evaluation and OPFOR	Various Locations	T-72M	A significant number of T-72M tanks remain in US military service for training purposes

Note: The exact models may not be entirely accurate on some locations due to limited photography.

LEFT A 2S19 self-propelled howitzer at the Artillery, Engineer and Communications Troops Museum, St Petersburg.

BELOW A 2S19 displayed next to the T-72 and T-80 tank chassis used in its development, Muzei Bronevoi Tekhniki, Prokharovka. The sheer size of the turret is evident when seen next to the gun tanks.

CONCLUSION

The T-72 entered service with the Soviet Army in 1973 against a background of political intrigue that had conspired to prevent its very existence, or at a minimum to limit its importance relative to the more advanced T-64 and the later T-80. In service the T-72 tank quickly established its workhorse main battle tank status, however, with a fine balance of firepower, armour and mobility combined with being relatively straightforward to operate and maintain in operational combat conditions. While initially deprived of some of the more advanced technology applied to the T-64 and T-80 design rivals, the tank was over many years in service gradually upgraded to such an extent that the latest T-72B3 and T-72B3M 'second generation' of rebuilt T-72 tanks actually replaced the tank's T-90 successor in production – a first in Soviet and Russian tank history. The T-72 tank was also widely exported, in some countries replacing technically superior but operationally less reliable designs supplied by NATO countries.

The T-72 remains in service today in large numbers domestically in the Russian Federation and in many countries worldwide. The T-72 tank is at present undertaking its most widespread combat role, as two former Soviet states both using the Soviet-era-origin tank fight a combined arms war on a scale unseen in Europe since 1945, with the tank again being honed and adapted by both sides in response to significant changes in warfare, not least the widespread use of drones as anti-tank weapons.

The T-72 tank has in its most recent combat use again proven its operational reliability as a workhorse main battle tank, as eminently suited for its design role in the third decade of the 21st century as when it entered service in 1973, more than half a century ago. When the T-72 entered service with the Soviet Army, the tank as a weapon of war had existed for less than six decades following its first deployment in action by the British in 1916. At the time of publication, the T-72 continues today to provide stellar performance in Russian and foreign service, now well into its own sixth decade of operational service, a major achievement by any measure. During all those years, the T-72 has seen combat action in myriad locations worldwide, and has also outlasted both the country of its birth and its own production replacement, with absolutely no sign that it will be completely replaced at any time in the near future.

The service record of the T-72 is an inarguable testament to the technical engineering and military competence behind its original design principles.

The remarkably long-lived T-72 tank remains today a premier example of a fit-for-purpose tough and reliable combat workhorse – precisely what any military, and any tank crew, ever needed from any tank design.

(A) T-72B tanks traverse Red Square during the final Soviet-era military parade held in Moscow on 7 November 1990, almost 30 years after the T-72 had entered service with the Soviet Army.

(B) T-72B3M tanks traverse Red Square in Moscow on 9 May 2019, almost 50 years since the T-72 entered service, a truly remarkable service history.

(C) A T-72M1 alongside an American M-60 at the recently closed Land Warfare Hall at the Imperial War Museum, Duxford. This photograph puts the relative size of the T-72 in perspective. (Peter Plume)

(D) A former NVA (DDR) service T-72M (M1) parked between British Chieftain and Challenger 1 tanks at the Tank Museum, Bovington, UK, during Tankfest 2025 gives perspective as to relative dimensions.

(E) A T-72B3 with 'Kontakt-5' KDZ armour, a V-84-1 engine and 'Sosna-U' based fire control system photographed in 2014. As with all tanks, it is crewed by young men who risk their lives for what they believe in. The strongest element of any tank, in any country.

A T-72B tank in three-colour camouflage passes through Red Square in Moscow on 7 November 1990. Though it was unknown at the time, this would be the last Soviet-era military parade to be held on Red Square. (Sergei Popsuevich)

APPENDICES

Appendix 1: T-72 Production Numbers

Year	Obiekt 172M	T-72	T-72A	T-72B	IRM-2	BREhM-1	MTU-72	Total Chassis
1970	3	-	-	-	-	-	-	3
1971	15	-	-	-	-	-	-	15
1972	15	-	-	-	-	-	-	15
1973	-	30	-	-	-	-	-	30
1974	-	220 / 3 K	-	-	-	-	-	220
1975	-	700 / 25 K	-	-	-	-	-	700
1976	-	1,017 / 50 K	-	-	-	-	-	1,017
1977	-	1,150 / 60 K	-	-	-	-	-	1,150
1978	-	1,200 / 40 K	-	-	-	-	-	1,200
1979	-	1,360* / 60 K*	-	-	-	-	-	1,360*
1980	-	-	1,350 / 80 K	-	-	-	-	1,350
1981	-	-	1,420 / 105 K	-	-	-	-	1,420
1982	-	-	1,371 / 80 K	-	10	-	-	1,371
1983	-	-	1,420 / N/A	-	23	-	-	1,443
1984	-	-	1,501 / N/A	-	42	1	-	1,544
1985	-	-	-	1,559 / N/A	53	5	-	1,617
1986	-	-	-	1,530 / N/A	90	30	-	1,650
1987	-	-	-	1,534 / N/A	85	60	-	1,679
1988	-	-	-	1,503 / N/A	105	76	-	1,684
1989	-	-	-	933 / N/A	122	75	5	1,135
1990	-	-	-	776 / N/A	129	95	20	1,020
Totals	33	5677 / 238 K	7062 / 265 K*	7835 / N/A	659	342	25	20,603†

K – Command Tank Variant
*UVZ changed over in midyear to produce the T-72A tank
† Note: 1,020 T-72 chassis were produced for use in other vehicles to include the MTU-72 bridge launcher, the TOS-1 Buratino rocket launcher, the BREhM-1 recovery vehicle, and the IRM-2 engineer vehicle. They were never gun tanks with turrets.

The IMR-2, BREhM-1 and MTU-72 hulls were shipped to Omsk for final assembly and were recorded in the 6XX series of Obiekt-number by that factory.

In addition, the ChTZ plant in Chelyabinsk produced another 1,894 T-72A, T-72B and T-72B1 tanks between 1982 and 1990, bringing the total Soviet production run of T-72 chassis to 22,497. Of that number 21,471 were either line tanks or command tanks.

Licence production of the tank was carried out by Poland, Czechoslovakia and Yugoslavia. Poland built around 1,500 tanks, Czechoslovakia had similar numbers, and Yugoslavia built around 600 of their M84 version of the tank. Total production of the T-72 was thus around 26,000 tanks and vehicles based on that chassis.

The T-90 continues in production as the direct successor to the T-72 tank, with the IMR-2MA (IMR-3), BREhM-1M, BMR-3M and the new MTU-90 bridge-launcher based on the later chassis.

Appendix 2: Soviet/Russian Standardized Life Cycle for Armoured Vehicles

All Soviet tank designs began with a recognized need for a certain class of combat vehicle and this would be assigned out as a project, often with a codename.

1 – All new projects started with a request from the Council of Ministers of the USSR (SM SSSR) and the Central Committee of the Communist Party (TsK KPSS). These were given to the relevant design and production facilities who decided if they could meet the project requirements. If they could, they were tasked with carrying out scientific research work on a project to determine its viability.
2 – Scientific Design Work (Nauchno-Issledivatalnaya Rabota or NIR). This was, and remains today, the scientific work that can determine the feasibility of a project and lay out possible solutions to the tasking. At this stage the project was either given a project name (e.g. 'Liven', 'Oka', 'Akatsiya', etc.) or a manufacturing plant internal designator. Once the NIR work is approved by the Scientific Committee for the Council of Ministers, the manufacturing plant is then authorized to carry out prototype design work.
3 – Prototype Design Work (*Opytno-Konstruktorskaya Rabota* or OKR). At this stage, the project was now given an article designator or Obiekt-number (e.g. Obiekt-137G2, Obiekt-482). This stage required at least one running prototype of the vehicle for assessment. Depending upon the problem at hand, as many as six prototypes might have been built, including one for destructive firing testing of its armour protection.

4 – Factory Testing. Once the prototype was ready, it underwent factory testing by the designers and engineers in concert with the 'Zakhazchik' – client or customer representative – the Ministry of Defence representative to the plant. Once the major bugs had been ironed out and approval granted by the Scientific Committee, the vehicle was then sent for State Polygon (range) Testing at Kubinka.

5 – State Range (Polygon) Testing. The military and members of the Ministry of Defence and Ministry of Defence Production authorities tested all major qualities of the new vehicle in a series of planned tests at the Kubinka Test Polygon. 'Findings' were made, which required the plant to repair or correct them as soon as possible. Once all corrections were made, permission was granted for troop testing.

6 – Troop Testing. This usually required an Establishment Lot (ustanovochnaya partiya / seriya) of vehicles to be built – usually a batch of three, five, ten or 25 tanks, depending on the viability of the product and requirements for thorough testing. Vehicles might then be sent to various parts of the Soviet Union for testing – the north for winter conditions, the Southern Republics such as Kazakhstan for desert conditions, the Urals for mountainous conditions, etc. Once the vehicle passed its troop testing phase, the Ministry of Defence and Ministry of Defence Production would recommend it for acceptance and full production.

7 – State Resolution. A joint resolution of the Central Committee of the Politburo of the Communist Party and the Council of Ministers of the USSR (many members holding positions in both) named the item (i.e. T-72) and announced it is accepted for service with the Soviet Army. Full production might then be ordered by the Ministry of Defence and Ministry of Defence Production (occasionally the project was tabled at this point due to extenuating circumstances, as for example the 100mm D-54TS armed T-62A tank) followed by the factory preparing to put the vehicle into full production. This might take place nearly immediately if only a modification of a vehicle in series production, or as much as a year and a half delay while the plant remodelled and retooled to produce the new machine.

All this might take up to ten years from the start of the project to first production model rollout.

Once the vehicles were in service, there were set times and levels of repairs needed called Technical Inspections (Tekhnichesky Osmotr or TO-1 and TO-2) and capital rebuilding. This varied from vehicle to vehicle but was around

2,500km and three years for TO-1, 5,000km and five years for TO-2, and ten years for capital rebuilding. (The mileage guarantee period for the T-72 was 5,000km.) That was also the point where any upgrades, changes or improvements were added to the tank. In the case of the T-72, that would mean improved radio sets, gunsights, laser rangefinders, through-the-bore ATGM systems, new engines, RMSh tracks, new OPVT equipment, and many other items. Later improvements would include explosive reactive armour.

While in service, there were four categories of serviceability for the tanks:

- Category I: vehicle is new, fully combat capable, all systems are fully operational, all spare parts and tools are in place, and the vehicle is ready to go.
- Category II: vehicle is used, mostly combat capable, needs some minor repairs to some systems, may be missing some spare parts and tools, but could stand in a combat formation.
- Category III: vehicle is in need of major repairs, some combat systems are inoperable or no longer present in the vehicle, it is missing most of its spare parts and tools, and would not be sufficiently capable of conducting combat.
- Category IV: vehicle is nearly inoperable, suffers from major failures of key systems (engine, driveline, gun, operating mechanisms) and needs capital repair or rebuilding.

There is a Category V, which signifies the vehicle has been written off (peacetime) or is a 'non-returning combat loss' (wartime). In some cases, vehicles in this condition were stripped of most running gear, supporting systems and electronics, and then dug in as pillboxes or firing points in fortified regions such as along the mainland Chinese border or on Sakhalin Island in the Pacific Ocean.

Appendix 3: Obiekt-Numbers of the T-72 and Related Developmental Tanks

Number	Year	Description
032	1986	Remotely controlled 'Klin-1' clearance vehicle based on IMR-2. Single prototype built.
033	1986	Control vehicle for the 'Klin-1' remotely controlled clearance vehicle.
140	1957	Completely new design of medium tank mounting the 100mm D-54TS gun in a new chassis with six road wheels, three return rollers, and the 'Vyuga' stabilizer.
142	2001	BREhM-1M armoured repair and recovery vehicle on later T-90 chassis.
146	2011	Proposed BREhM vehicle converted from early model T-72 tanks withdrawn from service.
151	1979	T-72-based self-propelled anti-tank gun prototype – 'Sprut-S' – with either a 152mm 2A58 gun or a 125mm 2A66.
153	2019	Proposed T-90-based Universal Armoured Engineer Vehicle (UBIM) (Robot-3).
166	1961	T-62 Medium Tank with a new 115mm U-5TS 'Molot' gun; modified twice during its production run and finally fitted with an AAMG.
166Zh	1963	T-62 tank fitted with the 115mm D-84 smoothbore gun and the 'Zhelud' cassette type autoloader with separate loading ammunition.
167M	1964	Obiekt-167 improved T-62 model fitted with the 115mm 2A21 separate loading ammunition gun and the 'Zhelud' autoloader; planned to fit the 2A26 gun and field as the T-62B but not accepted for service.
172	1968	Prototype of T-64A tank fitted with a V-45 diesel engine but retaining all T-64A components.
172M	1970	Prototype of a heavily modified T-64A with UVZ running gear, tracks, autoloader and other elements replacing the T-64A components. Accepted as T-72 'Ural' main battle tank in 1973.
172M1	1979	T-72 'Ural-1' with modified armour protection and 2A46 gun replacing 2A26.
172M2A	2009	T-72M1 tank upgraded with 'Sosna-U' fire control system and a remote-control machine-gun cupola.
172M2L	2009	T-72M1 upgraded for an order by India.
172M-Eh	1978	Export version of T-72 – also offered to Poland, Czechoslovakia and Yugoslavia to build under licence.
172M-Eh1	1978	Export version of T-72 – offered for sale to foreign customers.
172M-Eh2	1978	Export version of T-72 – T-72M variant with collective protection and monolithic armour turret; produced under licence in Poland and Czechoslovakia.
172M-Eh3	1981	Export version of T-72 – T-72M variant with collective protection and monolithic armour turret; 'Tucha' smoke grenade launchers fitted, standard sales model to Warsaw Pact nations.
172M-Eh4	1981	Export version of T-72 – T-72M variant with collective protection and monolithic armour turret; 'Tucha' smoke grenade launchers fitted; offered for sale to foreign customers.
172M-1	1979	Improved T-72A tank prototype.
172M-1-Eh5	1983	Export version of T-72A – T-72M1 variant with increased turret armour protection; 'Tucha' smoke grenade launchers fitted; produced under licence in Poland, Czechoslovakia and Yugoslavia (as M-84).
172M-1-Eh6	1983	Export version of T-72A – T-72M1 variant specifically built for India.
172M-Eh7/8	1987	T-72S 'Shilden' – export model of T-72B with reduced capability but ERA and the 'Svir' ATGM system; sold to Iran.
172MD	1975	T-72 fitted with a 125mm 2A49 high-power smoothbore gun (D-89T).
172MK	1974	T-72K command model.
172MK-Eh3	1981	T-72M command model for Warsaw Pact service.
172MK-Eh4	1981	T-72M command model for foreign customers.
172MK-1	1980	T-72A command tank variant.
172MN	1974	T-72 tank fitted with the 130mm LP-36E (2A50) rifled gun from SKB Perm.
172MP	1977	T-72 prototype fitted with the 125mm 2A46M gun.
172-2M	1972	Project 'Buyvol' with new glacis, new gun and other changes as well as V-67 engine; not accepted for service after test.
172-3M	1975	Improved T-72 prototype with 130mm 2A50 rifled gun and TPD-K1 laser rangefinder with Type 902 'Tucha' smoke grenade launcher system.
173	1969	T-64A tank variant fitted with the 'Zhelud' autoloader.
175	1976	T-72 prototype with improved combat characteristics including a 130mm D-85 rifled gun.
176	1975	Prototype with new turret and other changes to the T-72. Standardized as the T-72A in 1979.
176K	1980	T-72AK command model. Sub-designators (rarely seen) were 1 for company commander, 2 for battalion commander, and 3 for regimental commander, each with slightly different communications suites.
177	1981	T-72A prototype fitted with the 1A40-1 fire control system and 9K120 'Svir' guided weapons complex.
179	1981	T-72A prototype fitted with the 1A33 'Ob' fire control system and 9K122 guided weapons complex firing the 'Kobra' ATGM.
183	2013	Proposed BMPT-72 tank support combat vehicle based on withdrawn T-72 tank chassis.
184	1984	Prototype with new turret, fire control, 'Svir' through-the-bore ATGM and other changes. Standardized as the series production T-72B in 1984.
184-1	1984	T-72B1 tank without the 'Svir' missile system.
184-2	2012	T-72B3 tank with partial upgrades from T-72B2 'Rogatka' programme.
184-3	2013	T-72B3M tank with modernization features to include a commander's protected station.

184A	2005	T-72BA with new fire controls and other detail changes. Standardized as the T-72BA in 1989.
184A-1	2005	T-72B1A tank upgrade.
184K	1985	T-72B command model.
184K-1	1985	T-72B1K command model.
184M	2005	T-72B2 'Rogatka-1' upgraded T-72B with many improvements; while accepted for service, not placed in production due to high cost.
184M-3	2011	T-72B3 upgraded T-72B – retained key improvements from the T-72B2.
184-1MS	2012	'Beliy Orel' (White Eagle) T-72B1MS with new sights and optical control systems.
186	1985	Improved T-72B prototype with the 125mm 2A66 gun and a welded turret.
187	1988	Experimental 'Revolutionary' redesign of T-72 with new hull glacis, six different engine designs, and turret. Not accepted for service.
188	1987	T-90 main battle tank with cast turret – later designated T-90 Model 1992.
188-Eh1	1992	T-90S export model of the main battle tank.
188-1	1987	T-72BM tank accepted for production but not series produced and did not enter service.
188A	1995	T-90 tank prototype fitted with a welded turret.
188A1	2005	T-90A modernized tank with ESSA thermal sight.
188A1K	2009	T-90AK with PTK-T-1 battlefield management system.
188K	1994	T-90K command tank.
188M	2016	Modernized T-90 tank under OKR 'Proryv-3'.
188MS-1	2011	T-90MS tank with remote control machine gun, new turret with bustle ammo stowage, and other improvements under OKR 'Proryv-2'.
190	1981	Prototype self-propelled mine clearing vehicle – OKR 'Goboy'.
193	1999	IMR-3 engineer obstacle clearing vehicle.
195	2000	Obiekt-195 prototype next generation main battle tank.
197	1997	BRM-3M mine clearing vehicle.
197A	2003	BRM-3MA mine clearing vehicle on T-90 chassis – OKR 'Vepr'.
199	2000	Project 'Ramka' – a heavily armoured tank escort vehicle using a T-72 chassis and mounting four 'Ataka-T' ATGM, two 30mm 2A42 cannon, a machine gun and two AGS-17 grenade launchers; now being built on T-90 chassis and marketed as 'Terminator'.
316	1983	2S19 'Msta-S' 152mm self-propelled gun-howitzer; uses a T-72 chassis and drive train fitted with T-80 running gear.
327	1976–87	152mm 'Shaiba' self-propelled gun-howitzer prototype with 152mm 2A33/2A36 armament. Further developed into 2S19 'Msta-S'.
430	1960	Kharkov prototype for a new medium tank – four-man crew, new hull design, 100mm D-54TS gun, and 4TD two-cycle diesel engine; not accepted for service.
432	1963	Prototype new main battle tank with three man crew, 115mm 2A21 gun with mechanical loader, and 5TDF two-cycle diesel engine; standardized as the T-64 main battle tank in 1966.
434	1968	Improved T-64 with 125mm 2A26 gun and other detail improvements; standardized as the T-64A main battle tank.
436	1965	Prototype for fitting the V-36 four-cycle diesel engine to the T-64A tank; dropped in favour of Obiekt-439.
438	1965	Original designator for the UVZ project to fit a V-45 engine into the T-64A tank as a mobilization variant; redesignated as Obiekt-172.
439	1969	Kharkov effort to design a competing conversion of the T-64A with the V-45 four-cycle diesel engine and directed to replace Obiekt-172M; not accepted.
446	1979	T-64B main battle tank with 1A33 'Ob' fire control system and 9K112 'Kobra' guided weapons complex.
563	2001	TZM loader vehicle for the 'Buratino' or 'Solntsepyok' MRL vehicles.
608	1975	BREhM-1 armoured repair and recovery vehicle based on a T-72A chassis; the later BREhM-1M is based on a T-90 chassis.
632	1974	MTU-72 bridge-launcher vehicle based on a T-72A chassis with a 20 metre long bridge (when deployed).
634	1978 onwards	TOS-1 'Buratino' 30-round multiple rocket launcher system using a T-72A chassis.
634B	2001	TOS-1A 'Solntsepyok' 24-round multiple rocket launcher system using a T-72 or T-90 chassis.
637	1980	IMR-2 engineer obstacle clearing vehicle based on a T-72A chassis and similar in fitting and layout to the T-55 based IMR-1.
745	1995–96	Prototype BMPT with a single 30mm gun and four ATGMs on a T-72A chassis.
781	1987	Prototype BMPT with twin 30mm guns and four ATGMs on a T-72A chassis.
782	1987	Prototype BMPT with the armament of a BMP-3 in a low turret on a T-72A chassis.
785	1975	ChTZ (GSKB-2) bureau T-72 prototype with 125mm 2A82 or 130mm M-65 gun options, 2V-16 engine and T-80 running gear. Many features appeared a decade later on the UVZ Obiekt-187.
787	1995–96	Prototype BMPT with a flat turret and twin 30mm guns and four ATGM launchers on a T-72A chassis.

Note: The Soviets did not do incremental upgrade identifiers as used in the West and therefore both early and late variants of the same model of tank have the same designator and Obiekt-number. The T-72 'Ural' (Obiekt-172M) and T-72 'Ural-1' (Obiekt-172M1) are the only outliers here. However, due to changing requirements and various and ongoing new changes brought about by modern combat conditions, some vehicles now receive conditional identifiers such as T-72B3M Model 2022.

Appendix 4: Known Client Users of the T-72 Medium Tank

While most of the foreign clients that purchased or were given Soviet-built T-72 tanks also received either Polish or Czechoslovakian tanks at a later date, they were all treated as just T-72 tanks.

Only the Obiekt-172 and Obiekt-172M prototype tanks had a date of YYMM (year/month) followed by a letter, followed by a one-up monthly or summary production number of the vehicle. For example, 808V172-1 was one of the first two prototype Obiekt-172 tanks, built in August 1968 at Nizhny Tagil. In 1970 the codes were changed to a letter for the year, two digits for the month of production and a two-letter code for the manufacturing plant followed by the one-up number.

The early codes were Cyrilic В (transliterated as V in English) for UVZ, Е (E) for Kharkov, and Г (G) for Omsk; when in 1970 the system changed the codes became VT for UVZ (V – UVZ, T – tank); ET for Kharkov; and GT for Omsk. ShT is the code used for chassis produced by the Ural Transport Machinery Plant (Uraltransmash), AT is for ChTZ Chelyabinsk (A pre-1970) and NT (N pre-1970) is for the Chelyabinsk Metallurgical Plant, which produced castings and welded the hulls for T-72 assembly at ChTZ.*

After 1970, here are the known year codes used:

Year	Cyrillic Letter (English Letter)
1970	Л (L)
1971	Н (N)
1972	П (P)
1973	М (M)
1974	Р (R)
1975	А (A)
1976	Д (D)
1977	Г (G)
1978	Б (B)
1979	В (V)

In the following table are the known T-72 user countries and estimated numbers of tanks on hand and used over the years. It should be noted that Russian and Western data are often conflated; Russian numbers have been used (where known) for client/former client states on the basis that the country provides the parts for maintenance and thereby has a track of actual numbers of tanks still in

---

* There is no direct relationship between the Cyrillic and Latin-English alphabets; the transliterated letters above and in the table below are to show how the Cyrillic is written (but not pronounced) in English as it usually appears in translated texts.

service. With damaged tanks returned to service, modernizations and how they are accounted for etc., such numbers are always to be taken as a guide rather than a definitive number. The recent export of many T-72 tanks from Eastern European countries to Ukraine is not accounted for in the numbers below.

Country	Number	Remarks
Algeria	340–500	Mix of T-72, T-72M, T-72M1 and T-72AG conversions from Ukraine; also has some T-90
Angola	44	T-72M1 purchased from Belarus
Armenia	~250	T-72 mixture
Azerbaijan	400	T-72A, T-72B and improved models
Belarus	446	T-72B; had 1,797 before break-up of the USSR
Bulgaria	334	Czech T-72M2 and 350 Soviet-era tanks reported in reserve
Czech Republic	598	Remaining tanks from the ČSR – 30 T-72M4CZ in service
Democratic Republic of the Congo	100	T-72AV tanks purchased from Ukraine
Djibouti	42	T-72s purchased from Yemen
Estonia	184	Returned to Russia in 1994
Ethiopia	~220	50 T-72 purchased from Yemen, 171 T-72UA1 purchased from Ukraine
Finland	162	T-72M1, M1K, M1K1 from the USSR, Czechoslovakia and Poland. 63 delivered by the USSR 1984–88, 66 Czech- and 33 Polish-built tanks bought from Germany as ex NVA/DDR surplus. All written off in 2006.
Georgia	~191	Total of around 191 T-72 tanks in storage prior to the 2008 war
German Democratic Republic	452–549	T-72, T-72M, T-72M1 tanks from USSR, Poland and ČSR; now all scrapped, sold abroad or donated. 99 tanks sold to Finland 1992–94
Hungary	138	T-72A and T-72M1 types but most are either in reserve or being sold off
India	1100–1900	T-72M and T-72M1 tanks; now supplemented by T-90S and T-90SA tanks
Iran	563	538 T-72S and 25 T-72M1 tanks; with local conversions and upgrades being made to all tanks
Iraq	900	Over 1,000 purchased prior to August 1990; T-72, T-72M, T-72M1 and 'Lion of Babylon' (Polish T-72M1 tanks furnished in kit form); remaining tanks are now part of the new Iraqi Army
Kazakhstan	300	Former USSR tanks
Kenya	77	T-72AV purchased from Ukraine
Kyrgyzstan	215	Former USSR tanks
Kuwait	200	M-84 tanks purchased from Yugoslavia
Laos	50	T-72B1MS tanks
Latvia	114	Returned to Russia in 1994
Libya	~350	T-72s purchased before 2003; after 2012 civil war unknown
Lithuania	398	Returned to Russia in 1993
North Macedonia	31	T-72A and T-72AK battalion purchased from Ukraine
Morocco	148	136 T-72B and 12 T-72BK purchased from Belarus
Mongolia	100	Former USSR tanks
Myanmar	139	T-72S tanks
Nagorno-Karabakh	~500	T-72, T-72A, T-72AV, T-72B
Nicaragua	50	T-72B1MS tanks with some T-72B3 models noted
Nigeria	16	T-72AV purchased from Ukraine
Poland	~802	T-72 M1 and T-72M1D models including 135 T-72M1Z and 98 PT-91 upgraded tanks in service
Romania	30	T-72M1 tanks (ex-Syrian) purchased from Israel in 1986; now all scrapped or sold

Russia	2284+	Mostly T-72B and T-72B1 models; includes around 1,300 tanks upgraded to T-72BA and T-72B3 levels
Slovakia	299	T-72M1 tanks; had 272 at one time
Serbia	90	60 T-72M in reserve, 30 T-72S, 30 T-72B1MS
South Sudan	~100	T-72 models
Sudan	400	T-72AV purchased from Ukraine and Belarus; another 170 T-72 tanks may have also arrived
Syria	700	All models purchased from the USSR or former Warsaw Pact countries, some lost in 1982 war with Israel and now others due to the ongoing civil war; now also has T-72B and T-90 tanks
Tajikistan	44	Former USSR tanks
Turkmenistan	~700	Former USSR tanks
Uganda	50	T-72B tanks
Ukraine	~600	Mostly converted to T-72AV models and sold abroad
United States	<20	Former DDR tanks used for OPFOR training
Uzbekistan	70	Former USSR tanks
Venezuela	92	T-72B1 tanks purchased from Russia; 100 more on order
Yemen	39	Remaining tanks after selling stocks to other countries

Appendix 5: T-72 – Foreign Production & Service

The Soviet and foreign production and service history is such an extensive subject that only the briefest of summaries can be provided here. The number of variants built specifically for export and the local production and subsequent modification of original T-72 models is extensive, with the number of tanks in service in different armies varying significantly over time. Below is a brief introduction to what is an extensive subject in its own right. In the Soviet era, the T-72 was produced under licence in Czechoslovakia, Poland and Yugoslavia, and also assembled in India. Later local modifications of the T-72 were developed and produced in Czechia (the T-72CZ), in Poland (PT-91), Slovakia (T-72M1-A and T-72M2 Moderna) and Yugoslavia (M84). Localized variants based on the T-72 were subsequently produced in China (the Type 98), Iran (the Zulfikar) and Pakistan (Al Khalid), to name but a few examples.

Warsaw Pact Inventory

In 1991, several former Warsaw Pact countries retained significant inventories of T-72 tanks. The GDR (East Germany) had 549 T-72s in service in 1991, which in subsequent years were widely distributed to other countries. Hungary had 138 T-72 tanks in service, and Bulgaria had 334. Approximately 1,700 T-72 tanks had also by that time been exported to the Middle East by Czechoslovakia and Poland.

As of 2007, to take a single year as a point of reference, T-72 tanks had been delivered and remained in service with:

Algeria – 350
Angola – 50
Armenia – 246

Bulgaria – 432
Croatia – unknown
Czechia – 244 (T-72CZ)
China – unknown. It is known that China did purchase working drawings from the Soviets and may have received one or two tanks for evaluation but there is no solid evidence of their ever arriving in China.
Finland – 63
Georgia – 1,400
India – 1,400
Iran – 480
Kuwait – 150 (M84)
Libya – 200
Malaysia – 48
Morocco – 48
Poland – 586 T-72 & 233 PT-91
Romania – 5
Serbia – 62 T-72 & 206 M84
Slovakia – 247
Slovenia – 40 (M84)
Syria – 1,700
Vietnam – 120
Yemen – 60

Specific T-72 Production by Country

Croatia

Croatia developed the M-95 Degman tank from 2003, which traced its roots to the T-72 via the Yugoslavian M-84. The tank did not enter series production.

Czech Republic

After the division of Czechoslovakia, the Czech Republic did not retain tank-building capability, but did have capital rebuild facilities at Nový Jičín where modernized T-72, T-72M and T-72M1 tanks were rebuilt, and the T-72M3CZ and T-72M4CZ built for the Czech Army.

India

After India received significant direct deliveries of early T-72 tanks from the Soviet Union, the country opted to produce the T-72M1 export model locally in Avadi near Chennai. The licence agreement was agreed with Moscow and assembly of the first locally produced tank completed in late 1987. The first batch of 175 T-72M1 'Ajeya' tanks was built from Soviet-delivered component parts, with increasing localization thereafter. As of 2001, India was estimated to have 1,100 T-72-based tanks of various modifications in service. The tank was replaced in production by the licence-built T-90.

Iran

In the early 1990s, Iran was provided the documentation to licence-produce the T-72S in Iran. The tanks were provided with 'Kontakt-1' ERA and upgraded fire control systems.

Iraq

The T-72 was assembled in Iraq under what the Russians term 'otvertochnoe proizvodstvo' (screwdriver assembly) – in other words, the tanks were built in the USSR, disassembled into main components for shipment, and re-assembled in Iraq as local production.

Poland

Poland series-manufactured under licence the T-72, T-72M, T-72M1 and T-72M1 (K) at Zakłady Mechaniczne Bumar-Łabędy in Gliwice. Later, Poland developed its own variant, the PT-91 'Twardy', which was produced from late 1992, with around 200 PT-91 tanks in service by the late 1990s. The PT-91 was later modified as the PT-91M 'Twardy'.

Romania

In the late 1970s, Romania ordered 30 T-72M tanks for evaluation purposes with a view to establishing licence production, which was however declined by the Soviet Union. Romania thereby developed its own version of the tank, the TR-125 (Tanc Românesc 125 – Romanian Tank, 125mm armament). The TR-125 featured an elongated hull with seven road wheels and a 125mm A555 smoothbore gun and was powered by an 8VSA3 engine developing 900hp. Several prototypes were built in 1987–88 and tested until 1991, but the tank did not enter series production.

Slovakia (Czechoslovakia)

Czechoslovakia produced the export variant of the T-72 M-1975 and later the T-72M1 and T-72M2 at ZTS in Dubnitsa and Martin in Slovakia. Production ceased in 1985.

Yugoslavia

Yugoslavia was provided with production documentation by the Soviet Union in

1979, with approximately 50 tanks built from Soviet components. In 1983, the prototype of the locally developed M-84 was developed, which was subsequently put into series production with approximately 500 built in total. The BREhM version is designated M-874AB1. In 1991, when the civil war started in Yugoslavia, there were 502 M84 tanks in the country. The M-84 is externally similar to the T-72A but with many changes, such as the use of a DNNS-2 laser rangefinder. The later M-84A (A1) featured a new turret and modified armour layout. In 1989, Kuwait ordered 200 M-84A tanks including 15 command tanks and 15 M-874ABI BREhM recovery vehicles. Only 12 tanks were delivered before the start of the ground offensive in the First Gulf War. In 1990 Yugoslavia developed the V2001 'Vihor', which was not produced due to the break-up of the country.

Ukraine

Ukraine developed the T-72AG, T-72MP and T-72-120, none of which were successful in finding export markets. Ukraine had more success with the 'indigenous' T-80UD as built in Kharkov in the Soviet era, which was sold to Pakistan.

T-72AG

The T-72AG was a Ukrainian rebuild of the T-72 tank of which Ukraine inherited a substantial number after the break-up of the Soviet Union. The tank was powered by the 6TD engine, modified from the engine built for the Kharkov-built Soviet-era diesel powered T-80. The tank had significant other upgrades, including a 1G46 fire control sight, PNK-3S observation sight, new 'Nozh' ERA similar to the Russian 'Kontakt-5' ERA, steel reinforced rubber turret armour taken from the T-80U and a 12.7mm NSVT machine gun. The T-72AG was intended primarily for potential export sales (as were Russian tanks at the time) with the tank having its debut at the IDEX-95 exhibition in Abu Dhabi in the UAE.

T-72MP

The T-72MP was a KhBM (Ukraine) modification of the T-72 in collaboration with ZTM (Czechia) using a mix of local Ukrainian, Czech and French components. The tank was armed with a 125mm gun of undisclosed variant and powered by a 6TD diesel engine.

T-72-120

The T-72-120 was developed as a tank compatible with 120mm smoothbore fired NATO ammunition. The tank was first demonstrated at the IDEX-99 exhibition in the UAE.

Appendix 6: Soviet/Russian Communications Systems and Development

The T-72 arrived at a time when the Soviet Army was upgrading their first-generation VHF FM sets in service for better transmission characteristics on the battlefield.

T-72 tanks were initially fitted with the R-123 set, consisting of the transceiver, a power booster and the R-124 intercom system. The R-123 was a set with up to four frequency presets and increased output, but most welcome was its expanded frequency range of 20–51.5 MHz, which both permitted wider use and also easy coordination with motorized rifle and artillery units and their dedicated radio sets – the artillery used the R-108 from 28 to 36.5 MHz and motorized rifle the R-105 (36–46.1 MHz). These were fitted to new production T-72 tanks and T-72K commanders' tanks. The new radios provided communications of up to 25km in most situations.

Soviet communications doctrine required that commanders be able to communicate in a 'two down one up' network with subordinates and higher echelons. Therefore, a battalion commander was supposed to be able to call down to company commanders and platoon leaders and up to regimental command. With four preselected frequencies the R-123 filled the bill for this service.

Initially battalion commanders had two R-123 sets, but with the preset frequency option in the R-123 they soon received an HF set instead. They commenced with the R-130 HF AM/SSB (frequency range 1.5–10.99 MHz). The R-130 was optimized for what are referred to as single sideband 'skywave' communications where the signal is bounced off the ionosphere, and now a battalion commander could communicate up to 350km with the right antenna and weather conditions.

In the 1980s the Soviet Union began to adopt its first solid state radio sets, and of course that meant new radios for the tactical level. The new tactical set was the R-173 'Abzats', which was even more advanced with a frequency range of 30–79.90 MHz (similar to NATO and US sets). It could store up to ten preset frequencies and also could be used for both analogue and digital communications systems. It was paired with the improved R-174 intercom system. The HF command sets were upgraded to the R-134 HF AM/SSB series radios (frequency range 1.5–29.99 MHz). As older T-72 tanks were upgraded they also received these new radio sets.

Later some command vehicles received the newer R-163 'Arbalet' series of radios with improved operating characteristics and power outputs, but it was only with the introduction of the new R-168 'Akvedukt' series of radios that they joined the digital age. Current rebuilds and upgrades such as the T-72B3 are fitted with the R-168-25UE or R-168-25U-2 digital sets; the latter consists of twin 25 watt sets with a frequency range of 30–108 MHz and the ability to use digital signals or encryption as needed. Command vehicles can be fitted with R-168-50K sets using HF/SSB transmission.

Note that most Soviet tankers used the 'Shlemofon', which was a padded helmet with built-in headsets and a strap-on throat microphone; a chest switch was used for transmitting on the selected radio set. The throat microphone needed to be relatively tight to work properly, and if not adjusted correctly the user tended to sound somewhat like 'Donald Duck' when speaking!

Appendix 7: Soviet Ballistic Sets and Tables

While politically the Soviet Union witnessed some internal extremes and dynamic movements, when it came to engineering and science the Soviet Union and its designers were very methodical, thorough and practical. One such methodology was the determination of a set of ballistic standards and their application to all weapons of a given calibre and barrel specification.

Soviet weapon designers from the outset understood that all guns using similar ammunition and barrel length would have nearly identical ballistic tables and results. It made no difference if it was a machine gun, automatic cannon, mortar, howitzer or gun – all weapons of that calibre with that length barrel would fire with near identical performance. Also irrelevant was its platform – field gun, tank, railway, or ship. So tables were created based on the types of ammunition used and were therefore standardized by all arms plants to permit easier development of sights, equipment, accessories and most of all ammunition.

The sets were given a specific number and when developing sights or other accessories the relevant factory would have a set standard to use at once. For example, a 7.62mm machine gun firing 7.62x54mm cartridges, no matter whether it was a DT, SGM, SGMT, or PKT type, would use the same set of ballistics – Set 11 (or with new ammunition Set 23). Likewise, the 14.5mm KPV and KPVT would use Set 14. The T-54 and T-55 went through ballistic table Sets 20, 22 and 32, and the T-62 and early T-64s used ballistic table Set 41.

The T-72 started out with the new 125m D-81T gun, initially the 2A26M but then the D-81TM and 2A46, followed by successive versions of the 2A46 gun, all of which used Ballistic Table Set 49.

They had installed bespoke reticules that provided the deviation distance and lead percentage at range for each type of ammunition to cover the ballistic drop of the projectile and compensate for its velocity over distance. A different number and shift would be needed for each one.

The tanks also were provided with an artillery level to assist when called on to provide artillery fire at longer ranges with HE-FRAG ammunition. The tank commander had a table of elevation and range estimates and the gunner had an angle-measuring device he could use to determine the actual elevation of the gun (this generally required the tank to be sitting on a rise or hill to increase the range). Ranges of 14–15km could be reached in this indirect fire manner, but battlefield direct fire ranges were limited to about 3,000–3,500m due to gun elevation limits and sighting limitations.

The 125mm D-81 series guns use the following ammunition types:

Round	Projectile	Type	Muzzle Velocity	Armour Penetration
3VBM3	3BM9 3BM10	APFSDS	1,800mps	245mm/0 degrees*
3VBM6	3BM12 3BM13	APFSDS (Tungsten core)	1,800mps	280mm/0 degrees
3VBM7	3BM15 3BM16	APFSDS (Tungsten core)	1,785mps	310mm/0 degrees
3VBM8	3BM17 3BM18	APFSDS (export)	1,780mps	310mm/0 degrees
3VBM9	3BM22 3BM23	APFSDS (Tungsten core)	1,785mps	380mm/0 degrees
3VBM10	3BM29 3BM30	APFSDS (DU-nickel)	1,700mps	430mm/0 degrees
3VBM11	3BM26 3BM27	APFSDS (Tungsten core)	1,720mps	410mm/0 degrees
3VBM13	3BM32 3BM33	APFSDS (DU-nickel)	1,700mps	500mm/0 degrees
3VBM17	3BM42 3BM 44 'Mango'	APFSDS (double tungsten and alloy)	1,715mps	450mm/0 degrees
3VBM19	3BM42M 3BM44M 'Lekalo'	APFSDS (Tungsten core)	1,750mps	650mm/0 degrees
3VBM22	3BM59 'Svinets-1'	APFSDS (DU)**	1,650mps	830mm/0 degrees
3VBM23	3BM60 'Svinets-2'	APFSDS (Tungsten core)**	1,650mps?	740mm/0 degrees
3VBM?	3BM69 'Vakuum-1'	APFSDS (DU)**	2,050mps	1,000mm/0 degrees
3VBM?	3BM60 'Vakuum-2'	APFSDS (Tungsten core)**	?	900mm/0 degrees
3VBK7	3BK12	HEAT	905mps	420mm/0 degrees
3VBK10	3BK14	HEAT	905mps	450mm/0 degrees
3VBK16	3BK18	HEAT	905mps	500mm/0 degrees
3VBK16M	3BK18M	HEAT	905mps	550mm/0 degrees
3VBK17	3BK21	HEAT	905mps	550mm/0 degrees
3VBK17B	3BK21B	HEAT(DU shaper)	905mps	750mm/0 degrees
3VBK21	3BK25	HEAT	905mps	?
3VBK25	3BK29 'Breyk'	HEAT (Tandem Charge)	915mps	350–400mm behind ERA
3VBK25M	3BK29M	HEAT (Tandem Charge)	915mps	Est 800mm behind ERA
3VBK27	3VK31 'Start'	HEAT (Triple Charge)	915mps	Est 800mm behind ERA
3VOF22	3OF19	HE-FRAG	805mps	Charge 3.148kg
3VOF36	3OF26	HE-FRAG	850mps	Charge 3.4kg

3VOF128	30F82	HE-FRAG Programmable detonator	850mps	Charge 3.0kg 450 tungsten rod warhead
3VSh7	3Sh7 'Voron'	Shrapnel Programmable detonator	900mps	4,700 flechettes
3VSh8	3Sh8 'Ainet'	Shrapnel Remote detonator	900mps	4,700 flechettes
3UBK14 3UBK14M 3UBK14M1	9M119 "Svir" 9M119M 'Invar' 9M119M1 'Invar-M'	ATGM (M – tandem warhead)	Rocket propelled 350mps	900mm (after ERA)

* Range is 2,000m for all
** Requires modified autoloader with camming effect for use

One aspect that surfaced when these guns went into service was a massive increase in wear on the gun breech and barrel due to the very high muzzle velocity and chamber pressure needed by APFSDS projectiles to achieve velocities of 1,800mps. The early guns (2A26 and 2A46) reportedly only had a barrel life of 150 APFSDS rounds; due to the fact that HE-FRAG and HEAT had much lower velocities (about half that of the sabot rounds), the lifespan for use with HE-FRAG and HEAT ammunition was much higher.

Later guns (2A46M, M-1 etc.) were significantly modified, with increased barrel life to 300 rounds, and newer barrels with chromed bores and chambers to as much as 500. Due to the need to change barrels under operational field conditions these guns were designed so the barrels could be changed from the front; previously the turrets had to be removed or jacked up at the rear to pull out the gun and exchange the barrels. The gun breech on the later 2A46M, M1, etc. is fully enclosed (i.e. steel all around the breech opening); on the earlier 2A46 it has a distinct conventional style cut-out with sliding wedge on the right side. The recoil system on the later gun also has a second recoil brake, with the two recoil brakes now located symmetrically in the right upper and lower left corners.

The T-72 Ural, T-72A and export T-72M and T-72M1 tanks were fitted with the 2A46 gun. The T-72B and later were fitted with the 2A46M (and later M-1 etc.).

Appendix 8: OPVT Underwater Tank Driving Equipment

In the late 1950s Soviet industry fielded a useful and effective system for underwater driving with tanks. As water obstacles in the Belorussian, Russian and Ukrainian republics of the former Soviet Union were encountered roughly every 15–20km, with most being less than 5m deep, being able to wade across them was seen as essential to maintaining the offensive. The solution was introduced at UVZ in 1958 on the final production versions of the T-54B tank, and then immediately adapted for use on the later T-55 as it entered series production. Initially the T-62 Model 1961 used the OPVT-155 system then in production for the T-55.

RIGHT A Russian T-72B1 with operational OPVT snorkel at the Kubinka proving grounds in the 1990s.

BELOW Preparing a T-72B1 for OPVT wading with only the operational snorkel mounted, Kubinka, May 1996.

The equipment – Oborudovaniye dlya Podvodnogo Vozhdenniya Tanka (OPVT) or equipment for underwater driving of tanks – was to permit the tank to autonomously cross a water obstacle up to 700m wide and 5m deep and also permit the tank to emerge from the water combat ready with a safe crew. It provided air to the crew and engine, prevented water from flooding and stalling the engine while underwater, ensured the tank could move underwater in a given direction, and provided for the tank to be completely combat ready when it would egress from the water.

By the time the T-72 was developed, the Soviet tank industry had more than ten years' experience with the system and now developed a new variant that was built into the tank from the start. The OPVT system for the T-72 consisted of the following components:

- A three-section snorkel tube roughly 3.8m long when assembled;
- A bolt-on exhaust flapper valve providing one-way flow of the exhaust;
- Built-in covers for the radiator air intakes that were permanently mounted on the engine deck;
- Attached covers for the radiator exhaust grilles at the left rear of the tank (later permanently attached at the rear);
- Covers for the gun muzzle, gunner's sight aperture, machine gun port, and antenna feed and base;
- Cover for the air feed to the transfer case (guitara);
- Sealing for the turret, ventilator, ZIP bins and hatches;
- A bilge pump at the front left of the engine compartment fitted with a one-way valve on the tank's belly to bail out water collecting on the floor of the engine compartment;
- Life jackets and rebreathers for crew escape if necessary;
- A GPK-59 gyrocompass for underwater navigation.

All of the necessary components were now carried on the tank. The snorkel was mounted either on the rear of the turret or on the rear ZIP bin, and the flapper valve and radiator exhaust covers were carried inside the bins.

To prepare the tank for crossing, all of the seals were checked first and drain plugs installed in the hull floor of the tank. The one-way valve for the bilge pump was installed in place of a plug on the hull floor. The snorkel was removed, bolted together with seals between sections and base, and fitted to an opening in the gunner's hatch on the left side of the tank. This could be done best with the gunner's hatch opened, so the crew could swing it up into place when he closed his hatch. The covers were attached to their specific items with clamps and the flapper valve installed to the exhaust outlet.

Once the tank was prepared, the turret was swivelled about 10 degrees to the right to permit the driver to escape in case of an accident. A seal around the inside of the turret race was inflated to prevent water entry into the tank. Some leakage was expected and charts told the crew what was acceptable; once the tank began crossing, the bilge pump would be turned on to evacuate water that did seep into the tank, but it was only after the tank exited the water that it could fully clear the engine compartment.

The actual crossing usually required prepared banks on both sides of the obstacle or at least shallow approaches to the river or stream. The water obstacle

A Soviet-era Obiekt-172M with OPVT training snorkel at the Kiev Tank School. (Sergei Popsuevich)

TOP The T-72B1 with operational OPVT snorkel on the move is a curious sight. Note the turret hatch mounting and the float block tethered to the snorkel.

ABOVE The same T-72B1 tank as pictured above entering a lake during an exercise at Kubinka, May 1996.

could be no more than 700m wide, 5m deep, and have a current speed of no more than 1.5m per second. The tank would move into the water in first gear at an engine speed of 1,500rpm to make the crossing. The driver would use the GPK-59 gyrocompass to keep the tank heading in the right direction.

Once across, the tank could fire on targets immediately if needed, but this would destroy the muzzle and machine gun covers. The tank would start to overheat if the hatches over the engine deck were not opened soon after crossing, and the tanks could obviously not sit at idle for a long time with no air circulation. But unlike the earlier tanks this one had an automatic release for the radiator covers; by rotating the turret 29–33 degrees to the right with the manual traverse control, a lever activated the latches holding them in place and they sprang open. The crew still would have to manually remove the other covers and the 'flapper' valve when in a safe place.

In some cases guy lines could be rigged to the snorkel to provide stability, but these needed to be tethered to the turret (such as at the two front lifting hooks) in order for the turret to properly rotate and release the deck covers upon exiting the water.

For night crossings a cable would be dropped down the snorkel and a red light similar to the marker and tail lights fitted to the top so the commander could follow the progress of his tanks across the water.

There were, as might be expected, accidents during training and exercises, and usually tow cables would be run to the tanks to ensure that if they stalled they could be hauled out of the water. Often (as in East Germany) the places where training took place were purpose-built concrete basin-like structures to make it easy (and more predictable) to enter, cross and exit.

A larger training snorkel that bolted to the commander's cupola and allowed the crew easy exit if the tank stalled was developed for initial training. Another addition was an antenna feed to the top of the snorkel for an antenna allowing communications to the tank via radio. Both were developed for crew safety and also to reduce the number of accidents. If the driver-mechanic did not switch on the GPK-59 to give him a bearing, the worst scenario was that the tank would turn 90 degrees toward downstream and go with the flow rather than across it.

This system has remained in use since first developed for the T-72 and was also fitted to the later T-90.

Appendix 9: Statistical Data for T-72 Models Per UVZ (the Ural Railway Wagon Construction Plant) Data

Technical Characteristic	Ob. 172	Ob. 172-2M	T-72	T-72A	T-72B
General Data					
Status	Prototype (1968)	Prototype (1972)	Series	Series	Series
Year accepted for service	-	-	1973	1979	1984
Combat weight in metric tons	39	42	41	41.5	44.5
Crew	3				
Length, gun forward in mm	9,530				
Length of hull alone in mm	N/A	N/A	6,860	6,860	6,860
Overall width in mm	3,415	3,472	3,460	3,590	3,590*
Width over tracks in mm	3,270	3,370	3,370	3,370	3,370
Height to top of turret in mm	2,170	2,200	2,190	2,190	2,230
Control compartment volume m^3	2.0	N/A	2.0	2.0	2.0
Fighting compartment volume m^3	5.9	N/A	5.9	5.9	5.9
Engine compartment volume with/without fuel	3.1/3.1				
Power-to-weight ratio hp/mt (kWt/mt)	18.7 (13.8)	20 (14.7)	19 (14)	18.8 (13.8)	18.9 (13.9)
Exit hatch in belly	Yes				
Self-entrenching equipment	No	Yes			
Armament					
Main gun and mark	2A26	2A46	2A26/2A46	2A46	2A46M
Calibre in mm	125				
Type	Smoothbore				Smoothbore-Launcher
Length of barrel in mm (calibres)	6,000 (48)				
Recoil system disposition	Non-symmetrical				Symmetrical
Barrel purge system	Ejection				
Thermal shroud?	No	Yes	No	Yes	Yes
Loading	Automatic or Manual				
Basic load (number in autoloader)	39 (22)	45 (22)	39 (22)	44 (22)	45 (22)
Ammunition types fired	APFSDS, HEAT, HE-FRAG				All plus ATGM
Type of loading	Separate Projectile and Casing				

* Without dynamic protection.

Main armament stabilizer	Electro-Hydraulic in two planes	Electro-Mechanical Horizontal, Electro-Hydraulic Vertical	Electro-Hydraulic in two planes	Electro-Hydraulic in two planes	Electro-Mechanical Horizontal, Electro-Hydraulic Vertical
Additional armament	Coaxial Machine Gun				
Calibre	7.62mm				
Type	PKT				
Basic load – cartridges	N/A	2,000			
Additional armament Type and control	None	None	None	None	Autonomous Open Manual
Additional armament*	-	-	-	-	Machine gun
Calibre	-	-	-	-	12.7mm
Type	-	-	-	-	NSV-12.7
Basic load – cartridges	-	-	-	-	300
Guided armament	No	No	No	No	9K120
Guided missile	-	-	-	-	9M119
Type of missile guidance	-	-	-	-	Laser Beam
Maximum missile firing range	-	-	-	-	4,000 meters
Fire control system					
Maximum gun elevation in degrees	N/A	N/A	Up to 13.5		
Maximum gun depression in degrees	N/A	N/A	No more than 6		
Automatic sight check system	No	No	No	No	Yes
Main gunner's sight	Monocular Stereoscopic	Monocular† Stereoscopic	Monocular Stereoscopic	Periscopic‡ (EhOP) with Laser Rangefinder	Periscopic (EhOP) with Laser Rangefinder, Missile Guidance Channel
Gunner's sight stabilization	Independent vertical axis, dependent horizontal axis				
Gunner's night sight	Electro-optical monocular periscope			Combination (EhOP) binocular periscopic	Day/Night Combination (EhOP) binocular periscopic
Commander's sight complex	Combination electro-optical binocular periscopic			Combination Periscopic	Day/Night (EhOP) Binocular Periscopic
Rangefinder, type	Monocular Stereoscopic	Monocular§ Stereoscopic	Monocular Stereoscopic	Laser	Laser
Protection					
Armour Protection, Type	Combination	Hull – Combination; Turret – monolithic (with anti-cumulative shields)	Hull – Combination; Turret – monolithic		Combination - 21 sets of combination plates of 21mm steel, 6mm rubber and 3mm aluminium spaced 22mm apart per side of the gun
Turret Horizontal thickness of frontal armor (+/-30 degree sector)	N/A	435	410	530	~635
Equivalent protection in mm Against APDSFS Against HEAT	400 450	435 520	410 410	410 520	N/A N/A

* All T-72 tanks received this armament starting in December 1974.
† The monocular stereoscopic sight was installed in the first five prototype Obiekt-172-2M tanks. Starting with Number 6 they went to the TPD-K1 sight.
‡ EhOP – Electro-Optical Periscopic System.
§ The monocular stereoscopic sight was installed in the first five prototype Obiekt-172-2M tanks. Starting with Number 6 they went to the laser rangefinder.

Hull Horizontal thickness of frontal armour (0 degree sector)	550	630	550	580	N/A
Equivalent protection in mm Against APDSFS Against HEAT	305 450	N/A 520	305 450	360 500	N/A N/A
Glacis slope angle from vertical	68	70	68	68	68
Anti-cumulative skirts	No	Yes	No Flipper panels	Yes	Yes
TDA smoke system	Yes	Yes	Yes	Yes	Yes
Smoke grenade launchers	No	No	No	Yes	Yes
Dynamic protection	No	No	No	No	Attached*
Mobility					
Maximum highway speed (km/h)	60	60	60	60	60
Range on highways (km)	N/A	750	700	700	700
Fuel tank capacity (litres)	N/A	1,800	1,200+400	1,200+400	1,200+400
Average ground pressure, kg/cm^2	0.86	0.85	0.83	0.83	0.87
Ground clearance (mm)	500	495	470	470	490
Trench crossing distance (metres)	N/A	2.6-2.8	2.6-2.8	2.6-2.8	2.6-2.8
Step climbing height (metres)	N/A	0.85	0.85	0.85	0.85
Maximum side slope in degrees	N/A	N/A	30	30	30
Fording depth (unprepared/prepared) (metres)	N/A	1.2 (1.8)	1.2 (1.8)	1.2 (1.8)	1.2 (1.8)
Fording depth with OPVT (metres)	N/A	5	5	5	5
Engine-Transmission Installation					
Type of engine	V-45K	V-46F	V-46	V-46-6	V-84M
Type	Liquid-cooled multifuel diesel				
Cycles	4	4	4	4	4
Number of cylinders	12	12	12	12	12
Cylinder disposition	V type, 60 degrees				
Maximum power output in hp (kWt) under test stand conditions	730(537)	840(618)	780(574)	780(574)	840(618)
Weight of engine (kg)	N/A	N/A	980	980	1,020
RPM at maximum power	2,000	2,000	2,000	2,000	2,000
Engine dimensions (mm) Length Width Height	N/A N/A N/A	N/A N/A N/A	1,480 896 902	1,480 896 902	1,480 896 902
Piston stroke (mm)	N/A	N/A	180, 186.7	180, 186.7	180, 186.7
Piston diameter (mm)	N/A	N/A	150	150	150
Working volume (litres)	N/A	N/A	38.88	38.88	38.88
Boost system	N/A	N/A	Driven supercharger	Driven supercharger	Driven supercharger
Transmission type	Mechanical, Planetary				
Gearboxes	Two lateral, Planetary				
Number of speeds forward/reverse	7/1	7/1	7/1	7/1	7/1
MP type	Non-differential				
Service brakes, type	Disc, Oil Bath				
Final drives, type	Planetary				
Control type	Hydraulic				
Cooling system	Liquid, closed cycle with driven circulation and air drawn by radiator fan				

* Starting in 1988 the T-72B was fitted with built-in dynamic protection.

Fan Type	Centrifugal				
Number	1				
Air cleaner Type	1 stage*	2 stage			
1st stage	Cyclone	Cyclone			
2nd stage	-	Mesh type, crimped wire			
Number of air cleaners	1				
Starting system	Primary air, auxiliary electrical				
Running Gear					
Suspension type	Individual, Torsion bar				
Shock absorbers, type (Number)	Hydraulic, telescopic (6)	Hydraulic, blade (6)	Hydraulic, blade (6)	Hydraulic, blade (6)	Hydraulic, blade (6)
Tracks, type of connection	Parallel	Sequential			
Type of track link	T-64 twin pin	OMSh (initial) RMSh		RMSh	RMSh
Wheel track (mm)	2,730	2,790	2,790	2,790	2,790
Length of track on ground (mm)	4,242	4,270	4,270	4,270	4,270
Width of track (mm)	540	580	580	580	580
Number of track links per run	78–79	N/A	96	97	97
Number of road wheels per side	6	6	6	6	6
Diameter of road wheels (mm)	550	750	750	750	750
Type of amortization of road wheels	Internal	Rubber tyres on all wheels. Six lever-action shock absorbers on stations 1, 2 and 6 each side			
Number of return rollers per side	4	3	3	3	3
Track tension adjustment	Crank driven screw	Crank driven screw	Crank driven screw	Crank driven screw	Crank driven screw

Characteristic	T-72B2 'Rogatka'	T-72B1MS 'Beliy Orel'	T-72B3	T-72B3M
Status	Prototype 2006	Prototype 2012	In service 2012	In service 2016
Combat weight in metric tons	46.5	47.3	46	46.5
Crew	3	3	3	3
Length, gun forward in mm	9,530	9,530	9,530	9,530
Length of hull alone in mm	6,860	6,860*	6,860	6,860
Width in mm	3,590	3,770	3,770	3,780
Height to top of roof in mm	2,230	2,230	2,226	2,226
Ground clearance in mm	470	470–490	490	490
Average ground pressure in kg/cm^3	0.9	0.9	0.9	0.9
Obstacle Crossing Ability				
Grade in degrees	30	30	30	30
Step negotiated in metres	0.85	0.85	0.85	0.8
Trench crossing in metres	2.8	2.8	2.8	2.5
Fording depth in metres	1.2	1.2	1.2	1.2
Fording with OPVT in metres	5.0	5.0	5.0	5.0
Power Plant				
Engine type	V-92S2 (V-84-1) 12 cylinder multifuel	V-84MS 12 cylinder multifuel	V-84, V-93 or V-92S2F	V-92S2 12 cylinder multifuel
Power output in hp	1,000 (840)	840	840 (or 1,130)	1,130
Cooling system	Liquid	Liquid	Liquid	Liquid

* The first Article 172 tanks were fitted with a single stage air cleaner which was subsequently replaced with the more effective two-stage type.

Auxiliary power plant	VSU	DEhA10T		
Transmission type	Hydraulic	Hydraulic	Hydraulic	Hydraulic
Fuel capacity in litres (main tanks plus auxiliary)	1,200+400	-	1,200+400	-
Power-to-weight ratio hp/mt	21.5 (18.06)	19.53	18.3	24.6
Top speed in km/h	60	60	60	60-65
Highway range in km	700 (500)	700	500	500
Armour protection	Shell-proof combination with built-in ERA 'Relikt'	Shell-proof combination with attached ERA	Shell-proof combination with built-in ERA 'Kontakt-5'	Shell-proof combination with built-in ERA 'Relikt'
Smoke grenade system	Type 902A 12 tubes and TDA	Type 902B 8 tubes and TDA	Type 902B 8 tubes and TDA	Type 902B 8 tubes and TDA
Armament				
Main gun	125mm 2A46M-4	125mm 2A46M	125mm 2A46M-5 (2A46M-5-01)	125mm 2A46M-5
Basic load	-	42 rounds	41 rounds	41 rounds
Guided weapons type	-	-	'Refleks'	'Refleks'
Number and calibre of AA machine gun armament	12.7mm NSV	DPU with 12.7mm 6P49	12.7mm 6P50 'Kord'	12.7mm 6P50 'Kord'
Basic load in rounds	300	600	300	300
Coaxial machine gun type	7.62mm PKT	7.62mm PKT	7.62mm PKTM	7.62mm PKTM
Basic load	2,000	2,500	2,000	2,000
Fire control system	-	-	1A40-1 (1A40-4)	1A40-4
Rangefinder sight	'Sosna-U' Multichannel TPD-K1	PN-72K gunner's sight PKP-72 commander's sight PD-72 redundant controls	'Sosna-U' multichannel sight	'Sosna-U' multichannel sight, thermal camera and missile LKU
Guidance channel	-	-	ATGM guidance channel	ATGM guidance channel
Gun stabilizer	MKPH.462534.047			
Electro-optical suppression system	'Shtora'	-	-	-
Radio set installation	-	R-168-25UE-2	R-168-25U-2 'Akveduk' AVSKU	R-168-25U-2

All other items essentially remain the same from the T-72B.

Appendix 10: T-72 Related System Designators

Designator	Related Vehicle	Remarks
12ST85R	T-72B	Improved 27-volt lead-acid battery
172.10.026sb	T-72 Model 1975	Production model of the T-72 with a modified turret with new hatch and tourelle AA MG mounting
172.10.073sb	T-72 Ural 1, T-72A	'Kvarts' improved turret with silicon filler in cheeks
172.10.077sb	T-72B	Revised turret with 'bulge' stacked armor arrays
172.10.100sb	Late T-72B	Improved stacked array armor turret
172.50.001sb	Later production	Six-spoke cast aluminum road wheel
172.50.002sb	Early production	Eight-spoke cast aluminum road wheel
1A40	Early T-72B	Fire control system
1A40-1	T-72B	Fire control system including the 1K13 missile control sight
1A40-1M	T-72BA	Integrated fire control system with data sensors
1A40-4	T-72B3	Improved fire control system with commander's input
1K13-49	T-72B	Main sight with missile control
1K75	T-72B	9M119 missile control module

Code	Applicability	Description
2A26M2	T-72	D-81T 125mm smoothbore gun
2A46	T-72A	D-81T 125mm smoothbore gun
2A46M	T-72A, T-72B	D-81TM 125mm smoothbore gun with missile indexing
2A46M-5	T-72B3	D-81TM 125mm smoothbore gun
2A46M-5-01	T-72B3 UBKh	D-81TM-5 125mm smoothbore gun
2A66	T-72B2	D-91T 125mm improved smoothbore gun (proposed)
2Eh28M	T-72	'Siren' two-axis armament stabilizer system
2Eh42-2	T-72B	'Zhasmin' two-axis armament stabilizer system
2Eh42-4	T-72B3	'Zhasmin' two-axis armament stabilizer system
3BK12	All	125mm HEAT projectile – early
3BK12M	All	125mm HEAT projectile – improved
3BK14M	All	125mm HEAT projectile – new design principle
3BK18	All	125mm HEAT projectile – improved 3BK14M
3BM10	All	125mm APFSDA projectile – complete
3BM15	All	125mm APFSDS projectile – early (2A46)
3BM17	All	125mm APFSDS projectile – steel only penetrator
3BM22	All	125mm APFSDS projectile – better ballistic cap
3BM26	All	125mm APFSDS projectile – smaller penetrator
3BM32	All	125mm APFSDS projectile – depleted uranium
3BM42	All	125mm APFSDS projectile – jacketed tungsten
3BM9	All	125mm APFSDS projectile – early (2A26)
3D17	All	'Tucha' smoke grenade
3D6	All	'Tucha' smoke grenade
3D6M	T-72B3	'Tucha' smoke grenade
3EhTs11-2	All	Fire detection and prevention system
3EhTs13	T-72B3	'Iney' fire detection and prevention system
3OF19	All	125mm HE-FRAG projectile – early
3OF26	All	125mm HE-FRAG projectile – improved
3UBK14	T-72B	'Refleks' through-the-bore ATGM round – complete
3UBK20	T-72B	'Invar' through-the-bore ATGM round – complete
3VBK10	All	HEAT round – complete – new design principle
3VBK16	All	HEAT round – complete – improved 3BK14M
3VBK7	All	HEAT round – complete – early
3VBK7M	All	HEAT round – complete – improved
3VBM11	All	'Nadezhda' APFSDS round – complete – smaller penetrator
3VBM13	All	'Vant' APFSDS round – complete – depleted uranium
3VBM17	All	'Mango' APDSFS round – complete – jacketed tungsten
3VBM3	All	APFSDS round – complete – early (2A26)
3VBM7	All	APFSDS round – complete – early (2A46)
3VBM8	All	APFSDS round – complete – steel only penetrator
3VBM9	All	'Zakolka' APFSDS round – complete – better ballistic cap
3VOF22	All	HE-FRAG round – complete
3VOF26	All	HE-FRAG round – improved
4S20	T-72A onward	'Kontakt-1' Generation 1 explosive reactive armour
4S22	T-72B	'Kontakt-5' Generation 1.5 explosive reactive armour
4S23	T-72B3 UBKh	'Relikt' Generation 2 explosive reactive armour
4S24	T-72B3 UBKh	Bagged explosive reactive armour
4Zh40	All	Propellant charge – original
4Zh52	All	Propellant charge – newer generation
4Zh63	All	High velocity APDSFS propellant
613.44.22sb	All	RMSh rubber bushed tracks
6P49	T-72B3, T-72B3 UBKh	'Kord' 12.7mm heavy machine gun
6STEN-140M	All	27 volt lead-acid battery

902A	T-72A, T-72B	'Tucha' 12-tube smoke grenade launcher system
902B	T-72B3	'Tucha' 8-tube smoke grenade launcher system
9K120	T-72B	125mm bore launched ATGM system
9Kh949	T-72B	3UBK14 ejection charge
9M119	T-72B	'Svir' through-the-bore ATGM – HEAT warhead
9M119M	T-72B	'Invar' through-the-bore ATGM – tandem HEAT warhead
9S831	T-72B	9M119 missile electrical power converter
AK-150SV	All	Air compressor
AZ-172	All early tanks	Automatic loader control box for TPD-2-49 and TPD-K1
AZ-184	T-72B	Automatic loader control box for 1A40-1 system
DV-3	All	Rubber bladed individual cooling fan
DVE-BS	T-72BA	Mast mounted meteorological sensor system
FG-125	All	Infrared headlight
FG-127	All	Blackout headlight
GO-27	All	NBC protection system
GPK-48	Early models	Gyrocompass for night and underwater driving
GPK-59	All	Gyrocompass for night and underwater driving
GUV-7	All	Electrically fired primer
IP-5	All	Underwater escape rebreather system
K-10T	All	Collimator sight for anti-aircraft machine gun
KR-175	T-72B	Turret rotation circuit box
KSDTL-64	All	Interior small lights
L-2AG	Early T-72s	Main searchlight
L-4	T-72A, T-72B	Main searchlight
L-4A	T-72B	Main searchlight with xenon bulb & relocated power plug
MS-1	All	'Tsiklon' multistage air cleaner
NVST	All	12.7mm heavy machine gun
OPVT-72	All	T-72 underwater driving system
OU-3GA2	All tanks	Commander's IR searchlight
OU-3GK1	All tanks	Commander's IR searchlight
PKP-72	T-72B3M	Commander's all weather sight
PKTM	All	7.62mm coaxial machine gun
PKUZ-1A	T-72B3	NBC protection system
PN-72	T-72B3	'Sosna-U' thermal sight complex
PVM-71	All	Interior dome light
R-123	All early tanks	VHF FM radio set – 20–51.5 MHz
R-123M	All tanks	Improved VHF FM radio set – 20–51.5 MHz
R-124	All early tanks	Tank intercom system for the R-123/R-130M radio sets
R-130M	All command tanks	HF AM/SSB radio set – 1.5–10.99 MHz
R-134M	All later command tanks	Improved HF AM/SSB radio set – 1.5–10.99 MHz
R-168-25UE-2	T-72B3	Twin transceiver VHF FM radio set – 30–108 MHz with digital data capability and frequency hopping options
R-173	All later tanks	'Abzats' solid state VHF FM radio set – 20–79.999 MHz
R-173P	Command tanks	Solid state VHF FM radio receiver – 20–79.999 MHz
R-174	All later tanks	Tank intercom system for the R-173/R-134 radio sets
RP-377UVM1L	2022 and later	Frequency jammer against command detonated mines and guidance for drone systems
RTS-27-4A	All tanks	Glass vision block defogging system
RTS-27-4A	All	Periscope heater system
SET-5L	All tanks	Ballistic glass protection for main sights
SG-10-15	All	Starter/generator
'Sosna-U'	T-72B3	Main thermal integrated sight complex
TD-1	All	Flame detection sensor for PPO system

TKN-3	All early tanks	Commander's observation sight/periscope
TKN-3M	All later tanks	Commander's observation day/night sight/periscope with Gen 1 photocathode tube for passive night vision
TKN-3MK	All later tanks	Commander's observation day/night sight/periscope with Gen 2 photocathode tube for passive night vision
TN-28-10	All	Standard 28-volt 10 watt light bulb
TNPA-65A	All tanks	Commander's hatch periscopic rear vision block
TNPO-160	All tanks	Standard periscopic vision block
TNPO-165	All tanks	Gunner's periscopic vision block
TNPO-168V	All	Driver's periscope
TPD-1-49	Object 172	Original T-64 gunner's primary rangefinder sight
TPD-2-49	T-72	Gunner's primary rangefinder sight
TPD-K1	T-72 Ural-1, T-72A	Gunner's primary rangefinder sight
TPD-K1M	T-72B	1A40 primary rangefinder sight
TPN-1-49-23	T-72	Night sighting system
TPN-3	T-72A, T-72B1	Night sighting system
TVNE-4B	All	Driver's night driving periscope
UVBU	T-72B	1A40 series lead calculator
UVP	T-72B	Ammunition reset device
V-15	All	3BK14 piezoelectric fuse
V-429Ye	All	HE-FRAG point detonating fuse
V-46-4	T-72	780hp 12-cylinder diesel engine
V-46-6	T-72A	780hp 12-cylinder diesel engine
V-84-1	T-72B	840hp 12-cylinder diesel engine – early production
V-84MS	T-72B	840hp 12-cylinder diesel engine – late production with 'Silfon' heat suppressor system
V-92S1	T-72B	Prototype 12-cylinder diesel engine of 1,000hp with 'Silfon' heat suppressor system
V-92S2	T-72B2	1,000hp 12-cylinder diesel engine with 'Silfon' heat suppressor system
V-92S2F	T-72B3, T-72B3M	1,130hp 12-cylinder diesel engine with turbocharger and 'Silfon' heat suppressor system
VKU-330-4	T-72B	Turret autoloader circuit box
ZU-72	All	Turret mounted tourelle type anti-aircraft mount

Appendix 11: Summary of Main 'Obiekt-172M' Production Changes 1974–79

This list of design changes relates to the early Obiekt-172M and the modifications undertaken on T-72 production during the period 1974–79. The early production T-72 was from the very start of assembly subject to significant annual and ongoing changes in layout and equipment, as was the case with the subsequent main production models. In addition to production model changes, tanks were sent in batches for 'sredny remont' – medium rebuild (SR) and 'kapitalny remont' – capital rebuild (KR) after 8,000km and 14,000km respectively, during which, in addition to repairs including replacement of engine and running gear, upgrades were undertaken according to planned schedules. For tanks that had completed their first KR, the next SR was after a further 7,000km and the next KR at 12,000km. The appearance of a tank might thereby substantially change during its service life. (List provided courtesy of Alexander Koshchavtsev.)

1974

- KMT-6 minesweeper installed;
- From December, ZU-72 anti-aircraft machine gun mount introduced, including a new right hatch with 12.7mm NSV AAMG installation;
- Increased reliability of radiator mounting;
- Balancer bushings and brackets reinforced;
- Modification of crew working conditions (changing the location and design of control units, improving the layout of workplaces);
- ZEhTS11-3 fire-fighting system introduced, replacing (ZEhTS11);
- Built-in self-entrenching blade system introduced;
- Separate tow cable mounting points introduced (fore and aft).

1975

- From January, freon 114V2 gas introduced into the fire-fighting system instead of the 3.5 composition;
- In March, the 172.10.026sb-2 unified turret for line and command tanks introduced;
- In March, the TVNE-4PA driver's device introduced (replacing the TVNO-2BM);
- From May, the L-2AG IR illuminator was moved to the right side of the turret;
- In May, modifications related to the 2A46 gun with 'Tochnost' (accuracy) design improvements (new rollback brake compensator and heat shield);
- Changes made to improve the reliability of the automatic loader;
- From June, crew visibility increased due to the installation of additional TNPA-65 surveillance devices in the right (2 pcs) and left (1 pc) turret hatches;
- From November, the tow cable mountings on the hull glacis improved.

1976

- From June, the rear hull floor strengthened by welding external stiffeners;
- Mounting design of the roadwheel edge changed and its protrusion reduced, roadwheel weight reduced by 5kg;
- From September, a mechanical lock introduced to prevent engine damage from reverse starting, ensuring that the engine stalls before damage incurred;
- From September, driver's ventilation hatch cancelled (design simplification).

1978

- From January, new V-46-6 engine modification introduced;
- For tanks with 44 rounds of ammunition, a new front stowage rack 176.33.004sb was introduced instead of 175.33.004sb with fewer slots and a compartment for two boxes of PKT machine gun belts provided in the lower section;
- The TVN-4B device with the built-in power supply unit and heating regulator introduced (replacing the TVNE-4A);
- From October, the TPN-3-49 device for the L-4A IR illuminator introduced;
- A stop on the lower joint of the OPVT tube introduced to prevent damage when moving through light forests (the tube was positioned horizontally);
- Introduction of 275-litre fuel drums with separate brackets for standard 200 and 275-litre drums (275-litre drums were installed only on tanks undergoing military tests, i.e. not mass produced);
- From July, the 172.10.073sb turret with 'Quartz' type filler (i.e. sand rods) was introduced.

1979

- From January, rubber-fabric side screens introduced;
- From January, a set of 'Soda' (napalm protection) equipment introduced: flaps installed in the oil cooler rack, hose protection, instrument canopies, two cases for powder fire extinguishers installed on the turret;
- Traffic alarm system introduced;
- Yellow side marker lights introduced;
- From July, the 902A 'Tucha' system introduced;
- From July, a new driver's seat installed, with an increased level of personal safety;
- From October, hull glacis armour protection increased.

Appendix 12: Glossary

APFSDS	Armour-Piercing Fin-Stabilized Discarding Sabot projectile
APU	Auxiliary Power Unit
ATGM	Anti-Tank Guided Missile
BDD	Bronya Desantogo Deystviya – Assault Operations Armour
BM	Boevaya Mashina – Combat Vehicle
BMPT	Boevaya Mashina Podderzhki Tankov –

	Tank Support Combat Vehicle
BMR	Bronyevaya Mashina Razminiriovaniya – Armoured Mine Clearing Vehicle
BO	Boyevaya Otdel – fighting compartment
BREhM	Bronyevaya Remontirno-Ehvakuatsionnaya Mashina – Armoured Repair and Recovery Vehicle
BTRZ	Bronetankovy Remontny Zavod– Tank Repair Plant
BTS	Bronyevoy Tyagach Sredny or Sredny Tankovy Tyagach – Medium Tank Tractor
ChKZ	Chelyabinsky Kirovsky Zavod (ChTZ from 15.05.58)
ChTZ	Chelyabinsky Traktorny Zavod imeni V.I. Lenina (ChKZ before 15.05.58)
DZ	Dynamicheskaya Zaschita – Dynamic Protection (ERA)
ERA	Explosive Reactive Armour
GABTU	Gosudarstvennoye Avtomotivnoye Bronetankirovannoye Upravleniye – Main Automotive and Armoured Vehicle Directorate
GAU	Glavnoye Artilleriskoe Upravleniye – Main Artillery Directorate
GBTU	Glavnoye Bronetankovoe Upravleniye – Main Armoured Vehicle Directorate
GKOT	Gosudarstvennaya Kommissiya po Oboronnoy Tekhnike – State Committee on Defense Technology
Glavtank	12th Main Directorate for Tank Production of the Ministry of Transport Machinery Production
GMRD	Guards Motorized Rifle Division
GRAU	Glavnoye Raketno-Artilleriyskoye Upravleniye – Main Rocket and Artillery Directorate
HEAT	High Explosive Anti-Tank
HE-FRAG	High Explosive – Fragmentation
IMR	Inzhenirnaya Mashina Razgrazhdeniya – Engineer Vehicle for Obstacle Clearing
KhKBM	Kharkovskoe Konstruktorskoe Bureau po Mashinostroenniyu (ex KB-60M, later KhMDB) – Kharkov Machine Building Design Bureau
LKZ	Leningrad 'Kirov' Plant (Plant No. 185)
LVZ	Leningrad 'Voroshilov' Plant (Plant No. 174 in Omsk)
KAZ	Kompleks Aktivnoi Zashitni – Active Protection Complex
KB	Konstruktorskoye Byuro – design bureau
KBTM	Konstruktorskoye Byuro Transportivnoy Mashinoy – Design Bureau for Transport Vehicles (Omsk)

KMT	Koleiny Minniy Tral – Track Width Mine Trawl
KO	Kontrolnaya Otdel – control compartment
MBT	Main Battle Tank
MO	Ministerstvo Oboroni – Soviet (Russian) Ministry of Defence (MoD)
MOP	Ministerstvo Oboronoi Promishlennosti – Soviet (Russian) MoD Production
MRB	Motorized Rifle Brigade
MRD	Motorized Rifle Division
MRR	Motorized Rifle Regiment
MTO	Motorno-Transmissionaya Otdel – motor transmission compartment
MTrM	Ministerstvo Trasportivnoy Mashinikh Promishlennosti – Ministry of Transport Machinery Construction
MTU	Mostovaya Tankovaya Ustanovka – Tank Bridging Installation
NBC	Nuclear, Biological, Chemical
NII	Nauchno-Issledovatelniy Institut – Scientific Research Institute
NKVD	Narodny Kommisariat Vnutrenikh Del – People's Commissariat for Internal Affairs
NST	Novyy Sredny Tank – new medium tank
NTK	Nauchno-Tekhnicheskiy Komitet – Scientific Technical Committee
OKMO	Opytniy Konstruktorsko-Mekhanicheskiy Otdel – Prototype Design Mechanical Section
OPFOR	US Army Opposing Forces units
OPVT	Oborudovaniye Podvodnoy Vozhdeniya Tanki – underwater tank driving equipment
PAZ	Protivoatomnoi Zashiti – anti-nuclear protection
PPO	Protivo-Pozharnoye Oborudovaniye – fire suppression equipment
PTURS	Protivotankiy Upravlayushchiy Raketnyy Snaryad – ATGM
PU	Puskovaya Ustanovka (launch system)
RPG	Rocket Propelled Grenade (launcher)
SM SSSR	Sovet Ministerov SSSR – Council of Ministers of the USSR
TDA	Termalnaya Dymovaya Apparata – thermal smoke generation apparatus
TIUS	Tankovaya Informatsionno-Upravlayushchaya Sistema – tank information and control system
TO	Tankovyy Ognemet – tank flamethrower
TPU	Tankovoe Peregovornoe Ustroistvo - Tank voice communications system
TsK KPSU	Tsentralniy Komitet Kommunicheskoy Partii Sovetskogo Soyuza

	– Central Committee of the Communist Party of the Soviet Union
TsNII-6	Central Scientific Research Institutes for Flame Weapons, Moscow
TsNII-48	Central Scientific Research Institute for Armour, Leningrad
TsNII-173	Central Scientific Research Institute for Artillery Stabilizers, Moscow
TZM	Transportno – Zaryazhayushaya Mashina – Transport – Reload Vehicle
UAE	United Arab Emirates
UKBTM	Uralnoye Konstruktorskoye Byuro Transportivnoy Mashinoy – Urals Design Bureau for Transport Machinery (Nizhny Tagil)
UVBU	Ustroystvo Virabotky Bokovikh Uprezhdeny – lateral target tracking device
UVZ	Uralniy Vagonstroitelsviy Zavod – Urals Railway Wagon Construction Factory
VNII	Vsesoyuzniy Nauchno-Issledovatelsky Institut – All-Union Scientific Research Institute
VNII-100	Vsesoyuzny Nauchno-Issledovatelsky Institut – All-Union Scientific Research Institute No. 100 (later VNII Transmash)
VPK	Voenny Promishlennoi Kommissiei pri Soviet Ministrov SSSR – Military-Industrial Commissariat for the Council of Ministers of the USSR
VVS	Voenno-Vozdushnie Sili SSSR – the Soviet Air Force
Zavod No. 9	Artillery Plant No. 9, Perm (F. F. Petrov Bureau)
Zavod No. 75	Kharkov Tank Plant (formerly Kharkov Diesel Engine Construction Plant)
Zavod No. 174	Omsk Tank Plant (formerly in Leningrad)
Zavod No. 183	Urals Railway Wagon Construction Plant, Nizhny Tagil (formerly Kharkov Steam Locomotive Construction Plant in Kharkov) (today Kharkiv)
Zavod No. 393	Optical Plant, Krasnogorsk (the 'Zenit' Plant)
ZIP	Komplekt Zapasnykh Chastey, Instrumentov, i Prinadzhelnostey – set of spare parts, tools and accessories

ARTWORK

T-72 Ural, Syrian Arab Army, Aleppo region, 2016. The tank was modernized with the Galileo Avionica TURMS-T fire control system, with the apertures for the original TPD-2-49 sight on turret roof and TPN-1-49-23 gunsights welded shut. (Artwork by Andrey Aksenov)

T-72AK command tank, Karabakh Army, Third Karabakh War, September 2023. This tank was damaged and captured by the Azerbaijani Army, one of two such tanks captured. (Artwork by Andrey Aksenov)

T-72M, tank battalion of 65th Mechanized Brigade, Ukrainian Army (VSU), Zaporozhe area, autumn 2023. This T-72 was built in eastern Europe and modified before delivery to VSU in 2023. The yellow discs are unit quick identification signs. This tank was damaged and captured by the Russian Army. (Artwork by Andrey Aksenov)

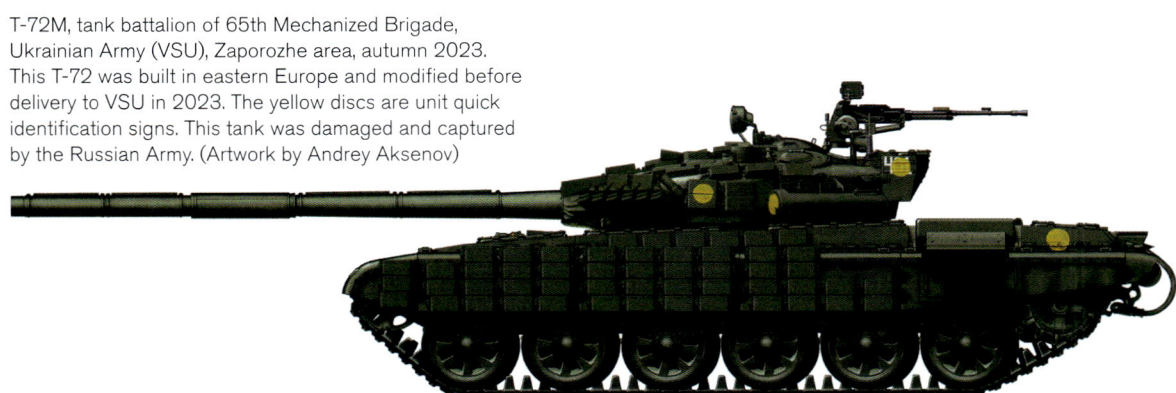

T-72M, 34th Brigade, 9th Armoured Division, Iraqi Army, Baghdad, January 2011. This tank was built in Czechoslovakia for the Hungarian People's army in the 1980s, then donated by Hungary to the new Iraqi Army in 2005. The ballistic protection cupola on the AAMG station is local modification. Late-style (post-2008) Iraq state flag sticker was applied on both sides of the cupola during an Army Day parade. (Artwork by Andrey Aksenov)

T-72B1V in camouflage for mountain areas, 201st Russian military base, Dushanbe, Tajikistan, 2016. (Artwork by Andrey Aksenov)

T-72B3M with KMT-6 mine ploughs attached, probably of the 26th Tank Regiment of the Russian Army, in temporary whitewash camouflage during the first days of the Russian-defined Special Military Operation, Kharkov area, Ukraine, February 2022. (Artwork by Andrey Aksenov)

BIBLIOGRAPHY

Books – Russian Language

Bachurin, N., Zenkina, V., and Roshchina, S., *Osnovnoy Boyevoy Tank T-80* (Gonchar Press, Moscow, 1993)

Baranov, I. N. (general editor), *Glavnyy Konstruktor V. N. Venediktov: Zhizn Otdannaya Tankam* (DiAl, Nizhny Tagil, 2009)

Baryatinskiy, Mikhail, *1945–2008: Sovetskiye Tanki v Boyu* (Yauza/Ehksmo, 2008)

Baryatinskiy, Mikhail, *Tanki v Chechnye – Sovetskaya Bronetankovaya Tekhika v 'Goryachikh Tochkakh' SSSR I SNG 1989–1998 gg.* (Zhelezhnodoroznoye Delo, Moscow, 1999)

Baryatinskiy, Mikhail, *Tanki XX Vek – Unikalnaya Ehtsiklopediya* (Yauza/Ehksmo, Moscow, 2010)

Baryatinskiy, Mikhail, *T-72 Uralskaya Bronya Protiv NATO* (Yauza/Ehksmo, Moscow, 2010)

Baryatinskiy, Mikhail, *T-72 i Ego Modifikatskii* (Yauza, Moscow, 2022)

Baushev, I. (editor), *Sozdateli Oruzhiya I Voyennoy Tekhniki Sukhoputnykh Voysk Rossii* (Pashkov Dom, Moscow, 2008)

Bezludko, A. V., Usovich, V. V., Sharipov, R. I., Yankovsky, I. N., Yurko, S. V., and Stefanovich, V. R., *Ustroistvo Tanka T-72B* (Voenno-Tekhnichesko Fakultet Kadera Bronetankovoe Vooruzhenie i Tekhnika, Ministerstvo Obrazavaniya Respubliki Belarus, Minsk, Belarus, 2011)

Bryukhov, Vasiliy P., *Bronetankovye Voyska* (Golos Press, Moscow, 2006)

Bryzgov, V. and Yermolina, O., *Bronetankovaya Tekhnika – Fotoalbom* (Gonchar, Moscow, 1994)

Chernyshev, Vladimir L. (editor), *Tanki I Lyudi: Dnevnik Glavnogo Konstruktora Aleksandra Aleksandrovicha Morozova* (internet version published on http://www.btvt.narod.ru, 2006/2007) (translated by author)

Chobitok, Vasiliy, *Osnovoi Boevoi Tank T-64* (Yauza, Moscow, 1964)

Drogovoz, Igor G., *Tankovyy Mech Strany Sovetov* (Kharvest, Minsk, 2001)

Feskov, V. I., Kalashnikov, K. A., and Golikov, V. I., *Sovetskaya Armiya v Gody 'Kholodnoy Voyny' (1945–1991)* (Tomsk State University, Tomsk, 2004)

Ionin, S. N., *Bronetankovye Voyska SSSR-Rossii* (Veche, Moscow, 2006)

Karpenko, A. V., *Obozreniye Otechestvennoy Bronetankovoy Tekhniki (1905–1995 gg.)* (Nevskiy Bastion, St Petersburg, 1996)

Karpenko, A. V., *Sovremennye Boyevye Tanki*; Series 'Orzhiye Otechestva' (St Petersburg, 2024)

Kholyavskiy, G. L., *Ehtsiklopediya Bronyetekhniki – Gusenichnye Boyevye Mashiny* (Kharvest, Minsk, 2001)

Krivosheyev, G. F., Andronikov, V. M., Burikov, P. D., and Gurkin, V. V., *Velikaya Otechestvennaya bez grifa secretnosti. Kniga Poter* (Veche, Moscow, 2009)

Lavrenov, S. Ya., *Sovetskiy Soyuz v Lokalnykh Voynakh I Konfliktakh* (Astrel', Moscow, 2003)

Minayev, A. V. (general editor), *Sovetskaya Voyennaya Moshch: Ot Stalina do Gorbacheva* (Voyennyy Parad, 1999)

Ministry of Defence USSR/RF Publications, *Inzhenernie Voiska Ministerstva Oboroni Rossiskoi Federatsii. Sredstva Inzhenernogo Vooruzheniya* (Moscow, 2000)

Ministry of Defence USSR/RF Publications, *Izdeliye 434: Rukovodstvo po Voyskovomu Remontu* (Moscow, 1969)

Ministry of Defence USSR/RF Publications, *Tanki T-64B I T-64B1: Tekhicheskoye Opisaniye i Instruktsiya po Ehksplutatsii* (TO) Book 1 (Moscow, 1983)

Ministry of Defence USSR/RF Publications, *Tank T-72A: Tekhicheskoye Opisaniye i Instruktsiya po Ehksplutatsii* (TO) Book 1 (Moscow, 1986)

Ministry of Defence USSR/RF Publications, *Tank T-72A: Tekhicheskoye Opisaniye i Instruktsiya po Ehksplutatsii* (TO) Book 2 (Moscow, 1988)

Ministry of Defence USSR/RF Publications, *Tank T-72B: Instruktsiya po Ehksplutatsii* (Moscow, 1997)

Ministry of Defence USSR/RF Publications, *Tank T-72B: Tekhicheskoye Opisaniye i Instruktsiya po Ehksplutatsii* (TO) Book 1 (Moscow, 1995)

Ministry of Defence USSR/RF Publications, *Tank T-72S: Katalog Detaley i Sbrochnykh Yedinitoy* Book 2 (Moscow, 1989)

Moskovskiy, A. G. (general editor), *75 Let Upravleniyu Nachalnika Vooruzheniya* (Voyennyy Parad, Moscow, 2004)

Popov, N. S., Yefremov, A. S., and Ashik, M. V., *Tank, Brosivshiy Vyzov Vremeni* (Kaskad Poligrafiya, St Petersburg, 2001)

Rogoza, S. L., and Achkasov, N. B., *Zasekrechennye Voyny 1950–2000 gg.* (AST, St Petersburg, 2004)

Safonov, B. S. and Murakhovskiy, V. I., *Osnovnye Boyevye Tanki* (Arsenal-Press, Moscow, 1993)

Shirokorad, A. B., *Ehtsiklopediya Otechestvennoy Artillerii* (Kharvest, Minsk, 2000)

Shirokorad, A. B., *Geniy Sovetskoy Artillerii* (AST, Moscow, 2002)

Solyankin, A. G., Zheltov, I .G., and Kudryashov, K. N., *Otechestvennye Bronirovannye Mashiny XX Vek: Tom 3 – Otechestvennye Bronirovannye Mashiny 1945–1965* (Tseykhgauz, Moscow, 2010)

Suvorov, S., *T-72: Vchera, Segodnya, Zavtra* (Tankomaster, Moscow, 2001)

Suvorov, S., *T-90: Pervyy Seriynyy Rossiyskiy Tank* (Tankomaster, Moscow, 2002)

Ustyantsev, S. and Kolmakov, D., *Boyevye Mashiny Uralvagonzavoda: Tank T-72*, Part 2 (Dom 'Media-Print', Nizhny Tagil, 2004) (translated by author)

Ustyantsev, S. and Kolmakov, D., *Boyevye Mashiny Uralvagonzavoda: Tanki 60-ikh*, Part 4 (Dom 'Media-Print', Nizhny Tagil, 2007) (translated by author)

Ustyantsev, S. and Kolmakov, D., *Boyevye Mashiny Uralvagonzavoda: T-72/T-90* (Dom 'Media-Print', Nizhny Tagil, 2013) (translated by author)

Vasilyeva (Kucherenko), L. and Zheltov, I., *Nikolay Kucherenko: Pyatdesyat Let v Bitve za Tanki SSSR* (Atlantida – XXI Vek/Moskovskiye Uchebniki, 2009) (translated by author)

Veretrennikov, A., Rasskazov, I., Sidorov, K., and Reshetilo, Y., *Kharkovskoye Konstruktorskoye Byuro po Mashinostroyeniyu imeni A. A. Morozova* (IRIS Press, Kharkov, 1998)

Veretrennikov, A., Rasskazov, I., Sidorov, K., and Reshetilo, Y., *Kharkovskoye Konstruktorskoye Byuro po Mashinostroyeniyu imeni A. A. Morozova* (Kharkov, 2007)

Zayets, A. R. and Bronya R., *Ehvolutsiya boyevikh I spetsialnykh bronirovannykh mashin v Sovetsvogo Soyuza I Rossii posle Vtoroy Mirovoy Voyny – Kratkiy Ocherk* (Gumanitarnyy Universitet, 2002)

Design Bureau & Manufacturer's Datasheets & Brochures

KBTM (Design Bureau of Transport Machine Building) – Omsk
KhKBM (Kharkov/Kharkiv Design Bureau) – Kharkiv
UKBTM (Urals Design Bureau of Transport Machine Building) – Nizhny Tagil
Uralvagonzavod (UVZ) – Nizhny Tagil
BTRZ No. 7 Kiev (Kyiv), BTRZ No. 17 Lvov (Lviv)

Books – English Language

Hull, A., Markov, D., and Zaloga, S., *Soviet/Russian Armor and Artillery Design Practices: 1945 to the Present* (Darlington Publications, Darlington, MD, 1999)

Kinnear, J., *The Russian Army on Parade 1992–2017* (Canfora Publishing, Stockholm, 2021)

Scott, H. F. and Scott, W. F., *The Armed Forces of the USSR* (Westview Press, Boulder, CO, 1979)

Periodicals – Russian Language

Arms – Russian Defence Technologies
M-Khobbi (Moscow)
Nevskiy Bastion (Leningrad)
Tekhnika i Vooruzheniye (pre-1991 Soviet issues)

Tekhnika i Vooruzheniye (post-1991 Russian issues)
Tekhnika-Molodezhi
Tankomaster
Voyennye Znaniye

Articles – Russian Language

Berezkin, V., 'Novoye Serdtse T-72' (The New Heart of the T-72), *Tankomaster*, Issue 2 (1997)

Gryankin, S., 'OSnovnoy Boyevoy Tank T-72' (T-72 Main Battle Tank), *Tekhnika-Molodezhi*, Issue 11 (1991)

Kirichenko, P. and Pasternak, G., 'Paradoksi Otechestvennogo Tankostroeniya', *Tekhnika i Vooruzheniye*, Issue 2 (2005), pp.17–24

Knyazkov, Col. (ret.) V., 'Ot Maloy T-34 na T-72' (From the Little T-34 to the T-72), *Voyennye Znaniye*, Issue 9 (1985)

Polikarpov, V. V., 'Ehksportnye Modifikatsii Tanka T-72' (Export Modifications of the T-72 Tank), *Nevskiy Bastion*, Issue 1 (1997)

Prishepo, Yu. P., 'O litsenziyakh i Vokrug Nikh', *Tekhnika i Vooruzheniye*, Issue 2 (2007), pp.2–9

Radvanskiy, Col. S., 'The T-27 Tank: Setting the Sight Angle', *Tekhnika i Vooruzheniye*, Issue 9 (1990)

Sutyagin, I., 'Srednyy Tank T-72M' (T-72M Medium Tank), *Tekhnika i Vooruzheniye*, Issue 11/12 (1992)

Suvorov, S.,'T-90 – Gordost Otechestvennogo Tankostroenniya', *Tekhnika i Vooruzheniye*, Issue 6 (2005), pp.18–21

Suvorov, S., 'Nuzhna Li Rossii Boevaya Mashina Podderzhki Tankov?', *Tekhnika i Vooruzheniye*, Issue 4 (2006), pp.41–45

Suvorov, S., 'Tanki T-72, Vchera, Segodnya, Zavtra', *Tekhnika i Vooruzheniye*, Issue 4 (2005), pp.24–31, 12 (2004), pp.27–29

Zayets, A., 'Luchshiy Tank Semidesyatykh' (Best Tank of the 1970s), *Voyennye Znaniye Issue N/K* (September 1995)

See also *Tekhnika i Vooruzheniye*, issues 5, 7–12 (2004) and 2, 3 (2005)

Periodicals – English Language

Armor (US Army)
International Defence Review
Jane's Defence Review
Jane's Intelligence Review
Jane's Soviet Intelligence Review

Online Sources

'Gur Khan Attacks' – http://gurkhan.blogspot.com/
'Soldat.ru' – http://www.soldat.ru/
'Yuri Pasholok's Journal' – http://yuripasholok.livejournal.com/
Stal i Ogon: Sovremennye i Perspektivnye Tanki – http://btvt.info
Tankograd blog post site – T-72 Parts 1 and 2 – https://thesovietarmourblog.blogpost.com

INDEX

Figures in **bold** refer to illustrations.

12th Main Directorate for Tank Production of the Ministry of Transport Machinery Production (Glavtank) 26, 31, 301

Abkhazia 183, 192, 197
Afghanistan 52, 139, 144, 153, **174**, 178–179, **183**, 185
air cleaners 23, 44, 59, 294, 297
air flow 22–23, 249
Alabino:
    garrison **104**, **152**
    polygon **54**, **116**, **117**, **118**, **165**, **170**
    proving grounds **160**, **172**
    training grounds **148**, **149**
Algeria 56, 279–280
ammunition 7, 14, 16, 22, 31, 37, 46, 55–56, 63–64, 67, 71–72, 76, 87–88, 91, 183–185, 188, 190, 195, 205, **213**, **215**, 235–236, 252, 274, 283, 285–287, 291, 298, 300
    3BM9 armour-piercing APFSDS rounds 191, 286, 296
    canisters 64, 67, 72, 91
antenna 69, 72, 284, 291
    feed 289, 291
Anti-Tank Guided Missile (ATGM) **15**, 42, 46, 69, 80, 87, 90, 97, 102, 105, 118, 125, 131, 133, 154, **155**, **156**, 157, 190, 194, 205–206, 243, 277, 291, 295, 300, 302
    9K112 Kobra 33–34, 36, 274–277
    9K120 Svir 41–42, 49, 83, 90–91, 96, **102**, **108**, **111**, **205**, 237, **264**, 274, 287, 292, 297
    9K122 Kobra-U 81, 274

9M111: 116, 195
9M112 Kobra 91
9M119 Svir 91, 287, 292, 295, 297
9M119M Invar 105, 250, 287, 297
Kornet 155
Refleks 102, 105, 295–296
through-the-bore 33, 41, 81, 90, 250, 275–276, 296–297
armament 11, **13**, 16, 37, 64, 67, 71, 87–88, 91, 103, 127, 131, 154, **156**, **157**, **159**, **166**, 187, 243, 252, 277, 282, 291–292, 295–296
    2A20: 14, 16
    2A21: 14, 16, 20, 276–277
    2A26 (D-81) smoothbore gun 16, 31, 33, 63, 276–277, 287, 291, 296
    2A26M 67, 285
    2A33: **166**, 277
    2A36: **166**, 277
    2A46: 33, 36, 46, 76, 88, **212**, 250, 274, 285, 287, 291, 296, 299
    2A46M 74, 76, 81, 91, 103, 123, **249**, 250, 255, 274, 287, 291, 295–296
    2A46M-5: 53, 55, 122, **124**, 127, 295–296
    2A46M-5-01: 131, 295–296
    2A66: 46, 99–100, 103, 276–277, 296
    D-54TS 274, 276–277
    D-81: **13**, 16, 19–20, 22, 31, 33, 286
    D-81T 63, 67, 285, 296
    D-81TM 36, 71, 285, 296
    D-85 rifled gun 34, 73, 274
armour:
    glacis 93, 235–236, 300
    panels 16, 69, 76, 80, 97, 110, **112**, **113**, **114**, **117**, 128, 132,

293
    penetration 55, 195, 286
    protection 7, 14, 38, 41, 46, 71, 76, 84, 88, 90, 93, 116, 119, **124**, **162**, 165, 184, 235, 237, 273, 274, 292, 295, 300
    'Reshotka' slat armour grilles 53, 57, 116, **120**, **123**, **124**, 125, 127–128, **129**, **131**, 132, **184**, 200–201, **207**, **249**
Armour-Piercing Fin-Stabilized Discarding Sabot projectile (APFSDS) 42, 46, 55, 64, 76, 80, 110, 125, 188, 191, 237, 252, 286–287, 291, 296, 300
    Svinets-2: 46, 55, 286
armoured vehicles 27, 44, 116, **153**, 174, 190, 193, 195, **250**, 266, 273
autoloaders 14, 16, 22, 24, **38**, 55, 64, 83, **89**, 100, 103, 105, 183–184, **212**, **213**, 243, **245**, 252, 274, 287, 291, 298
    Zhelud cassette 20–22, 24–25, 31, 63, 67, 183, 274
Auxiliary Power Unit (APU) 11, 101, 194, 256, 300
    AB-1 series 72, 101

Belarus 53, 118, 123, 130, 187, **235**, 265, 279–280
Belorussia 27, 49, 118, **238**, **239**, 287
blocks 99, 132, **240**, **246**
    Kontakt-1: **8**, **41**, 43, **44**, **48**, 52, 84, **92**, 93, **94**, **95**, 96–97, 110, 119, 156, 194, **197**, 200, 237–238, **240**, **246**, **247**, 249, 255–256, **263**, 282, 296
Boevaya Mashina (BM – Combat Vehicle) 50, **53**, 95, 162, **175**, **176**, 178–180, **251**, 300
Boevaya Mashina Podderzhki Tankov (BMPT – Tank Support

Combat Vehicle) 119, **126**, 131, 153, **154**, 155, **156**, **157**, **158**, **160**, **161**, **162**, **264**, 266, 277, 300
    BMPT-72: 157, **159**, **162**, 274
Boyevaya Mashina Ognemetov (BMO-T – tyazhelaya or heavy armoured flamethrower vehicle) **162**, **163**, **164**, **165**
Boyevaya Otdel (BO – fighting compartment) 300
Brezhnev, Leonid 28, 34
Bronetankovy Remontny Zavod (BTRZ – Tank Repair Plant) 84, 96, **245**, **246**, **248**, **249**, 255, 301
    No. 7: 247
    No. 17: 247
    No. 103: 144
    No. 143: 221
Bronya Desantogo Deystviya (BDD – Assault Operations Armour) 108, 300
Bronyevaya Mashina Razminiriovaniya (BMR – Armoured Mine Clearing Vehicle) **181**, 301
    BMR-1: 144
    BMR-2: 144
    BMR-3: 136, **144**, **145**, **146**
    BMR-3M **146**, 273
Bronyevaya Remontirno-Ehvakuatsionnaya Mashina (BREhM – Armoured Repair and Recovery Vehicle) **146**, **181**, 274, 283, 301
    BREhM-1: 146, **147**, **148**, **149**, **150**, **151**, **152**, **153**, **252**, **253**, **254**, **264**, 272–273, 277
    BREhM-1M: **152**, 153, 273, 276–277
Bronyevoy Tyagach Sredny or Sredny Tankovy Tyagach (BTS – Medium Tank Tractor) 146, 301
    BTS-2: 153
    BTS-4: 153
    BTS-5: **254**
    BTS-5B **254**
Bumar-Łabędy **242**, 282

cannon 74, 154, 285
    2A42: 155–157, 277
    2A72: 154, **155**, **156**, **157**, **158**, **159**
capremont (capital rebuild) 57, 59, 104
casing 14, 31, 61, 63–64, 178, 291
Caucasus mountains 27, 193
Central Committee of the Communist Party of the Soviet Union (TsK KPSS) 12–13, 22, 25–26, 29, 32, 273, 303
Central Scientific Research Institutes for Flame Weapons, Moscow (TsNII-6) 303
Central Scientific Research Institute for Armour, Leningrad (TsNII-48) 303
Central Scientific Research Institute for Artillery Stabilizers, Moscow (TsNII-173) 303
chassis 19, **22**, 25, 44, 61, 70, **88**, 135, **136**, 137, 141, **142**, 144, 146, 153–154, 156–158, 162–163, 165, **166**, 171, 173, 178–179, **180**, **181**, 183, 185, **249**, 252, **254**, 256, **267**, 272–273, 276–278
    BMP 135
Chechnya 52, 55, 116, 125, 128, 183, **184**, 193–196, 205, 259, **264**, 266
    First Chechen War 158, 162, **183**, 193, 195
    Second Chechen War 179, 193, 195
Chelyabinsky Kirovsky Zavod (ChKZ) (ChTZ from 15.05.58) 62, 301
Chelyabinsky Traktorny Zavod imeni V.I. Lenina (ChTZ) (ChKZ before 15.05.58) 13, 16, 21, 25–26, 42, 46, 57, 59, 62, 87, **90**, 154, **155**, **156**, 273, 277–278, 301
    KB 154
China 6, 37, 56, 243, 275, 280–281
clearance vehicle 274
    Klin-1: 141, 274
Coalition forces 47–48, 189–191, 197

Cold War 19, 50, 119, 135, **240**, 259
communications 11, 65, 69, 123, 130, **218**, 255, **267**, 274, 284, 291, 300
components 7, 11, 24, 44, 53, 59–60, 63, 65, 68, 70, **112**, **114**, 122, 127, **135**, 136, 141, 171, 178, 189, 209, **218**, **249**, **250**, 255, 274, 282–283, 288–289
cooling system 25, 44, 89, 99, 194, 249, 256, 293–294
    extraction 14, 22, 60, 65
    Silfon 52–53
Crimea 201
Croatia 192, 281
Czechoslovakia 6, 9, 37, 47–48, 55–56, 187, 236, **241**, 242, **263**, 265, 273, 274, 278–282, **305**

Dagestan **48**, **100**, **186**, **189**, **190**, 195, 266
destruction simulator complex 125
    1K713 firing 125
Donetsk 55, 201
doubler plants 16, 18
dozer blade 128, 141, **217**
driver-mechanic 14, 22, **29**, 45, 89, 103, 108, 130, 137, 140, 142, 163, 183, 209, **214**, 241, 291
    control panel 209, **214**
    seat 52, 81, 87, **214**
Dudayev, General-Major Dzhokar 193, 195
dual receiver 123
    GLONASS/GPS 123, 127, 157
Dynamicheskaya Zaschita (DZ – Dynamic Protection (ERA)) 43, 84–85, 93, 96–97, **102**, 110, **117**, **119**, **120**, **121**, **123**, **124**, 125, **126**, **131**, **247**, 301
    Nozh system **249**, 252, 255–256, 283

Ekaterinburg **65**, 165, 194, **261**, **262**, **265**, 266
engines:
    5TDF two-cycle diesel 14, 16, 31, 59, 247, 256, 277
    A-68: 116

turbine 7, **14**, 21, 27–28, 31, 101, 135
V-2 diesel 7, 19, 21, 23, 46, 122, 135, 247
V-26: **13**
V-36: **11**, 19–20, 277
V-45: **17**, 19–22, 24, 59, 61, 276–277
V-45K 23, 26, 62, 67, 293
V-46: 7, 31, 67, 156, 183, **215**, 256, 293
V-46-6: 80, 180, 247, 293, 298, 300
V-84: 44, 80, 108, 157, 247, 294
V-84-1: 93, 103, 127, 141, 255, **269**, 294, 298
V-84M 93, 127, 293
V-84MS 52, 55, 102, 105, 108, **181**, **215**, **216**, 294, 298
V-86: 100
V-92S 53, 157
V-92S1: 117, 298
V-92S2: 55, 108, **112**, **114**, 117, 122, 127, 153, 156, 237, 294, 298
V-92S2F **126**, 130–131, 294, 298
Ethiopia 252, 256, 279
Ethiopian-Somali Border War 188
Explosive Reactive Armour (ERA) 42, 52, 84–85, 91, **93**, 96–99, **100**, 103, **108**, **109**, 110, 128, 132, **144**, **146**, 184, 194–195, 206, 266, 275–276, 286–287, 295–296, 301
Blazer 42–43, 97, 188
Kontakt-1: **8**, **41**, 43, **44**, **48**, 52, 84, **92**, 93, **94**, **95**, 96–97, 110, 119, 156, 194, **197**, 200, 237–238, **240**, **246**, 247, 249, 255–256, **263**, 282, 296
Kontakt-5: 46, 52, 93, 110, **111**, **112**, **114**, **117**, 119, 127, 158, 165, 250, 252, **269**, 283, 295–296
Nozh **249**, 252, 255–256, 283
Relikt Dynamic Protection 53, **112**, **114**, 119, **120**, **122**, **123**, **124**, 125, 130, **131**, 295–296

Finland **209**, **240**, **241**, **242**, **263**, 265, 279, 281
Finnish Army 9, **241**
fire controls 11, 34, 46, 53, 67, 76, 90–91, 99, 102, 105, 122–123, 127, 157, **168**, 171, **210**, 236, 247, 249–250, 256, 276–277, 282–283, 292, 295, **304**
1A33 Ob 36, 40, 81, 83, 91, 255, 276–277
1A40: 36, 41, 76, 81, 295, 298
1A40-1: 83, 91, 103, 274, 295, 297
Sanoyet-2: 118
flamethrowers 163, **164**, 178, 300
RPO-A Shmel (bumblebee) hand-held 163, **164**
TOS-1 (TOC-1) Buratino heavy 165, **174**, 178–179, 183, 185, 272, 277
TOS-1A (TOC-1A) Solntsepyok heavy 163, 165, **174**, **175**, **176**, **177**, **178**, **179**, 180, **198**, 277
flyer plates 194
4S20: 97, 119, 194, 296
Fort IX Czerniaków 236, 266
France 39, 53, 118, 123, 249–250, 252, 265, 283
fuel capacity 12, 67, 295

Gamsakhurdia, Zviad 192
Georgia 49, 55, **93**, **94**, 183, **191**, 197–198, **200**, **240**, 259, 267, 279, 281
Georgian Civil War 192, 197
Germany 42, 97, 141, 205, 235, **236**, **240**, **241**, **242**, 265, **262**, **263**, 267, 279
East 47, 55–56, 259, 279–280, 290
Glavnoye Artilleriskoe Upravleniye (GAU – Main Artillery Directorate) 301
Glavnoye Bronetankovoe Upravleniye (GBTU – Main Armoured Vehicle Directorate) 13, 19, 25, 235, 301
Glavnoye Raketno-Artilleriyskoye Upravleniye (GRAU – Main Rocket and Artillery Directorate) 301
Gorbachev, Mikhail 47, 50, 193
Gosudarstvennoye Avtomotivnoye Bronetankirovannoye Upravleniye (GABTU – Main Automotive and Armoured Vehicle Directorate) 155, 301
Gosudarstvennaya Kommissiya po Oboronnoy Tekhnike (GKOT – State Committee on Defense Technology) 301
Great Britain **68**, **238**, **243**, **262**, **264**, 265
Great Patriotic War 7, 11, 22, 42
Grechko, Andrey 7, 15, 25, 27, 34
Group of Soviet Forces Germany (GSFG) 55
Grozny 116, 193–195
Guards Motorized Rifle Division (GMRD) 301
Gulf War:
First 48–49, 191, 197, **238**, 259, 283
Second 197, 259
gunsights 275, **304**
gyrocompass 72, 297
GPK-48: 297
GPK-59: 289–291, 297

heat signature 53, 108
High Explosive Anti-Tank (HEAT) 31, 42, 64, 69, 76, 80, 97–98, 125, **252**, 286–287, 291–293, 296–297, 301
High Explosive (HE-FRAG – Fragmentation) 157, 188, 286–287, 291, 296, 298, 301
Hungary 47, 55, 279–280, **305**
Hussein, Saddam 47, 188, 197, 203

illuminators **62**, **77**, **99**, **111**, 299–300
Imperial War Museum 265, **269**
India 37–38, 56, **108**, 188, 238, 274, 279–282
infrared 11, 16, 45, 53, 76, 117, **262**, 297
searchlights 36, 87
Inzhenirnaya Mashina

Razgrazhdeniya (IMR – Engineer Vehicle for Obstacle Clearing) 22, 44–45, 136–137, 141, **181**, 185, 301
   IMR-1: 44, 136–137, 139–141, 277
   IMR-2: 135, **136**, **137**, 138–141, **183**, 266, 273, 276–277
   IMR-2M 135, 136, **138**, **139**, **140**, 141, **252**
   IMR-2M2: 141
   IMR-2MA 141, 273
   IMR-3: **135**, 141, 273, 277
Iran 38, 47, 52, 56, 185–189, 203, **237**, 266, 274, 279–282
   Iran–Iraq War 43, 185–187
Iraq 47–48, 56, 185–187, 190, 197, 203, 235, **237**, 242, **264**, 265–267, 279, 282, **305**
   Iraq War 43, 185–187
   Iraqi Army 188, 197, 203, 279, **305**
   Iraqi Civil War 203
Israel 37, 158, 187, 266, 279–280
Israel Defence Forces 42, 97

Kantemirovskaya Tank Division 49, **109**, **167**
Kartsev, Leonid 12–13, 22–25, 45, 60–62, 183, 235
Kazakhstan 128, 156, 180, 252, 274, 279
Kharkov/Kharkiv 7, 12–13, 16, **17**, 18–28, **29**, 31–32, 34, 38, **41**, 50, 57, 59, 61, 67–69, 75–76, **245**, 247, **248**, **249**, 277–278, 283, 301, 303, **305**
Kharkovskoe Konstruktorskoe Bureau po Mashinostroenniyu (KhKBM (ex KB-60M, later KhMDB) – Kharkov Machine Building Design Bureau) 35, 88, 245, 249, 301
Kiev/Kyiv 201, **204**, **205**, **246**, 247, **248**, **249**, **256**, 289
   Kyiv Tank Plant **249**, 255
Kodori Gorge 183, 197
Koleiny Minniy Tral (KMT – Track Width Mine Trawl) **217**, 300
   KMT-6: 146, **240**, 299, **305**
   KMT-6M2: **40**, 157, **263**
   KMT-7: **144**, 145, **146**, 157
   KMT-8: 146, 157
   KMT-RZ 141
Kompleks Aktivnoi Zashitni (KAZ – Active Protection Complex) 88, 301
   Arena-Eh 118
Komplekt Zapasnykh Chastey, Instrumentov, i Prinadzhelnostey (ZIP – set of spare parts, tools and accessories) 44, 68–69, 84, 237, 289, 303
Konstruktorskoye Byuro (KB – design bureau) **11**, **17**, 21, 24, 35, 87, 154, 301
Konstruktorskoye Byuro Transportivnoy Mashinoy (KBTM – Design Bureau for Transport Vehicles (Omsk)) 142, 153–154, 158, 162–163, 178, 301
Kontrolnaya Otdel (KO – control compartment) 300
Kotin, Zhosef 12, 23
Krutyakov, Ivan F. 23–26, 34, 37
Kubinka **11**, 26, **39**, 43, 50, 71, 75, **77**, **101**, 110, 131, **151**, **154**, **156**, **157**, **184**, **262**, 266, 274, **288**, **290**
Kubinka Tank Museum **15**, **18**, **92**, **110**, 154, 188, 266
Kucherenko, Nikolay 26–28, 34, 39
Kursk Oblast 55, 132, 185, 204, 259
Kutuzovsky Prospekt **108**, **148**, **167**, 171
Kuwait 47, 188, 191, 197, 279, 281, 283

Laos 241, 279
Lebanon 42–43, 85, 97, 187
Leningrad 'Kirov' Plant (LKZ) (Plant No. 185) 12–13, 21, 24, 27, 31, 50, 62, 301
Leningrad 'Voroshilov' Plant (LVZ) (Plant No. 174 in Omsk) 301
Libya 56, 198, 200, 279, 281
Libyan Civil War 198, 200
logistics 32, 39, 194–195
Lugansk 55, 57, 201
Lvov/Lviv 140, 247

machine guns 195, 276–277, 285, 289–290, 295, 297, 299
   7.62mm 64, 139, 154, **155**, **156**, 255, 285, 292, 295, 297
   12.7mm 16, 27, 67, 102, 128, 141, 144, 153, **156**, 162–163, 180, 241, 255, 283, 292, 295, 296–298
   14.5mm 243
   coaxial 64, 67, 155, **157**, 292, 295, 297
   heavy 16, 144, 162, 243, 296–297
   Kord 141, 295–296
   NSVT 141, 144, **156**, 255, 283
   NVST 153, 180, 297
   PKT 64, 139, 154, **155**, **156**, 255, 285, 292, 295, 300
   PKTM 154, 156, 295, 297
   Utes 16, 102, 255
Main Battle Tank (MBT) 7–8, 13, **20**, 21, **22**, 28, **29**, **32**, 36, **38**, 39, 42, 45, 50, 67, 70, 90–91, 96, 102–104, 118–119, 125, 129, 137, **149**, 183, 187, 206, 235, 243, 245, 268, 276–277, 300
manipulator 139, 141
   universal work element (URO) 141
meteorological sensor mast DVE-BS 53, 102, 105, **112**, **113**, **114**, 297
Middle East 47–48, 188, 191, 200, 235, 242–243, 259, 280
mine clearance/clearing system 139, 141, **181**, 217, 301–302
   BMR-1: 144
   BMR-2: 144
   BMR-3: 136, **144**, 145, **146**
   BMR-3M 146, 273
   EhMT **144**, **146**
   EhMT-1: 145–146, 157
   KMT 6: 146, **240**, 299, 305
   KMT-6M2: **40**, **157**, **263**
   KMT-7: **144**, 145, **146**, 157
   KMT-8: 146, 157
   KMT-RZ 141
   UR-83: 138–139
mine detonation **144**, **146**

mine ploughs 141, **240**, **305**
Ministerstvo Oboroni (MO – Soviet (Russian) Ministry of Defence (MoD)) 21, 25–27, 34, 36, 39, 49, 84, 103, 155–156, 179, 274, 300
Ministerstvo Oboronoi Promishlennosti (MOP – Soviet (Russian) MoD Production) 6, 19–21, 24–28, 31–34, 36, 39–41, 45, 49, 54, 59, 61, 87, 274, 300
Ministerstvo Trasportivnoy Mashinikh Promishlennosti (MTrM – Ministry of Transport Machinery Construction) 300
Minsk 118, 125, **238**, **239**, 265
Minsk II Agreements 201
Morov, A. A. 136, 142, 178
Morozov, Aleksandr 12–14, 16, 19, 21, 34–35, 87
Moscow **6**, **9**, 21, 23, **32**, **36**, 39, 43, 49–50, 52, **53**, **54**, 55, **56**, **73**, **74**, **86**, **98**, **108**, **119**, **122**, **126**, 129–130, **133**, **140**, **148**, **149**, **150**, **151**, 153–154, **159**, **161**, **162**, **164**, **167**, **168**, **171**, **173**, **177**, **181**, 188, 193, 196, 221, **230**, **250**, **260**, **263**, 266, **269**, 281, 303
    August 1991 Putsch 193
Mostovaya Tankovaya Ustanovka (MTU – Tank Bridging Installation) 22, 300
    MTU-2: 88
    MTU-12: 142
    MTU-20: 142
    MTU-55: 142
    MTU-72: 136, **142**, **143**, 144, 272–273, 277
    MTU-90: 144, 273
Motorized Rifle Brigade (MRB) 195, 300
    Maikop 194–195
Motorized Rifle Division (MRD) 49–50, 171, 193, 197, 301–303
Motorized Rifle Regiment (MRR) 183, 194–195, 300
Motorno-Transmissionaya Otdel (MTO – motor transmission compartment) 71, 128, 300
Muzei Bronevoi Tekhniki (Vadim Zadorozhny Museum) 9, 181, **230**, **260**, **262**, 266, **267**
muzzle reference system 53, 122
    UUI-2: 53
    VVS-2: 122

Nagorno-Karabakh 192, 279
    Nagorno-Karabakh Conflict 192
Nakidka thermal blanketing system 53, 125, 132
Narodny Kommissariat Vnutrenikh Del (NKVD – People's Commissariat for Internal Affairs) 300
NATO 6, **31**, 37, 48, 54, 69, 132–133, 188, 192–193, 204, 252, 268, 283–284
Nauchno-Issledovatelniy Institut (NII – Scientific Research Institute) 71, 97, 119, 300
    NII-38: **110**, **262**
    Staly 71, 97, 119
Nauchno-Tekhnicheskiy Komitet (NTK – Scientific Technical Committee) 25, 300
Nevsky Pyatachok **70**, **259**, 267
Nizhny Tagil 6–7, 12–13, **17**, 19, 21–22, 24, 26–27, **29**, 31–32, 50, 57, 59, **62**, **113**, 127–128, **129**, 137, **138**, 141–142, **143**, 154, **155**, **158**, **159**, **174**, **176**, **179**, 201, **209**, **215**, 245, **260**, **261**, **262**, **264**, 266, 278, 303
North Korea 6, 243
Novyy Sredny Tank (NST – new medium tank) 12–13, 67, 300
Nuclear, Biological, Chemical (NBC) 44, **69**, 101, 136, 181, **219**, 235–237, **243**, 297, 300

Oborudovaniye Podvodnoy Vozhdeniya Tanki (OPVT – underwater tank driving equipment) 16, 25, 64, 68–69, **101**, **152**, 249, **253**, 275, 287, **288**, **289**, **290**, 293–294, 300, 300
    OPVT-72: 297
    OPVT-155: 287
Okunev, Ivan V. 12, 23
Omsk 26, 127, 136, 142, 153–154, 158, **162**, **164**, **174**, **175**, 178, **179**, **181**, **263**, 266, 273, 278, 301, 303
Operation *Desert Storm* 188–191
Operation *Iraqi Freedom* 197
Operation *Peace for Galilee* 42, 187
Opytniy Konstruktorsko-Mekhanicheskiy Otdel (OKMO – Prototype Design Mechanical Section) 302
Opytno-Konstruktorskaya Rabota (OKR) 273
    Anker 100
    Goboy 277
    Kotlas-KZ 125
    Motobol 104
    Otryazayemost-2: 85
    Proryv-2: 277
    Proryv-3: 277
    Sovershenstvovaniye-72B 100
    Velizh 101
    Vepr 277
    Zhelud 67

Padikovo 9, 209, 221, **259**, 266
Pakistan 56, 280, 283
Partizanskaya Polyanna Museum/ memorial complex **84**, **86**, **232**, **261**, 266
Patriot Park **15**, **86**, **113**, **116**, **119**, **121**, 131, 154, **156**, **157**, **163**, **179**, **262**, 266
podboy 44–45, 81, 137
Poland 6, 9, 37, 47–48, 55–56, 186–187, 189, **236**, **240**, **242**, **243**, **262**, 266, 273, 274, 278–282
Politburo 7, 12, 25, 32, 34, 274
projectiles 14, 22, 31, 41–42, 45, 61, 63–64, 69, 83, 85, 90–91, 98, 105, 110, 118, 133, 171, 174, 178–179, 194, 237, 285–287, 291, 296, 300
Prokhorovka **262**, 266
propellant 14, 22, 31, 61, 63–64, 183, 296
Protivo-Pozharnoye Oborudovaniye (PPO – fire suppression equipment) 139, **216**, 297, 302
Protivoatomnoi Zashiti (PAZ – anti-nuclear protection) 139–140, 185, 302

Protivotankiy Upravlayushchiy Raketnyy Snaryad (PTURS) 302
Puskovaya Ustanovka (PU) (launch system) 302
    TOS-1A PU **176**, **177**

radiation lining/protection 6, **35**, **39**, 42, 44–45, **70**, 77, 81, **82**, 84, 93, **99**, 137, 140–141, 221, **260**
radiators 14, 23, 44, 60, 99, 249
    air exhaust 65
    air intakes 25, 65, 289
    covers 290
    exhaust covers 289
    exhaust grilles 289
    fan 293
    mounting 299
radio sets 72, 93, 275, 284–285, 291, 295
    HF AM/SSB 72, 96, 284, 297
    K-2RB 'Libid' radio communications 255
    R-105: 284
    R-108: 284
    R-112: 72
    R-123: 65, 69, 72, **218**, 284, 297
    R-123M **218**, **242**, 297
    R-124: 65, 69, **218**, 284, 297
    R-130: 284
    R-130M 72, 96, 297
    R-134: 96, 284, 297
    R-134M 297
    R-163: 53, 284
    R-168: 53, 130, 157, 284
    R-168-50K 284
    R-168-25U-2: 123, 127, 285, 295
    R-168-25UE 285
    R-168-25UE-2: 295, 297
    R-173: 53, 93, 96, 284, 297
    R-173P 96, 297
    RP-377UVM1L radio signal jamming system 128
    VHF FM 11, 65, 69, 93, 123, 284, 297
rangefinders 14, 16, **24**, 27, 31, **36**, 46–47, 53, 61, 63, 67, **70**, 73, 76, **86**, 90, **99**, 123, 157, 174, 185, **191**, **209**, 236, 275–276, 283, 292, 295, 298

reconnaissance vehicles 135, 181
    RKHM (PXM) NBC 181
Red Square 6, **9**, **32**, **33**, 39, 43, 49, 54–55, **56**, **72**, **78**, **96**, **97**, **122**, **127**, 129, **148**, 157, **161**, **167**, **168**, **169**, **170**, **172**, 180, 241, **269**
Republican Guards 185–186, 188
Republican Guards Forces Command (RGFC) 188, 190
resolutions 21, 26, 47, 103–104, 274
    No. 141-58: 13, 16
    No. 326-113: 26
    No. 360-137: 22
    No. 554-172: 29
    No. 635-188: 40
    No. 729-305: 16
    No. 733-244: 36
    No. 741-208: 45
    No. 759-58: 50, 102
    No. 982-321: 21
    No. 1043-361: 36
road wheels 11, **13**, 14, **18**, 20, 23, 27, 37, 60–61, 69, **72**, 105, 150, 153, 243, 256, **261**, **264**, 274, 282, 294–295
    8-bolt **35**, 61, 81, **260**, **261**
Rocket Propelled Grenade (RPG) (launcher) 42, 69, 80, 97, 116, 118, 125, 133, 154, 158, 184, 194–195, 205, 302
Romania 47, 279, 281–282
running gear 11, 14, **15**, **18**, 19, 21, **22**, 23–24, 31, 60–61, 80, 87, 93, 122, 171, 173, 275–277, 294, 298
Russia 23, 49, 57, 71, 125, 130, 132, 180, 197, 200–201, 203–204, 206, 259, 279–280
Russian Army 38, 50–52, 54–55, 57, 102, **109**, 121, 125, 127, **129**, 131, 156, 158, 165, 179, 181, 193–194, 196, 237, **240**, **304**, **305**
Russian constitutional crisis, 1993: 196–197
Russian Federation 9, 47–52, 54–56, 103–104, 121–122, 125, 185, 187, 193, 196, 198, 206, 239, 241, 247, 259, 265–266, 268

Russo-Ukrainian conflict 6, **105**, 132, **162**, **185**, **202**, 203–206, **207**, 259

Scientific Technical Council of the Main Armoured Vehicle Directorate (NTK GBTU) 25
searchlights **62**, **66**
    L-2: 61, 63, **262**
    L2AG 67, **99**, 297, 299
    L2G 73
    L-4: **77**
    L-4A 36, 74, 76, **205**, 297, 300
self-propelled gun-howitzer 165, 277
    2S3 Akatsitya **167**, 171
    2S35 Koalitsiya-SV: **172**, **173**
    2S5 Giasint **167**, 171
    2S19: 87, **165**, **166**, **167**, **168**, **169**, 170, **171**, **173**, **180**, **198**, **254**, **255**, **256**, **265**, 266, **267**, 277
    2S19M 165, 171
    2S19M1: **168**, **169**, 171
    2S19M2: **169**, **170**, **171**
    2S35 Koalitsiya-SV **172**, **173**
    MSTA-B 165
    MSTA-S 87, **165**, **167**, **168**, 173, 180, 277
    MSTA-SM **169**, 171
    Shaiba 277
self-propelled laser weapons system 180
    1K17 Szhatiye **180**, 181
Serbia 192, 241, 280–281
Sholokovo **36**, **70**, **260**, 266
    T-34 Museum **36**, **70**, **260**, 266
Shrivenham Defence Academy **243**, **263**, 265
side skirts **35**, **70**, 71, 84, 98, **99**, **112**, **113**, **114**, **116**, **117**, **120**, **121**, **122**, **123**, 128, **129**, 131, 132, **162**, **163**, **169**, **247**
sights/sighting system 11, 16, 27, 35–36, 41, 45–46, 52, **66**, 76, 81, 83, 98, **108**, **111**, 118, 127, 130, 132, 156–157, 163, **191**, **247**, 249–250, 255, 275, 277, 283, 285–286, 289, 292, 295, 297–298

1K13: 90, 96, 237, 295
1K13-49: 49, 52, 105, **205**, 255, **264**, 295
PKP-72: 241, 295, 297
PNK-4M **112**, **114**
Sosna-U 53, 55, **112**, **113**, **114**, **117**, 118, **122**, 123, **124**, 127, **213**, 241, **264**, **269**, 276, 295, 297
thermal 45–46, 123, 130, 132, 250, 277, 297
TKN-3: 63, **209**, **211**, 298
TKN-3MK 127, 298
TPD-K1: 73, 76, **86**, 96, 123, **209**, 276, 292, 295, 297–298
TPD1-49: **24**, 298
TPD-2-49: **24**, **36**, 63, **66**, 67, **70**, 76, 185, **210**, **211**, 297–298, **304**
TPN-1-49: 60, 63
TPN-1-49-23: 298, **304**
TPN-3-49: 36, 74, 76, **86**, 300
Slovakia 56, 280–282
smoke grenade system/launchers 27, **39**, 47, 87, **117**, 132, 276, 293, 296
    Type 902A Tucha 73–74, 80, 156, 295, 297, 300
    Type 902B Tucha 84, 295, 297
snorkels 25, 64–65, 69, **101**, **152**, 157, 249, **253**, **288**, **289**, **290**, 291
Soda anti-napalm and fire suppression system 65, 69, 80, 300
South Ossetia 183, **191**, 197, 259
    South Ossetia and Abkhazia (Georgian) War 197–198
Sovet Ministerov SSSR (SM SSSR – Council of Ministers of the USSR) 12–13, 16, 21–22, 24–26, 29, 34, 36, 40, 45, 89, 273, 302
Soviet Union 7–9, 11, 13, 16, 21–22, 25, 33–34, 36–39, 43, 45, 47–50, 54–56, 59, 84, **85**, 87, 96–97, 103–104, 119, 121, 135, **166**, 171, 174, 178, **180**, 181, 186, 188, 191–192, 196, 201, 209, 237, 241, 243, **245**,

252, **253**, 274, 281–285, 287, 303
Special Military Operation 131, **162**, **198**, 201, **202**, 203, **305**
Sri Lankan Civil War 1987: 188
St Petersburg **51**, **111**, **259**, **267**
stabilizers **177**, 276
    2Eh28M Siren two-axis hydro-electric armament stabilizer 67, 296
    2Eh42-2 Zhasmin gun stabilizer 250, 296
    2Eh42-4 Zhasmin gun stabilizer 102, 105, 296
    2Eh42M 250, 252
    dual axis gun 11
    gun 295
    jacks **177**
    main armament 292
    Siren 296
    vertical axis gun 11
    Vyuga 276
    Zhasmin-2 armament 71
stowage (ZIP) 16, 44, 64, 67–69, 72, 76, 84, **89**, **152**, 153, **189**, **213**, **219**, 237, 277, 289, 300, 303
Sudan 201, 280
    South Sudan 201, 280
    Sudan-South Sudan conflict 201
Syria 56, 128, 157, 184, 200–201, 203, 242, 280–281
    Syrian Civil War 200–201

Tadjikistan Civil War conflict 196
Tankovaya Informatsionno-Upravlayushchaya Sistema (TIUS – tank information and control system) 53, 123, 302
Tankovoe Peregovornoe Ustroistvo (TPU – tank voice communications system) 69, 302
    TPU-A1: 65
    TPU-A2: 65
Tankovyy Ognemet (TO – tank flamethrower) 302
    TO-1: 274–275
    TO-2: 274–275
tank chassis 44, 70, 135, 153, 158, 162, **254**, **267**, 276

tank destroyers 16
    M18: 193
    M36: 193
Tank Museum, Bovington **68**, **262**, 265, **269**
tanks:
    M1A1 Abrams 45, 189
    M1A2 Abrams 203
    Abrams 205
    Challenger 1: 45, 189, **269**
    Challenger 2: 205
    Chieftain 185, 187, **269**
    Chon'ma 75, 243
    KV-1: 18
    KV-3: 18
    M4: 11, 153
    M31: 153
    M32: 153
    M48: 42, 97, 153, 187–188
    M51: 153
    M60: 153, 185, 187
    M60A1: 187
    M84: 191, 193, 273, 280–281, 283
    M88: 153
    M-95 Degman 281
    Obiekt-032: 141, 276
    Obiekt-033: 141, 276
    Obiekt-140: 13, 276
    Obiekt-142: 276
    Obiekt-146: 276
    Obiekt-151: 276
    Obiekt-153 UBIM (Robot-3) 141, **181**, 276
    Obiekt-166M **11**, **13**, **31**, 276
    Obiekt-166M1: 11
    Obiekt-166Zh 276
    Obiekt-167: **31**
    Obiekt-167M 19–20, 24, 276
    Obiekt-167T **14**
    Obiekt-172: 21, 23–24, 26, **40**, 59, 61, 266, 277–278
    Obiekt-172-2M Buyvol 27, 34, 71, 274, 291–292
    Obiekt-172-3M 73, 276
    Obiekt-172M **14**, 15, **17**, **18**, **20**, **22**, **24**, 25–28, **29**, **32**, **33**, **35**, **36**, 38–39, **51**, **59**, **60**, 61, **62**, **63**, **64**, **65**, 67–69, **70**, 71, 74–75, 81, 85, **88**, **89**, **99**, 101, 209, **210**, **213**, **214**, **215**, **216**, **217**, **218**, **219**, 235, **245**,

259, **260**, **261**, 266–267, 276–278, **289**, 298
Obiekt-172M-1: 81, 83, 85, 87, 276–277
Obiekt-172M1M **112**, **114**
Obiekt-172MD 73
Obiekt-172M-Eh 38, 235
Obiekt-172M-Eh1: 235, 276
Obiekt-172M-Eh3: 236, 276
Obiekt-172M-Eh4: 236, 276
Obiekt-172M-Eh5: 236–237
Obiekt-172M-Eh6: 236–237
Obiekt-172M-Eh7: 276
Obiekt-172M-Eh8: 38, 237, 276
Obiekt-172MK 276
Obiekt-172MK-1: 276
Obiekt-172MK-Eh3: 276
Obiekt-172MK-Eh4: 276
Obiekt-172MN 72, 276
Obiekt-172MP 74, 276
Obiekt-173: 25, 67, 276
Obiekt-175: 34, 70, 73, 276
Obiekt-176: 37, 76, 276
Obiekt-176K 276
Obiekt-177: 83, 276
Obiekt-179: 81, 83, 276
Obiekt-183: 276
Obiekt-184: 90, 100, **102**, 116–119, 276
Obiekt-184-1: **102**, 276
Obiekt-184-2: 127, 276
Obiekt-184-3: **53**, **113**, 276
Obiekt-184-4: 130
Obiekt-184A 52, 110, 277
Obiekt-184A-1: 52, 277
Obiekt-184K 101, 277
Obiekt-184K-1: 277
Obiekt-184M 122, 277
Obiekt-184M-3: 277
Obiekt-184-1MS 277
Obiekt-185: 100
Obiekt-186: 89, 99, 277
Obiekt-187: 45–46, 88, 90, 100–101, 103, 277
Obiekt-188: 45–47, 49–50, 93, 102–103
Obiekt-188-1: 102–103, **111**
Obiekt-188-Eh1: 277
Obiekt-188A 277
Obiekt-188A1: 277
Obiekt-188A1K 277

Obiekt-188K 277
Obiekt-188M 277
Obiekt-188MS-1: 277
Obiekt-190: 277
Obiekt-193: 154, 277
Obiekt-195: 88, 277
Obiekt-197: 277
Obiekt-197A 277
Obiekt-199 Ramka 153–155, **158**, **159**
Obiekt-219: 21, 24, 27–28, **29**, 31, 46
Obiekt-219sp1: 27
Obiekt-219sp2: 27–28, 36, 235
Obiekt-277: 13
Obiekt-316: **165**, 277
Obiekt-327: **165**, **166**, 277
Obiekt-430: 13, 25, 277
Obiekt-432: 13–16, 19–21, 25, **31**, 277
Obiekt-434: 16, 19, 21–22, 25, **31**, 75, 277
Obiekt-435: 22
Obiekt-436: 19–21, 277
Obiekt-438: 19, 21, 277
Obiekt-439: 20, 24, 277
Obiekt-446: 277
Obiekt-447A 34, 36
Obiekt-477: 88
Obiekt-563: 179, 277
Obiekt-608: 153, 277
Obiekt-632 Triton **142**, 277
Obiekt-634: 178–179, 277
Obiekt-634B 179, 277
Obiekt-637: 136, 277
Obiekt-745: 154, 277
Obiekt-770 (ChTZ Chelyabinsk) 13
Obiekt-781: **154**, **155**, **157**, **264**, 266, 277
Obiekt-782: 154, **157**, 266, 277
Obiekt-785: 87–88, **90**, 277
Obiekt-787: 154, **156**, 266, 277
Pokpo'ong 243
BMT-72: **251**, 256
Ps264-122: 209, **263**, 265
Ps264-231: **263**
T-14 Armata 57, 125, 129
T-15: 129

T-16: 129
T-26: 18
T-34: 7, 11, 18, 32, **36**, **70**, 146, 247, **260**, 266
T-34-85: 49, 241
T-34M medium 18
T-50 light 18
T-54: 6, 11–13, 16, 37, 39, 49, 61, 122, 285
T-54B 144, 287
T-55: 6, 16, 19, 22–23, 37, 39, 44, 49, 52, 60–61, 65, 69, 108, 122, 136, 139–141, 144, 158, **164**, 187, 277, 285, 287
T-62 Medium Tank 6, **11**, 14, 16, 19–20, 23, 37, 40, 49, 52, 60–61, 64–65, **69**, 108, 183, 185, 187–188, 193–194, 198, 204, 243, **257**, 276, 285, 287
T-62A 274
T-62B 24, 276
T-64: 7, 15, **18**, 19, 21–23, 25, 28, **29**, **31**, 32, 34–35, 37, **38**, 39, 43, 45, 55, 57, 76, 83, 103, 121, 133, 135, **149**, 183, 185, 196, 201, 245, 247, 249, **260**, 268, 277, 285, 294, 298
T-64A **17**, **20**, 21–23, **24**, 25–28, 31–33, 36, 38, 40, 59–64, **65**, 67, 69, 81, **88**, **89**, 235, **245**, 266, 276–277
T-64B 36, 40–42, 81, 90–91, 96, 277
T-64B1: 36, 43
T-64B1V 43
T-64BV 43
T-72: 6–9, **11**, 13, **14**, **15**, 19, **20**, 21, **22**, **24**, 28, **29**, **31**, **32**, **33**, 34, **35**, **36**, 37, **38**, 39, **40**, 42–50, **51**, 52, **53**, 55–57, 59, **60**, **64**, 67, **68**, **69**, **70**, 71–76, 80–81, 83–84, **85**, 87, **88**, 90–91, 96–97, **99**, 101, 103, **108**, 110, 115, **121**, 122, 125, 127, 131–133, **135**, 137, 142, 146, 154–155, **156**, **157**, **161**, 162–163, 165, **166**, 171, 178, 180, **181**, 183, **184**, 185–198, 200–201, 203–206, **207**, 209, **210**, **211**, **215**, **217**, **218**, 221, **235**, 237, **238**, 242–243, **245**, **246**, 247, **248**, **249**, 250, **251**,

254, 255–256, **259**, **260**, **261**,
262, **264**, 265–266, **267**, 268,
269, 272–285, 287–288,
291–292, 295–298, **304**
T-72-120: 252, 283
T-72A 9, **35**, 37–38, **39**, **40**,
41–43, 55–56, 59, **68**, **69**, **70**,
72, **73**, **74**, **75**, 76, **77**, **78**, **80**,
81, **82**, **83**, **84**, **85**, **86**, 87, 92,
98, **99**, 116, **117**, **136**, 137,
142, 144, 154, 156–157,
178–179, 184, 192–193, 209,
210, **212**, **214**, **216**, **217**, **219**,
230, **232**, 236, **246**, **247**, 249,
255–256, **260**, **261**, **262**, **264**,
265, 266–267, 272–273,
276–277, 279, 283, 287, 291,
295–298
T-72AG **249**, **250**, 252, 279,
283
T-72AK 81, 276, 279, **304**
T-72AM Banan 249
T-72AMT **249**, 255
T-72AV **41**, 43, 55, 84–85,
92, **93**, **94**, **95**, 96, 98, **102**,
191, **197**, **198**, **200**, **235**, **238**,
240, **245**, **246**, **248**, **262**, 266,
279–280
T-72B Rogatka 6–9, **11**, 13,
14, **15**, 19, **20**, 21, **22**, **24**, 28,
29, **31**, **32**, **33**, 34, **35**, **36**, 37,
38, 39, **40**, 42–50, **51**, 52, **53**,
55–57, 59, **60**, **64**, 67, **68**, **69**,
70, 71–76, 80–81, 83–84, **85**,
87, **88**, 90–91, 96–97, **99**,
101, 103, **108**, 110, 115, **121**,
122, 125, 127, 131–133, **135**,
137, 142, 146, 154–155, **156**,
157, **161**, 162–163, 165, **166**,
171, 178, 180, **181**, 183, **184**,
185–198, 200–201, 203–206,
207, 209, **210**, **211**, **215**, **217**,
218, 221, **235**, 237, **238**,
242–243, **245**, **246**, 247, **248**,
249, 250, **251**, **254**, 255–256,
259, **260**, **261**, **262**, **264**,
265–266, **267**, 268, **269**,
272–285, 287–288, 291–292,
295–298, **304**
T-72BA **53**, 55, 95, 104–105,
108, 110, **111**, 115, 122, **205**,
277, 280, 295, 297

T-72BK 96, 279
T-72BKA 104
T-72BK1A 104
T-72B1: **6**, **8**, 42, **43**, **44**, **48**,
49, 52, **53**, 87, **96**, **97**, 98,
100, **101**, **102**, **104**, **105**, **186**,
190, **204**, 237, 239, **240**, **246**,
263, 266, 273, 276, 280, **288**,
290, 298
T-72B1A 104, 277
T-72B1K 96, 277
T-72B1MS Belly Orel 239,
277, 279–280, 294
T-72B1V 43, **305**
T-72B2 Rogatka: 52, **53**,
54–55, 119, 125, 127, 130,
238, 276–277, 294, 296, 298
T-72B3 Urban 43, **53**, **54**, 55,
83, 95, 108, **111**, **113**, **115**,
116, **117**, **118**, **119**, **120**, **121**,
122, **124**, 125, **126**, **127**, **129**,
130–132, **162**, 200, **203**, 206,
213, 268, **269**, 276–277,
279–280, 284, 294–298
T-72B3M **9**, 55, **56**, **117**,
121, **122**, **123**, **124**, **126**, **127**,
128, 129, **130**, **131**, 132, **133**,
206, 268, **269**, 276–277, 294,
297–298, **305**
T-72B4: 129–130
T-72BM 8, 49–50, **53**, 93,
102–103, **111**, 206, 277
T-72BM3: 130
T-72BU 8, 50, 103, 105
T-72E 252
T-72Eh-1: 55
T-72K 72, 81, 276, 284
T-72M 42, 48, 55–56, **66**, **74**,
153, 186, **236**, **237**, 242,
265–267, **269**, 276, 279–282,
287, **304**, **305**
T-72M1: 48, 53, 56, 85, 186,
189, 191, **209**, **212**, **214**, 236,
237, 238, **240**, **242**, **243**, **262**,
263, 265–267, **269**, 276,
279–282, 287
T-72M1K **241**
T-72M1K1: **242**
T-72M1M 53, **112**, **114**, 128,
238
T-72M1Z 279
T-72M3CZ 281

T-72M4CZ 279, 281
T-72MP 250, 252, 283
T-72S Shilden 38, 43, 52, 56,
108, **109**, **110**, 187, 237, 256,
276, 279–280, 282
T-72UA1: 252, 256, 279
T-72UA4: 252
T-80: 7, 15, 19, **29**, 31–34,
36–37, **38**, 39–40, 43, 49–50,
52, 55, 57, 87, 103, 105, 121,
135, 137, 171, 183, 194, 235,
239, **249**, 255, **267**, 268, 277,
283
T-80B 41–42, 91, 96, 118
T-80B1V 43
T-80BV 43
T-80BVM 207
T-80U 46, 105, 250, 283
T-80UD 46, 49, 105, 107,
245, 247, 249, **250**, 283
T-84: 245, 249
T-90 Vladimir 8, 50–54, 57,
83, 87, 93, 101–103, 105,
112, **113**, **114**, **116**, 122, 125,
135, 141, 146, 153, 156, 180,
184–185, 200, 206, 252, 268,
273, 276–277, 279–280, 282,
291
T-90M 57, 141, **181**
T-90S 50, 108, 277, 279
T-90SA 279
Termalnaya Dymovaya Apparata
 (TDA – thermal smoke
 generation apparatus) 80, 139,
 293, 295, 302
test polygons 50, 75
 Kubinka **101**, 274
 NIIBT 26
Third World 7, 19, 38, 184, 235
Tito, Josef Broz 192
tracks 11, 14, 16, 23, 60, 105,
 110, 153, 183, **217**, 255, 276,
 291, 294
 guards **100**, 138
 OMSh 61
 RMSh 24, 27, 61, 105, 275,
 296
 UMSh 52–53, 55, 105, 122
transfer case 23, 60, 62, 289
 guitara 60, 62, 289
Transmash 26, 46, 59, 303
transmissions 60–62, 99, 130, 150,

153, 183, 293, 295
  4-speed 31
  7-speed 7, 14, 23, 31, 62, 183
  assemblies 171
  Chrysler 'Dynaflow' 31
  hydromechanical 88
  Morse 72
Transnistria 183, 196
  Moldova-Transnistria conflict 1992: 196
Transportno – Zaryazhayushaya Mashina (TZM – Transport – Reload Vehicle) 178–179, 277, 303
  TZM-T **179**, 180
Tsentralniy Komitet Kommunicheskoy Partii Sovetskogo Soyuza (TsK KPSU – Central Committee of the Communist Party of the Soviet Union) 89, 302–303
TTTs (design parameters) **29**, 31, 36
Turkmenistan 27, 280
turrets **6**, 14, **15**, 16, **20**, 22, **24**, 25, 31, **35**, **36**, 37, **38**, **39**, 41–42, 44, 46–47, 53, 55, **59**, 60–61, 63–64, **65**, 67–69, **73**, **74**, 75–76, 80, **82**, 84–85, 87, **88**, **89**, 90–91, **92**, **93**, **94**, **97**, 98, **99**, 102–103, 105, 110, **112**, **113**, **114**, 116, **117**, **119**, **121**, **122**, 125, **129**, 130, **131**, 132, **133**, 137, 139, 142, 144, 146, 154, **156**, **157**, 163, 165, **168**, **172**, **173**, **180**, 185, 188, 192, 195, **197**, **198**, 200, 205–206, **207**, 235–237, **240**, 242, **243**, **245**, **247**, 250, **251**, 252, 255–256, **260**, 266, **267**, 272, 276–277, 283, 287, 289, **290**, 291–292, 295, 297–300, **304**
Tverskaya Ulitsa **56**, **124**, **152**, **169**, **175**

Ukraine 6, 9, 27, 34, 49–50, 52, 54–57, **64**, **85**, **105**, 132, 140, **162**, 180, 185, **198**, 201, **202**, 203–206, **207**, **238**, **245**, **246**, **247**, **248**, **250**, **252**, **253**, **254**, 255, 259, 279–280, 283, **305**
Ukrainian Army (VSU) 57, **137**,
  152, **198**, 201, 204, **252**, **253**, **254**, **256**, 295, **304**
Ulitsa Tverskaya **150**, **168**
United Arab Emirates (UAE) 283, 303
United States 200, 267, 280
Ural Mountains 18, 48–49
Ural Transport Machinery Factory (Uraltransmash) 165, 173, 180, 278
Uralniy Vagonstroitelsviy Zavod (UVZ – Urals Railway Wagon Construction Factory) 12, 16, **17**, **20**, 21, **22**, 23–28, 31, 34, 36–38, 40–41, 45, 49–50, 52, 57, 59–61, **62**, 67–68, 71, 73, 83–84, 87, **89**, 90–91, 99, **113**, 125, 127–128, **129**, 131, 137, **139**, 142, 144, 154, **155**, 156–157, 173, **179**, **181**, 196, 209, **215**, 221, **230**, **232**, 239, 245, **254**, **260**, **261**, **262**, **263**, **264**, 266, 272, 276–278, 287, 291, 303
  KB **11**, **17**, 24
Uralnoye Konstruktorskoye Byuro Transportivnoy Mashinoy (UKBTM – Urals Design Bureau for Transport Machinery (Nizhny Tagil)) 83, 103, 118, 125, 128, 141, 155, 201, 302–303
Uralvagonzavod 21, 57, 173
US Army Opposing Forces units (OPFOR) 267, 280, 302
USSR 6, 12–13, 27, 34, 49, 97, 105, 186, 188, 193, 235, 242, 245, 265–266, 273–274, 279–280, 282, 302–303
Ustinov, Dmitriy Fedorovich 6, 13, 15, 19, 21, 25–28, 31–34, 36–41, 55, 71, 83, 91, 104, 180, 235
Ustroystvo Virabotky Bokovikh Uprezhdeny (UVBU – lateral target tracking device) 76, 298, 303

Venediktov, Valeriy N. 12, 23–25, 36, 38, 61, 183
Verkhnyaya Pyshma **262**, 266
Victory Day 54, **168**, **170**
viewers 16, 44, 46
  MK-4: 65
  thermal 46, 130, 157, 250
  TVN-5 night-driving 108
Voenno-Vozdushnie Sili SSSR (VVS – the Soviet Air Force) 193, 303
  VVS-2: 122
Voenny Promishlennoi Kommissiei pri Soviet Ministrov SSSR (VPK – Military-Industrial Commissariat for the Council of Ministers of the USSR) 303
Vsesoyuzniy Nauchno-Issledovatelsky Institut (VNII – All-Union Scientific Research Institute) 42, 303
Vsesoyuzny Nauchno-Issledovatelsky Institut (VNII-100 – All-Union Scientific Research Institute No. 100 (later VNII Transmash)) 42, 303

Warsaw Pact 37–38, 47, 56, 185, 192, 209, 235–237, 242, 274, 280
World War II 9, **11**, 43, 49, 54, 118, 133, 146, 153, 192–193, 205

Yeltsin, Boris 8, 47, 50–51, 193, 195–196
Yugoslavia 6, 9, 56, 192, 236, 242, 273, 274, 279–280, 282–283
  break-up of 192–193

Zverev, S. A. 15, 19, 24